THIS IS YOUR **PASSBOOK**® FOR ...

CERTIFIED MASTER OF BUSINESS ADMINISTRATION (MBA)

NATIONAL LEARNING CORPORATION®
passbooks.com

PASSBOOK® SERIES

THE *PASSBOOK® SERIES* has been created to prepare applicants and candidates for the ultimate academic battlefield – the examination room.

At some time in our lives, each and every one of us may be required to take an examination – for validation, matriculation, admission, qualification, registration, certification, or licensure.

Based on the assumption that every applicant or candidate has met the basic formal educational standards, has taken the required number of courses, and read the necessary texts, the *PASSBOOK® SERIES* furnishes the one special preparation which may assure passing with confidence, instead of failing with insecurity. Examination questions – together with answers – are furnished as the basic vehicle for study so that the mysteries of the examination and its compounding difficulties may be eliminated or diminished by a sure method.

This book is meant to help you pass your examination provided that you qualify and are serious in your objective.

The entire field is reviewed through the huge store of content information which is succinctly presented through a provocative and challenging approach – the question-and-answer method.

A climate of success is established by furnishing the correct answers at the end of each test.

You soon learn to recognize types of questions, forms of questions, and patterns of questioning. You may even begin to anticipate expected outcomes.

You perceive that many questions are repeated or adapted so that you can gain acute insights, which may enable you to score many sure points.

You learn how to confront new questions, or types of questions, and to attack them confidently and work out the correct answers.

You note objectives and emphases, and recognize pitfalls and dangers, so that you may make positive educational adjustments.

Moreover, you are kept fully informed in relation to new concepts, methods, practices, and directions in the field.

You discover that you arre actually taking the examination all the time: you are preparing for the examination by "taking" an examination, not by reading extraneous and/or supererogatory textbooks.

In short, this PASSBOOK®, used directedly, should be an important factor in helping you to pass your test.

The Certified MBA Exam

The Certified MBA Exam, developed by the National Certification Institute, is a new criteria in ranking and hiring new M.B.A.'s. It is pass-fail, but students will receive a ranking of their results in different subjects. It will last 5 hours and contain 300 multiple-choice questions, in areas including: organizational behavior, strategy, marketing, operations, macro- and micro-economics, finance, managerial accounting, financial accounting, and quantitative methods. A sample question: A company's net income in its entire life totaled $10 million. It paid dividends of $3 million, built a new plant for $4 million, and increased its inventory by $2 million. What are its retained earnings? (The answer is $7 million.)

HOW TO TAKE A TEST

You have studied long, hard and conscientiously.

With your official admission card in hand, and your heart pounding, you have been admitted to the examination room.

You note that there are several hundred other applicants in the examination room waiting to take the same test.

They all appear to be equally well prepared.

You know that nothing but your best effort will suffice. The "moment of truth" is at hand: you now have to demonstrate objectively, in writing, your knowledge of content and your understanding of subject matter.

You are fighting the most important battle of your life—to pass and/or score high on an examination which will determine your career and provide the economic basis for your livelihood.

What extra, special things should you know and should you do in taking the examination?

I. YOU MUST PASS AN EXAMINATION

A. WHAT EVERY CANDIDATE SHOULD KNOW

Examination applicants often ask us for help in preparing for the written test. What can I study in advance? What kinds of questions will be asked? How will the test be given? How will the papers be graded?

B. HOW ARE EXAMS DEVELOPED?

Examinations are carefully written by trained technicians who are specialists in the field known as "psychological measurement," in consultation with recognized authorities in the field of work that the test will cover. These experts recommend the subject matter areas or skills to be tested; only those knowledges or skills important to your success on the job are included. The most reliable books and source materials available are used as references. Together, the experts and technicians judge the difficulty level of the questions.

Test technicians know how to phrase questions so that the problem is clearly stated. Their ethics do not permit "trick" or "catch" questions. Questions may have been tried out on sample groups, or subjected to statistical analysis, to determine their usefulness.

Written tests are often used in combination with performance tests, ratings of training and experience, and oral interviews. All of these measures combine to form the best-known means of finding the right person for the right job.

II. HOW TO PASS THE WRITTEN TEST

A. BASIC STEPS

1) Study the announcement

How, then, can you know what subjects to study? Our best answer is: "Learn as much as possible about the class of positions for which you've applied." The exam will test the knowledge, skills and abilities needed to do the work.

Your most valuable source of information about the position you want is the official exam announcement. This announcement lists the training and experience qualifications. Check these standards and apply only if you come reasonably close to meeting them. Many jurisdictions preview the written test in the exam announcement by including a section called "Knowledge and Abilities Required," "Scope of the Examination," or some similar heading. Here you will find out specifically what fields will be tested.

2) Choose appropriate study materials

If the position for which you are applying is technical or advanced, you will read more advanced, specialized material. If you are already familiar with the basic principles of your field, elementary textbooks would waste your time. Concentrate on advanced textbooks and technical periodicals. Think through the concepts and review difficult problems in your field.

These are all general sources. You can get more ideas on your own initiative, following these leads. For example, training manuals and publications of the government agency which employs workers in your field can be useful, particularly for technical and professional positions. A letter or visit to the government department involved may result in more specific study suggestions, and certainly will provide you with a more definite idea of the exact nature of the position you are seeking.

3) Study this book!

III. KINDS OF TESTS

Tests are used for purposes other than measuring knowledge and ability to perform specified duties. For some positions, it is equally important to test ability to make adjustments to new situations or to profit from training. In others, basic mental abilities not dependent on information are essential. Questions which test these things may not appear as pertinent to the duties of the position as those which test for knowledge and information. Yet they are often highly important parts of a fair examination. For very general questions, it is almost impossible to help you direct your study efforts. What we can do is to point out some of the more common of these general abilities needed in public service positions and describe some typical questions.

1) General information

Broad, general information has been found useful for predicting job success in some kinds of work. This is tested in a variety of ways, from vocabulary lists to questions about current events. Basic background in some field of work, such as sociology or economics, may be sampled in a group of questions. Often these are principles which have become familiar to most persons through exposure rather than through formal training. It is difficult to advise you how to study for these questions; being alert to the world around you is our best suggestion.

2) Verbal ability

An example of an ability needed in many positions is verbal or language ability. Verbal ability is, in brief, the ability to use and understand words. Vocabulary and grammar tests are typical measures of this ability. Reading comprehension or paragraph interpretation questions are common in many kinds of civil service tests. You are given a paragraph of written material and asked to find its central meaning.

IV. KINDS OF QUESTIONS

1. Multiple-choice Questions

Most popular of the short-answer questions is the "multiple choice" or "best answer" question. It can be used, for example, to test for factual knowledge, ability to solve problems or judgment in meeting situations found at work.

A multiple-choice question is normally one of three types:

- It can begin with an incomplete statement followed by several possible endings. You are to find the one ending which *best* completes the statement, although some of the others may not be entirely wrong.
- It can also be a complete statement in the form of a question which is answered by choosing one of the statements listed.
- It can be in the form of a problem – again you select the best answer.

Here is an example of a multiple-choice question with a discussion which should give you some clues as to the method for choosing the right answer:

When an employee has a complaint about his assignment, the action which will *best* help him overcome his difficulty is to
- A. discuss his difficulty with his coworkers
- B. take the problem to the head of the organization
- C. take the problem to the person who gave him the assignment
- D. say nothing to anyone about his complaint

In answering this question, you should study each of the choices to find which is best. Consider choice "A" – Certainly an employee may discuss his complaint with fellow employees, but no change or improvement can result, and the complaint remains unresolved. Choice "B" is a poor choice since the head of the organization probably does not know what assignment you have been given, and taking your problem to him is known as "going over the head" of the supervisor. The supervisor, or person who made the assignment, is the person who can clarify it or correct any injustice. Choice "C" is, therefore, correct. To say nothing, as in choice "D," is unwise. Supervisors have and interest in knowing the problems employees are facing, and the employee is seeking a solution to his problem.

2. True/False

3. Matching Questions
Matching an answer from a column of choices within another column.

V. RECORDING YOUR ANSWERS

Computer terminals are used more and more today for many different kinds of exams.

For an examination with very few applicants, you may be told to record your answers in the test booklet itself. Separate answer sheets are much more common. If this separate answer sheet is to be scored by machine – and this is often the case – it is highly important that you mark your answers correctly in order to get credit.

VI. BEFORE THE TEST

YOUR PHYSICAL CONDITION IS IMPORTANT
If you are not well, you can't do your best work on tests. If you are half asleep, you can't do your best either. Here are some tips:

1) Get about the same amount of sleep you usually get. Don't stay up all night before the test, either partying or worrying—DON'T DO IT!
2) If you wear glasses, be sure to wear them when you go to take the test. This goes for hearing aids, too.
3) If you have any physical problems that may keep you from doing your best, be sure to tell the person giving the test. If you are sick or in poor health, you relay cannot do your best on any test. You can always come back and take the test some other time.

Common sense will help you find procedures to follow to get ready for an examination. Too many of us, however, overlook these sensible measures. Indeed, nervousness and fatigue have been found to be the most serious reasons why applicants fail to do their best on civil service tests. Here is a list of reminders:

- Begin your preparation early – Don't wait until the last minute to go scurrying around for books and materials or to find out what the position is all about.
- Prepare continuously – An hour a night for a week is better than an all-night cram session. This has been definitely established. What is more, a night a week for a month will return better dividends than crowding your study into a shorter period of time.
- Locate the place of the exam – You have been sent a notice telling you when and where to report for the examination. If the location is in a different town or otherwise unfamiliar to you, it would be well to inquire the best route and learn something about the building.
- Relax the night before the test – Allow your mind to rest. Do not study at all that night. Plan some mild recreation or diversion; then go to bed early and get a good night's sleep.
- Get up early enough to make a leisurely trip to the place for the test – This way unforeseen events, traffic snarls, unfamiliar buildings, etc. will not upset you.

- Dress comfortably – A written test is not a fashion show. You will be known by number and not by name, so wear something comfortable.
- Leave excess paraphernalia at home – Shopping bags and odd bundles will get in your way. You need bring only the items mentioned in the official notice you received; usually everything you need is provided. Do not bring reference books to the exam. They will only confuse those last minutes and be taken away from you when in the test room.
- Arrive somewhat ahead of time – If because of transportation schedules you must get there very early, bring a newspaper or magazine to take your mind off yourself while waiting.
- Locate the examination room – When you have found the proper room, you will be directed to the seat or part of the room where you will sit. Sometimes you are given a sheet of instructions to read while you are waiting. Do not fill out any forms until you are told to do so; just read them and be prepared.
- Relax and prepare to listen to the instructions
- If you have any physical problem that may keep you from doing your best, be sure to tell the test administrator. If you are sick or in poor health, you really cannot do your best on the exam. You can come back and take the test some other time.

VII. AT THE TEST

The day of the test is here and you have the test booklet in your hand. The temptation to get going is very strong. Caution! There is more to success than knowing the right answers. You must know how to identify your papers and understand variations in the type of short-answer question used in this particular examination. Follow these suggestions for maximum results from your efforts:

1) Cooperate with the monitor

The test administrator has a duty to create a situation in which you can be as much at ease as possible. He will give instructions, tell you when to begin, check to see that you are marking your answer sheet correctly, and so on. He is not there to guard you, although he will see that your competitors do not take unfair advantage. He wants to help you do your best.

2) Listen to all instructions

Don't jump the gun! Wait until you understand all directions. In most civil service tests you get more time than you need to answer the questions. So don't be in a hurry. Read each word of instructions until you clearly understand the meaning. Study the examples, listen to all announcements and follow directions. Ask questions if you do not understand what to do.

3) Identify your papers

Civil service exams are usually identified by number only. You will be assigned a number; you must not put your name on your test papers. Be sure to copy your number correctly. Since more than one exam may be given, copy your exact examination title.

4) Plan your time

Unless you are told that a test is a "speed" or "rate of work" test, speed itself is usually not important. Time enough to answer all the questions will be provided, but this does not mean that you have all day. An overall time limit has been set. Divide the total time (in minutes) by the number of questions to determine the approximate time you have for each question.

5) Do not linger over difficult questions

If you come across a difficult question, mark it with a paper clip (useful to have along) and come back to it when you have been through the booklet. One caution if you do this – be sure to skip a number on your answer sheet as well. Check often to be sure that you have not lost your place and that you are marking in the row numbered the same as the question you are answering.

6) Read the questions

Be sure you know what the question asks! Many capable people are unsuccessful because they failed to *read* the questions correctly.

7) Answer all questions

Unless you have been instructed that a penalty will be deducted for incorrect answers, it is better to guess than to omit a question.

8) Speed tests

It is often better NOT to guess on speed tests. It has been found that on timed tests people are tempted to spend the last few seconds before time is called in marking answers at random – without even reading them – in the hope of picking up a few extra points. To discourage this practice, the instructions may warn you that your score will be "corrected" for guessing. That is, a penalty will be applied. The incorrect answers will be deducted from the correct ones, or some other penalty formula will be used.

9) Review your answers

If you finish before time is called, go back to the questions you guessed or omitted to give them further thought. Review other answers if you have time.

10) Return your test materials

If you are ready to leave before others have finished or time is called, take ALL your materials to the monitor and leave quietly. Never take any test material with you. The monitor can discover whose papers are not complete, and taking a test booklet may be grounds for disqualification.

VIII. EXAMINATION TECHNIQUES

1) Read the general instructions carefully. These are usually printed on the first page of the exam booklet. As a rule, these instructions refer to the timing of the examination; the fact that you should not start work until the signal and must stop work at a signal, etc. If there are any *special* instructions, such as a choice of questions to be answered, make sure that you note this instruction carefully.

2) When you are ready to start work on the examination, that is as soon as the signal has been given, read the instructions to each question booklet, underline any key words or phrases, such as *least*, *best*, *outline*, *describe*

and the like. In this way you will tend to answer as requested rather than discover on reviewing your paper that you *listed without describing*, that you selected the *worst* choice rather than the *best* choice, etc.

3) If the examination is of the objective or multiple-choice type – that is, each question will also give a series of possible answers: A, B, C or D, and you are called upon to select the best answer and write the letter next to that answer on your answer paper – it is advisable to start answering each question in turn. There may be anywhere from 50 to 100 such questions in the three or four hours allotted and you can see how much time would be taken if you read through all the questions before beginning to answer any. Furthermore, if you come across a question or group of questions which you know would be difficult to answer, it would undoubtedly affect your handling of all the other questions.

4) If the examination is of the essay type and contains but a few questions, it is a moot point as to whether you should read all the questions before starting to answer any one. Of course, if you are given a choice – say five out of seven and the like – then it is essential to read all the questions so you can eliminate the two that are most difficult. If, however, you are asked to answer all the questions, there may be danger in trying to answer the easiest one first because you may find that you will spend too much time on it. The best technique is to answer the first question, then proceed to the second, etc.

5) Time your answers. Before the exam begins, write down the time it started, then add the time allowed for the examination and write down the time it must be completed, then divide the time available somewhat as follows:
    - If 3-1/2 hours are allowed, that would be 210 minutes. If you have 80 objective-type questions, that would be an average of 2-1/2 minutes per question. Allow yourself no more than 2 minutes per question, or a total of 160 minutes, which will permit about 50 minutes to review.
    - If for the time allotment of 210 minutes there are 7 essay questions to answer, that would average about 30 minutes a question. Give yourself only 25 minutes per question so that you have about 35 minutes to review.

6) The most important instruction is to *read each question* and make sure you know what is wanted. The second most important instruction is to *time yourself properly* so that you answer every question. The third most important instruction is to *answer every question*. Guess if you have to but include something for each question. Remember that you will receive no credit for a blank and will probably receive some credit if you write something in answer to an essay question. If you guess a letter – say "B" for a multiple-choice question – you may have guessed right. If you leave a blank as an answer to a multiple-choice question, the examiners may respect your feelings but it will not add a point to your score. Some exams may penalize you for wrong answers, so in such cases *only*, you may not want to guess unless you have some basis for your answer.

7) Suggestions
   a. Objective-type questions
      1. Examine the question booklet for proper sequence of pages and questions
      2. Read all instructions carefully
      3. Skip any question which seems too difficult; return to it after all other questions have been answered
      4. Apportion your time properly; do not spend too much time on any single question or group of questions
      5. Note and underline key words – *all, most, fewest, least, best, worst, same, opposite,* etc.
      6. Pay particular attention to negatives
      7. Note unusual option, e.g., unduly long, short, complex, different or similar in content to the body of the question
      8. Observe the use of "hedging" words – *probably, may, most likely,* etc.
      9. Make sure that your answer is put next to the same number as the question
      10. Do not second-guess unless you have good reason to believe the second answer is definitely more correct
      11. Cross out original answer if you decide another answer is more accurate; do not erase until you are ready to hand your paper in
      12. Answer all questions; guess unless instructed otherwise
      13. Leave time for review

   b. Essay questions
      1. Read each question carefully
      2. Determine exactly what is wanted. Underline key words or phrases.
      3. Decide on outline or paragraph answer
      4. Include many different points and elements unless asked to develop any one or two points or elements
      5. Show impartiality by giving pros and cons unless directed to select one side only
      6. Make and write down any assumptions you find necessary to answer the questions
      7. Watch your English, grammar, punctuation and choice of words
      8. Time your answers; don't crowd material

8) Answering the essay question

Most essay questions can be answered by framing the specific response around several key words or ideas. Here are a few such key words or ideas:

M's: manpower, materials, methods, money, management
P's: purpose, program, policy, plan, procedure, practice, problems, pitfalls, personnel, public relations
   a. Six basic steps in handling problems:
      1. Preliminary plan and background development
      2. Collect information, data and facts
      3. Analyze and interpret information, data and facts
      4. Analyze and develop solutions as well as make recommendations

5. Prepare report and sell recommendations
6. Install recommendations and follow up effectiveness

b. Pitfalls to avoid
1. *Taking things for granted* – A statement of the situation does not necessarily imply that each of the elements is necessarily true; for example, a complaint may be invalid and biased so that all that can be taken for granted is that a complaint has been registered
2. *Considering only one side of a situation* – Wherever possible, indicate several alternatives and then point out the reasons you selected the best one
3. *Failing to indicate follow up* – Whenever your answer indicates action on your part, make certain that you will take proper follow-up action to see how successful your recommendations, procedures or actions turn out to be
4. *Taking too long in answering any single question* – Remember to time your answers properly

EXAMINATION SECTION

EXAMINATION SECTION
TEST 1

DIRECTIONS: Each question or incomplete statement is followed by several suggested answers or completions. Select the one that BEST answers the question or completes the statement. *PRINT THE LETTER OF THE CORRECT ANSWER IN THE SPACE AT THE RIGHT.*

1. In production and operations control, choosing the site of the production facility is a function of the _____ process. 1.____

    A. production design
    B. selection
    C. production planning
    D. production evaluation

2. Each of the following is an advantage associated with high job specialization EXCEPT for 2.____

    A. facilitating scientific method study
    B. saving time in switching from one task to another
    C. being well–suited to small, entrepreneurial companies
    D. increasing worker dexterity

3. A statement of the duties, working conditions, and other significant requirements associated with a particular job is termed a 3.____

    A. replacement chart
    B. job specification
    C. job description
    D. job analysis

4. A _____ organizational plan is illustrated by a company's method for figuring overtime pay. 4.____

    A. short–term
    B. long–term
    C. single–use
    D. standing

5. Which of the following files lists the names and quantities of all items that are required to produce one unit of product? 5.____

    A. Inventory
    B. Output
    C. MRP
    D. Bill of materials

6. Which of the following is NOT a branch of the quantitative management approach? 6.____

    A. Behavioral science
    B. Management information systems
    C. Operations management
    D. Management science

7. During a staff development meeting, several employees are asked to view some video-tapes that illustrate a process related to job performance, and are then asked to tape and observe their own performance of this activity.
This is an example of 7.____

    A. understudy
    B. socialization
    C. behavior modeling
    D. apprenticeship

8. _____ is a statistical technique that involves evaluating random samples from a group of produced materials to determine whether the group meets agreeable quality levels.   8.____

   A. Statistical process control
   B. Acceptance sampling
   C. Raw materials sampling
   D. AQL

9. A formal business group, consisting of a manager and all the subordinates who report to that manager, is known as a(n)   9.____

   A. strategic business unit
   C. command group
   B. reference group
   D. module

10. Which of the following ideas was contributed by the classical viewpoint of management?   10.____

   A. The visualization of organizations as systems of interrelated parts
   B. The managerial importance of leadership
   C. There is no one best way to manage
   D. The importance of pay as a motivator

11. Each of the following is a component of quality control EXCEPT   11.____

   A. marketability
   C. aesthetics
   B. function
   D. safety

12. The human resource needs of a company are determined *primarily* by   12.____

   A. a human resource audit
   B. the company's goals and strategies
   C. the legal environment
   D. a replacement chart

13. If an employee is terminated as a result of _____, this is an example of *due cause*.   13.____

   A. layoff
   C. retirement
   B. incompetence
   D. plant closing

14. According to the systems approach to management, there are four major components to an organizational system. Which of the following is NOT one of these components?   14.____

   A. Inputs
   C. Feedback
   B. Transformation processes
   D. Raw materials

15. Tactical problems are *primarily* the responsibility of   15.____

   A. workers
   C. middle–level managers
   B. low–level managers
   D. executives

16. Robert Owens' (1771–1858) contribution to management theory involved   16.____

   A. human resources
   C. work specialization
   B. cognitive theory
   D. behaviorist theory

2

17. The _____ dimension of quality involves the degree to which a product's design or operating characteristics meet established standards.

   A. reliability
   C. serviceability
   B. conformance
   D. durability

17.____

18. Which type of technology is illustrated by a commercial bank?

   A. Long–linked
   C. Long–term
   B. Intensive
   D. Mediating

18.____

19. According to situational leadership theory, the technique of *telling* is used when followers are

   A. able to take responsibility but are unwilling or too insecure to do so
   B. able and willing to take responsibility
   C. unable to take responsibility but are willing to do so
   D. unable and unwilling or too insecure to take responsibility for a given task

19.____

20. The principles of management by objectives (MBO) include each of the following EXCEPT

   A. executive–proposed goals
   B. managerial–subordinate discussion
   C. mutual goal–setting
   D. performance feedback

20.____

21. Each of the following is considered to be a valuable characteristic of layout design EXCEPT

   A. reduction of material transport cost, but not time
   B. bottleneck–free floor design
   C. employee safety provisions
   D. minimizing travel distance required for worker to reach materials

21.____

22. What stage of group development deals with accomplishing assigned tasks?

   A. Internal problem–solving
   B. Growth and productivity
   C. Orientation
   D. Evaluation and control

22.____

23. Typically, which of the following steps in the budgetary process would occur FIRST?

   A. Unit manager formulation of unit's operating plans
   B. Top management outlines resource restraints
   C. Top management combines information
   D. Unit managers determine resource needs

23.____

24. In a matching analysis, what has occurred when an external opportunity matches the internal strength of a company?   24.____

    A. Problem   B. Vulnerability
    C. Leverage   D. Constraint

25. What type of reinforcement schedule is illustrated by a weekly paycheck?   25.____

    A. Variable interval   B. Variable ratio
    C. Fixed interval   D. Fixed ratio

KEY (CORRECT ANSWERS)

1.	B		11.	A
2.	C		12.	B
3.	C		13.	B
4.	D		14.	D
5.	D		15.	C
6.	A		16.	A
7.	C		17.	B
8.	B		18.	D
9.	C		19.	D
10.	D		20.	A

21.	A
22.	B
23.	B
24.	C
25.	C

TEST 2

Each question or incomplete statement is followed by several suggested answers or completions. Select the one that BEST answers the question or completes the statement. *PRINT THE LETTER OF THE CORRECT ANSWER IN THE SPACE AT THE RIGHT.*

1. A management approach that is oblivious to ethical considerations is described as   1.____

   A. unethical   B. amoral   C. libertine   D. immoral

2. Informal leaders could serve a valuable role in a company when   2.____

   A. they defer to organizational power
   B. their influence is compatible with the company's goals
   C. they make other people feel satisfied with their own performance
   D. their activity receives praise from higher management

3. Moving from marketing to production is an example of a(n) _____ of career path.   3.____

   A. vertical   B. circumferential
   C. radial   D. cone

4. Each of the following is a DISADVANTAGE associated with the use of a rational model for decision–making in a company EXCEPT   4.____

   A. preferences cannot be ranked in a permanent way
   B. payoffs are difficult to estimate
   C. not all necessary information is available
   D. environmental conditions cannot be accurately forecast

5. The MAIN advantage to product departmentalization is   5.____

   A. duplication of efforts
   B. adaptability
   C. achieving economies of scale
   D. innovation

6. The decision to hire a new employee is a(n) _____ decision.   6.____

   A. programmed   B. nonprogrammed
   C. detail   D. under certainty

7. Which of the following are concerned with departmental or interdepartmental activities?   7.____

   A. Policies   B. Procedures
   C. Rules   D. Goals and strategies

8. Each of the following is a legal concern associated with job testing EXCEPT   8.____

   A. length of the test
   B. reliability of the test
   C. relation of test to the job
   D. whether test measures what it professes to measure

9. The settling of disputes over contract language during collective bargaining is known as _____ arbitration.   9.____

   A. interest   B. verbal   C. rights   D. contract

10. In an oligopolistic economic environment, there are _____ sellers and _____ buyers.   10.____

    A. many; few
    B. many; many
    C. few; many
    D. few; few

11. What term would be used to describe a company whose decision–making power is dispersed among lower–level managers?   11.____

    A. Thin
    B. Decentralized
    C. Flat
    D. Fat

12. The effort to solve problems by beginning with a problem and attempting to move logically to a solution is known as   12.____

    A. the rational model
    B. convergent thinking
    C. the incremental model
    D. divergent thinking

13. If a manager determines that controls are needed but the control process will be too costly, each of the following is an alternative to controls EXCEPT   13.____

    A. changing the dependence relationship
    B. implementing horizontal integration
    C. changing organizational goals and objectives to eliminate dependence
    D. changing the nature of the dependence

14. Each of the following is an advantage associated with the use of internal recruitment in the management of human resources EXCEPT   14.____

    A. availability of reliable candidate information
    B. rewarding of good performance
    C. increased internal morale due to upward mobility opportunities
    D. increased likelihood of new ideas being introduced

15. A company uses an organizational design in which a product structure overlays a functional structure. What type of design structure is being used?   15.____

    A. Functional
    B. Matrix
    C. Contingency
    D. Classical

16. The allocation of a company's financial resources is known as the _____ process.   16.____

    A. capital development
    B. financial evaluation
    C. budgeting
    D. equity sourcing

17. Developing plans, setting goals, and making decisions are part of   17.____

    A. coordination
    B. influencing
    C. formulation
    D. implementation

18. Generally, the consumerism movement is concerned with each of the following EXCEPT   18.____

    A. price fixing
    B. retail complaint–handling
    C. equal opportunity employment
    D. deceptive labeling

19. A company's management sets a goal of achieving a 12% return on investment capital from the sale of a company's product line. What type of goal has the company set?

    A. Operative   B. Official
    C. Operational   D. Short–term

19.____

20. When a company's turnover rate is too low,

    A. replacement costs are too high
    B. there has been blocking of lower–level personnel
    C. insufficient weeding out has taken place
    D. a shortage of capable managers exists

20.____

21. A ratio that compares the owner's financial contributions to a company with creditors' contributions is called the _____ ratio.

    A. leverage   B. profitability
    C. liquidity   D. operating

21.____

22. The production evaluation process is primarily concerned with _____ control.

    A. input   B. output   C. marginal   D. process

22.____

23. _____ is considered a structural barrier to managerial automation.

    A. Incompatible systems
    B. Uncertainty avoidance
    C. Resistance
    D. A reward system that emphasizes quick and dramatic results

23.____

24. After an affirmative action plan has been written by a reporting company, a copy is required to be forwarded to the

    A. Department of Labor
    B. Equal Employment Opportunity Commission (EEOC)
    C. National Labor Relations Board
    D. Department of Human Service

24.____

25. Historically, the management theory that first focused on principles that could be used by managers to coordinate the internal activities of organizations was the theory of_____ management.

    A. behaviorist   B. quantitative
    C. administrative   D. bureaucratic

25.____

KEY (CORRECT ANSWERS)

1.	B		11.	B
2.	B		12.	B
3.	B		13.	B
4.	C		14.	D
5.	B		15.	B
6.	A		16.	C
7.	B		17.	C
8.	A		18.	C
9.	A		19.	A
10.	C		20.	C

21.	A
22.	B
23.	D
24.	A
25.	C

TEST 3

DIRECTIONS: Each question or incomplete statement is followed by several suggested answers or completions. Select the one that BEST answers the question or completes the statement. *PRINT THE LETTER OF THE CORRECT ANSWER IN THE SPACE AT THE RIGHT.*

1. Which of the following is a financial resource for a company? 　　　　1._____

   A. Raw material reserves 　　　　　B. Reputation for quality
   C. Bond issues 　　　　　　　　　　D. Warehouses

2. Discretionary expense centers are LEAST likely to be used with _____ departments. 　　2._____

   A. finance
   B. human resources
   C. research and development
   D. public relations

3. _____ managerial power is said to come from the individual, rather than from the company. 　　3._____

   A. Coercive 　　　　　　　　　　　B. Reward
   C. Expert 　　　　　　　　　　　　D. Legitimate

4. The data inputs to computer–based executive support–systems are probably 　　4._____

   A. transactions 　　　　　　　　　B. aggregate data
   C. high–volume data 　　　　　　　D. analytic models

5. What type of audit involves the evaluation and assessment of an entire company's operations? 　　5._____

   A. Management 　　　　　　　　　B. Social
   C. External 　　　　　　　　　　　D. Internal

6. Performance feedback that is NOT evaluative is described as 　　6._____

   A. informal 　　　　　　　　　　　B. reinforcing
   C. dispersed 　　　　　　　　　　　D. informational

7. Which type of leader power stems from a position's placement in the managerial hierarchy and the authority vested in the position? 　　7._____

   A. Legitimate 　　　　　　　　　　B. Referent
   C. Expert 　　　　　　　　　　　　D. Reward

8. In matrix organizations, the BEST strategy for conflict resolution is typically 　　8._____

   A. conciliation 　　　　　　　　　B. consensus
   C. confrontation 　　　　　　　　　D. aversion

9. Which of the following is a destructive force that is MOST likely to affect the implementation phase of the development of a quality circle? 　　9._____

   A. Disagreement on problems
   B. Raised aspirations
   C. Prohibitive costs
   D. Burnout

10. An accountant who audits a company's books would use the _____ style of decision–making.

    A. intuitive   B. systematic
    C. compensatory   D. preceptive

10.____

11. Which functional area of a company involves equity ratio?

    A. Finance   B. Marketing
    C. Operations   D. Development

11.____

12. A company's plan for the acquisition or divestiture of major fixed assets is the

    A. profit budget
    B. balance sheet
    C. expense budget
    D. capital expenditures budget

12.____

13. The main DISADVANTAGE associated with job simplification is

    A. higher training costs
    B. lack of quality control mechanism
    C. lowered employee motivation
    D. loss of production efficiency

13.____

14. A company uses a compensation system in which employees throughout the organization are encouraged to become involved in solving problems, and are given bonuses tied to organizational performance improvements.
This is an example of

    A. skill–based pay   B. gainsharing
    C. benchmarking   D. expanded commission

14.____

15. A task force formed by a company is responsible to

    A. the local community   B. top–level management
    C. union leaders   D. stockholders

15.____

16. What is the term for the identification of a trend and smoothing its pattern?

    A. Segmentation   B. Moving average
    C. Time–series analysis   D. Replacement analysis

16.____

17. _____ is a term for grouping jobs horizontally.

    A. Aggregation   B. Departmentalization
    C. Formalization   D. Dispersion

17.____

18. Which type of power, if exercised by a manager, is MOST likely to result in resistance by subordinates?

    A. Reward   B. Expert   C. Coercive   D. Referent

18.____

19. In manufacturing, MRP systems use three major inputs. Which of the following is NOT   19.____
    one of these three?

    A. Bill of materials information
    B. Investment information
    C. Inventory status information
    D. Master production schedule

20. What type of quality control is concerned *primarily* with the quality of raw input materials?   20.____

    A. Output   B. Feed–forward
    C. Feedback   D. Work in process

21. When groups are slow to reach a decision, they are demonstrating   21.____

    A. assembly effect   B. entropy
    C. process loss   D. synergy

22. ____ costs are those associated with acquiring raw materials.   22.____

    A. Storage   B. Contingency
    C. Order   D. Carrying

23. An effective managerial control system is each of the following EXCEPT   23.____

    A. focused   B. flexible
    C. future–oriented   D. timely

24. During what stage of orientation does an employee acquire technical skills that are likely   24.____
    to improve her current job performance?

    A. Induction   B. Implementation
    C. Socialization   D. Training

25. In a bureaucracy, the practice of adding unnecessary subordinates is likely to create   25.____

    A. red tape   B. position protection
    C. dominance of authority   D. inflexibility

_____

KEY (CORRECT ANSWERS)

1.	C	11.	A
2.	A	12.	D
3.	C	13.	C
4.	B	14.	B
5.	A	15.	B
6.	D	16.	C
7.	A	17.	B
8.	C	18.	C
9.	C	19.	B
10.	B	20.	B

21.	C
22.	C
23.	A
24.	D
25.	C

EXAMINATION SECTION
TEST 1

DIRECTIONS: Each question or incomplete statement is followed by several suggested answers or completions. Select the one that BEST answers the question or completes the statement. *PRINT THE LETTER OF THE CORRECT ANSWER IN THE SPACE AT THE RIGHT.*

Questions 1-2.

DIRECTIONS: Questions 1 and 2 refer to the information below.
An automobile manufacturer estimates a total annual demand of 60,000 axles for use in the manufacturing process, ordering costs of $30 per order, and holding costs of $20 per unit per year. The lead time for obtaining axles from a nearby producer is 8 days. The equation for determining EOQ is as follows:

$$EOQ = \frac{\sqrt{2(\text{ demand })(\text{ ordering costs })}}{(\text{ holding costs })}$$

1. Using the economic order quantity of (EOQ) equation for inventory control, what is the company's approximate EOQ?   1.____

   A. 225   B. 425   C. 90,000   D. 180,000

2. The reorder point, or inventory level at which a new order should be placed, is determined by the following equation:
ROP = (lead time)(demand ÷ 365).
According to the information above, an inventory manager should place a new order when the stock of axles reaches approximately   2.____

   A. 425   B. 658   C. 1315   D. 2630

3. When speed and accuracy are important and a task is complex, _____ communication is probably the best method.   3.____

   A. circle   B. chain
   C. wheel   D. all-channel

4. When a job selection rate for a protected group is less than 80 percent of the rate for the majority group, _____ has occurred.   4.____

   A. adverse impact   B. affirmative action
   C. adverse selection   D. discrimination

5. Which of the following is NOT an advantage associated with functional job grouping?   5.____

   A. Establishes cost centers for easier financial control
   B. Allows for specialization
   C. Facilitates coordination by top managers
   D. Demonstrates clearly-marked career paths

6. The Taft-Hartley Act is a piece of federal legislation that regulates   6.____

   A. equal employment opportunities
   B. employee compensation
   C. labor-management relations
   D. insider stock trading

7. A company's manufacturing and shipping departments usually exhibit _____ interde-pendence.

    A. sequential   B. integrated
    C. tangential   D. applied

7.____

8. Which type of plant layout pattern is illustrated by an airplane production plant?

    A. Product   B. Process
    C. Fixed-position   D. Input

8.____

9. The purpose of an ombudsperson is to

    A. initiate single-action plans
    B. coordinate market research data
    C. alleviate channel conflict
    D. handle employee grievances and ethical problems

9.____

10. A raw materials inventory is a stock of

    A. items that are currently being transformed into a final product or service
    B. parts, ingredients, and other basic inputs to a production or service process
    C. materials that are used to facilitate production or to satisfy customer demand
    D. items that have been produced and are awaiting sale or transit

10.____

11. In Herzberg's theory, fringe benefits are an example of a(n) _____ factor.

    A. satisfying   B. motivating
    C. physiological   D. hygiene

11.____

12. Market research data suggest that a company's product is no longer competitive in qual-ity or price. However, the company still hopes to maintain its current sales for the product. What type of strategy would be BEST for this product?

    A. Shrink   B. Defense
    C. Turnaround   D. Growth

12.____

13. Each of the following is a physical resource for a company EXCEPT

    A. managerial personnel
    B. raw material reserves
    C. manufacturing plant efficiency
    D. location of physical plants

13.____

14. The diagram showing the authority and responsibility relationships within a company is the _____ chart.

    A. Gantt   B. replacement
    C. organization   D. succession

14.____

15. Which of the following is not typically classified as a carrying cost?

    A. Breakage   B. Spoilage   C. Postage   D. Insurance

15.____

16. *External equity* is the term for the extent to which   16._____

    A. pay rates allocated to specific individuals within the organization reflect variations in individual merit
    B. pay rates for particular jobs correspond to rates paid for similar jobs on the entire job market
    C. pay rates for various jobs inside the organization reflect the relative worth of those jobs
    D. compensable factors will be used to rate the worth of particular jobs

17. The PRIMARY goal of an amoral manager is   17._____

    A. optimum market share   B. public service
    C. profitability   D. organizational success

18. What is the term for a predetermined standard against which random samples of pro-   18._____
duced materials are compared in acceptance sampling?

    A. Statistical product control
    B. Acceptable quality level
    C. Quality circle
    D. Finished goods inventory

19. As the need for coordination increases within a company, what type of job grouping   19._____
becomes most beneficial?

    A. Functional   B. Geographic
    C. Process   D. Product

20. Which of the following is not one of a company's human resources?   20._____

    A. Sales representatives
    B. Engineers
    C. Customers
    D. Computer systems analysts

21. Which of the following types of interdependency is emphasized by long-linked technol-   21._____
ogy?

    A. Reciprocal   B. Pooled
    C. Sequential   D. Applied

22. At the managerial level, the mentoring relationship is an example of the _____ tech-   22._____
nique for learning technical skills.

    A. OJT   B. understudy
    C. socialization   D. induction

23. Which of the following is NOT an element of MacGregor's Theory Y concerning manage-   23._____
rial assumptions?

    A. When conditions are favorable, the average person will seek responsibility.
    B. Commitment to goals is the function of available rewards.
    C. The average person wants to be directed, and seeks security above all.
    D. The intellectual potential of most workers is only partially utilized in most companies.

24. Which of the following is a DISADVANTAGE associated with group decision-making?   24.____

    A. High cost
    B. Less careful evaluation of alternatives
    C. Deterioration of group member skills
    D. Less thorough problem identification

25. What is another term for an operating plan?   25.____

    A. SBU plan   B. Daily plan
    C. Functional plan   D. Tactical plan

KEY (CORRECT ANSWERS)

1.	B		11.	D
2.	C		12.	A
3.	B		13.	A
4.	A		14.	C
5.	C		15.	C
6.	C		16.	B
7.	A		17.	C
8.	C		18.	B
9.	D		19.	D
10.	B		20.	C

21.	C
22.	B
23.	C
24.	A
25.	D

TEST 2

DIRECTIONS: Each question or incomplete statement is followed by several suggested answers or completions. Select the one that BEST answers the question or completes the statement. *PRINT THE LETTER OF THE CORRECT ANSWER IN THE SPACE AT THE RIGHT.*

1. According to the contingency model of leadership, which of the following factors is MOST significant in affecting a leader's favorability?   1.____

    A. Leader-member relations   B. Personality traits
    C. Task structure   D. Position power

2. Each of the following is an element of organization structure EXCEPT the   2.____

    A. various mechanisms needed to foster vertical coordination
    B. clustering of individual positions into units, and of units into departments, to form a hierarchy
    C. assignment of tasks and responsibilities that define individual and unit jobs
    D. working capital available for expansion of unit and departmental functions

3. _____ analysis centers on what a company is able to do.   3.____

    A. Regression   B. Internal resource
    C. P&L   D. Trend

4. Which of the following leadership theories emphasizes the individual characteristics of leaders?   4.____

    A. Situational   B. Actualization
    C. Behavioral   D. Trait

5. Which of the following management theories is NOT a classical perspective?   5.____

    A. Bureaucratic   B. Scientific
    C. Quantitative   D. Administrative

6. For the production of high-cost, low-volume products, the _____ layout is probably best.   6.____

    A. product   B. fixed-position
    C. process   D. conveyor

7. Which of the following is not a type of *responsibility center* that is used as a managerial control?   7.____

    A. Production center   B. Profit center
    C. Revenue center   D. Investment center

8. During the appraisal of an employee's performance, a human resources manager uses a general impression based on a few characteristics of the employee in order to judge other characteristics of the employee.
What type of rating error has occurred?   8.____

    A. Recency   B. Severity
    C. Halo effect   D. Contrast

9. As plans become more short-range, their   9.____

    A. function increases   B. scope broadens
    C. specificity decreases   D. specificity increases

10. According to Mintzberg's typology, an *adhocracy* is a management structural configura-   10.____
tion that is characterized by each of the following EXCEPT

    A. high formalization
    B. various forms of matrix departmentalization
    C. expertise dispersed throughout
    D. emphasis on mutual adjustment

11. Each of the following is an advantage associated with low job discretion EXCEPT   11.____

    A. allowing management to establish performance standards
    B. encouraging innovation and creativity of employees
    C. reducing loss of time through consultation
    D. greater management control over work methods

12. In the management of human resources, the MAIN difference between replacement   12.____
planning and succession planning is that

    A. replacement planning focuses on specific candidates who could fill designated
       managerial positions
    B. in replacement planning, age is used to track possible retirements
    C. succession planning focuses on specific candidates who could fill designated man-
       agerial positions
    D. in succession planning, age is used to track possible retirements

13. Of the following strategic role stages involved in operations management, which is per-   13.____
formed FIRST?

    A. Support overall organizational strategy
    B. Achieve parity with competition
    C. Pursue operations management-based strategy
    D. Minimize negative potential

14. The top-down method of budgeting works particularly well in each of the following situa-   14.____
tions EXCEPT when

    A. unit managers have limited knowledge of the current situation
    B. the budgeting process must be expediently performed
    C. business needs necessitate close coordination among units
    D. there is an economic crisis

15. A company's _____ policy will decide the control and scheduling of production.   15.____

    A. financial   B. personnel
    C. marketing   D. product

16. Each of the following is an example of a carrying cost for raw materials EXCEPT   16.____

    A. spoilage costs   B. taxes
    C. bid preparation time   D. storage

17. Which of the following is a qualitative measure of goal achievement? 17.____

    A. Morale   B. Market share
    C. Gross income   D. Turnover

18. When production components are arranged according to the steps involved in producing 18.____
a product, _____ layout occurs.

    A. fixed-position   B. input
    C. process   D. product

19. Technological change in a company's environment typically causes the company to 19.____
develop

    A. control   B. recruitment
    C. marketing   D. monitoring

20. An MRP file is intended to control each of the following EXCEPT 20.____

    A. personnel requirements   B. priorities for materials
    C. inventory   D. capacity planning

21. The goal of management by objectives (MBO) is to stimulate better performance through 21.____
_____ management.

    A. reactive   B. proactive
    C. authoritarian   D. synectic

22. In Vroom's expectancy theory, what is the term for the perceived relationship between 22.____
effort and performance?

    A. Valence   B. Instrumentality
    C. Expectancy   D. Halo

23. The behavioral perspective on management includes 23.____

    A. the managerial importance of group dynamics
    B. the development of quantitative tools to assist in providing products and services
    C. the improvement of work methods through study
    D. identification of circumstances that will influence which particular approach will be
       effective in a given situation

24. _____ layout is the term for a production layout that groups similar work components 24.____
and equipment.

    A. Fixed-position   B. Conveyor
    C. Product   D. Process

25. In organizational management, *span of control* refers to 25.____

    A. the number of people reporting to one manager
    B. formalized rules and procedures
    C. the separation of operating units
    D. the centralization of decision-making

KEY (CORRECT ANSWERS)

1.	A	11.	B
2.	D	12.	A
3.	B	13.	D
4.	D	14.	B
5.	C	15.	D
6.	B	16.	C
7.	A	17.	A
8.	C	18.	D
9.	D	19.	D
10.	A	20.	A

21.	B
22.	C
23.	A
24.	D
25.	A

TEST 3

DIRECTIONS: Each question or incomplete statement is followed by several suggested answers or completions. Select the one that BEST answers the question or completes the statement. *PRINT THE LETTER OF THE CORRECT ANSWER IN THE SPACE AT THE RIGHT.*

1. When a manager's decision-making model is described as *incremental,* the manager('s)   1.____

    A. seeks alternatives only until a satisfactory solution is found
    B. approach is geared toward achieving short-term results
    C. is seeking an optimal decision
    D. is behaving in a random pattern, making nonprogrammed decisions

2. _____ is an example of task change.   2.____

    A. On-the-job training   B. Automation
    C. Survey feedback   D. Job enlargement

3. Which of the following is MOST likely to influence the complexity of a company's environ-   3.____
   ment?

    A. Number of customers
    B. Amount of sophisticated knowledge available
    C. Size of the market
    D. Degree of government regulation

4. Each of the following is a stage involved in group development EXCEPT   4.____

    A. orientation   B. growth
    C. cohesion   D. evaluation

5. Which of the following is LEAST likely to be among the positive effects of the budgeting   5.____
   process?

    A. Encouraging innovative thinking to meet resource allocation
    B. Keeping managers informed about organizational activities
    C. Enhancing coordination across units
    D. Providing standards against which managers' performance can be evaluated

6. During the planning stage, a manager uses several years of historical data on sales to fit   6.____
   a line to predict future sales. This is an example of

    A. regression analysis   B. time-series analysis
    C. causal modeling   D. trend projection

7. When developing a management information system, a company is likely to implement   7.____
   system development during the _____ phase.

    A. testing   B. operation
    C. integration   D. planning

8. In production operations and control, quality control is a function of   8.____

    A. production design   B. selection
    C. production planning   D. production evaluation

9. A company decides to perform an internal social audit in which the company's social activities and resources and expenses used to participate are listed. After these numbers are compiled, the company assesses the extent to which it has reached its goals for each program.
What type of assessment has been made?

    A. Cost approach
    B. Inventory approach
    C. Program management approach
    D. Cost-benefit analysis

9.____

10. In reinforcement theory, the successive rewarding of behaviors that closely approximate the desired response, until the actual desired response is made, is known as

    A. negative reinforcement   B. shaping
    C. behavior modification   D. extinction

10.____

11. A middle-level manager appoints a staff member to serve on a committee in the surrounding community. In terms of forming responses to social issues, the manager is practicing

    A. implicit change   B. structural change
    C. tokenism   D. functional change

11.____

12. The chain of command and problems of authority are issues of

    A. grouping   B. coordination
    C. organizing   D. influence

12.____

13. Which of the following is an example of reciprocal interdependence?

    A. Ordering and manufacturing
    B. Airline operations and maintenance
    C. A Dodge plant and a Plymouth plant
    D. Shipping and accounting

13.____

14. Each of the following is considered to be an element in a company's economic environment EXCEPT

    A. competitors   B. investors
    C. suppliers   D. demographic trends

14.____

15. A decision support system is a computer-based system that is used to

    A. execute and record day-to-day routine transactions
    B. aid the decision-making process in situations that are not well-structured
    C. automate certain office tasks
    D. allow on-line access to information needed by managers mainly at the middle and first-line levels

15.____

16. An operating budget that indicates anticipated revenues is the

    A. profit budget   B. balance sheet
    C. sales budget   D. cash budget

16.____

17. On an organization chart, a dotted line represents a   17.____

    A. vertically integrated distribution channel
    B. staff authority relationship
    C. horizontally integrated distribution channel
    D. direct authority relationship

18. Which dimension of quality involves supplements to the basic functioning characteristics   18.____
    of a product or service?

    A. Reliability   B. Serviceability
    C. Performance   D. Features

19. Each of the following is an advantage associated with conducting a social audit EXCEPT   19.____

    A. tangibility of results
    B. fostering a greater concern for social issues among organization members
    C. provision of data for comparing effectiveness of various programs
    D. illumination of areas in which the organization is vulnerable to public pressure

20. Which of the following types of management structures is most compatible with a stable   20.____
    environment?

    A. Matrix   B. Functional
    C. Product   D. Geographic

21. _____ characteristics are NOT a situational factor for a leader.   21.____

    A. Personality   B. Managerial
    C. Subordinate   D. Organizational

22. _____ is the term for the rules governing group behavior.   22.____

    A. Command modules   B. Norms
    C. Functions   D. Fronts

23. Of the following, top-down budgeting BEST incorporates   23.____

    A. information on competition
    B. alternative courses of action
    C. operational plans
    D. overall resource availability

24. Each of the following is likely to be a purpose of a company's strategic plan EXCEPT   24.____

    A. making future decisions
    B. generating options for consideration
    C. improving coordination of activities
    D. developing management

25. A stock of items that are currently being transformed into a final product or service is   25.____
    known as a(n) _____ inventory.

    A. input   B. output
    C. work-in-process   D. finished-goods

KEY (CORRECT ANSWERS)

1.	B	11.	C
2.	D	12.	D
3.	B	13.	B
4.	C	14.	D
5.	A	15.	B
6.	D	16.	C
7.	A	17.	B
8.	D	18.	D
9.	C	19.	A
10.	B	20.	B

21.	A
22.	B
23.	D
24.	A
25.	D

EXAMINATION SECTION
TEST 1

DIRECTIONS: Each question or incomplete statement is followed by several suggested answers or completions. Select the one that BEST answers the question or completes the statement. *PRINT THE LETTER OF THE CORRECT ANSWER IN THE SPACE AT THE RIGHT.*

1. An environmental analysis serves as the basis for

    A. leading   B. organizing
    C. controlling   D. planning

1.____

2. Which of the following is an advantage associated with product job grouping?

    A. Achieving coordination of efforts
    B. Facilitating development of functional expertise
    C. Broadening managerial perspectives
    D. Eliminating cost duplication

2.____

3. Each of the following is an internal information source for a company EXCEPT

    A. sales data for previous year
    B. information on competitor's activities
    C. annual reports
    D. records of company performance

3.____

4. _____ is a control principle which suggests managers should be informed of a situation only if control data show a significant deviation from standards.

    A. Goal incongruence   B. Management by exception
    C. Tactical control   D. Management by objectives

4.____

5. On which of the following does an analysis of the internal environment direct its focus?

    A. Government regulations   B. Demographic changes
    C. Organizational resources   D. Availability of funds

5.____

6. A retail cosmetics store develops a plan for store expansion. What type of plan is being developed?

    A. Standing plan   B. Budget
    C. Program   D. Project

6.____

7. According to the path–goal theory of leadership, which of the following is one of the main functions of a leader?

    A. Redesigning work
    B. Motivation of subordinates
    C. Noninterference of subordinates
    D. Developing organizational goals

7.____

8. Each of the following is an advantage associated with the systems approach to manage-   8.____
   ment EXCEPT

   A. considering how an organization interacts with its environment
   B. providing a framework for assessing how well an organization's parts interact to
      achieve a common purpose
   C. emphasizing the diagnosis of problems within individual units
   D. used to analyze the organization at many levels

9. In a _____ environment, a problem–seeking style is most likely to succeed.   9.____

   A. predictable   B. simple
   C. dynamic   D. stable

10. An example of process technology is   10.____

    A. ship building   B. chemical manufacturing
    C. neurosurgery   D. textile manufacturing

11. According to _____ theory, an employee's behavior can be modified by changes in the   11.____
    external environment.

    A. cognitive   B. social learning
    C. reinforcement   D. self–actualization

12. Which of the following steps in deciding whether to expand or contract available facilities   12.____
    would be performed FIRST?

    A. Generating and evaluating alternatives
    B. Comparing current capacity with probable future demand
    C. Considering risks
    D. Using forecasts to determine probable future demand

13. Each of the following is considered to be a use of an organization chart EXCEPT   13.____

    A. communicating with people outside the organization
    B. showing informal working relationships
    C. showing intended reporting relationships between people
    D. illustrating where people are positioned in the structure

14. The Hawthorne studies of the 1920s and 1930s ultimately led to the _____ view of   14.____
    management.

    A. administrative   B. systems
    C. contingency   D. human relations

15. The settling of disputes over the interpretation of an agreement during collective bargain-   15.____
    ing is known as _____ arbitration.

    A. interest   B. verbal   C. rights   D. contract

16. The purpose of social scanning is to   16._____

    A. detect evidence of impending changes that will affect the organization's social responsibilities

    B. detect areas in which an organization is vulnerable to public pressure

    C. evaluate the social performance of the company

    D. evaluating the organizational importance of social trends

17. Which of the following is true when a company's replacement ratio is too low?   17._____

    A. There has been blocking of lower–level personnel.

    B. Insufficient weeding out has taken place.

    C. Replacement costs are too high.

    D. A shortage of capable managers exists.

18. What stage of group development deals with public communication programs?   18._____

    A. Evaluation and control   B. Growth and productivity

    C. Orientation   D. Internal problem–solving

19. According to situational leadership theory, the technique of *participating* is used when followers are   19._____

    A. able to take responsibility but are unwilling or too insecure to do so

    B. able and willing to take responsibility

    C. unable to take responsibility but are willing to do so

    D. unable and unwilling or too insecure to take responsibility for a given task

20. Which of the following are concerned with boundaries for decision–making and standing guidelines?   20._____

    A. Policies   B. Procedures

    C. Rules   D. Goals and strategies

21. Referent leader power   21._____

    A. results in a greater freedom to punish others

    B. relies on a possession of expertise that is admired by others

    C. generates greater control over information

    D. results from being admired or liked by others

22. Which of the following steps in the strategic planning process would be performed FIRST?   22._____

    A. Identifying the company's mission

    B. Setting the bottom line

    C. Developing a management succession plan

    D. Determining the capital equipment purchase plan for the coming year

23. A line worker checks the metal finish of new motorcycles. This is an example of _____ 23.____
quality control.

    A. input   B. feedforward
    C. feedback   D. output

24. Which of the following is an example of *upward* communication?   24.____

    A. Suggestion boxes   B. Bulletin boards
    C. Supervisory meetings   D. Posters

25. Each of the following is considered a subordinate characteristic in the path–goal theory   25.____
of leadership EXCEPT the employee's

    A. ability   B. confidence
    C. needs   D. task

KEY (CORRECT ANSWERS)

1. D		11. C	
2. A		12. D	
3. B		13. B	
4. B		14. D	
5. C		15. C	
6. C		16. A	
7. B		17. D	
8. C		18. A	
9. C		19. A	
10. B		20. A	

21. D
22. A
23. B
24. A
25. D

TEST 2

DIRECTIONS: Each question or incomplete statement is followed by several suggested answers or completions. Select the one that BEST answers the question or completes the statement. *PRINT THE LETTER OF THE CORRECT ANSWER IN THE SPACE AT THE RIGHT.*

1. A characteristic of an organic management system is

    A. centralized control
    B. nonprogrammed decision–making
    C. stable environment
    D. formal structure

1.____

2. A manager decides that three years of supervisory experience in the company qualifies an employee for promotion. What type of decision has the manager made?

    A. Conjunctive
    C. Disjunctive
    B. Subjunctive
    D. Compensatory

2.____

3. Charles Babbage's (1792–1871) contribution to management theory involved

    A. bureaucratic management
    C. work specialization
    B. cognitive theory
    D. management–as–science

3.____

4. What is the term for a data bank containing basic information about each employee that can be used to assess the likely availability of individuals for meeting current and future human resource needs?

    A. Job description
    C. Job specification
    B. Skills inventory
    D. Replacement chart

4.____

5. Each of the following would be a likely entry barrier into the iron ore industry EXCEPT

    A. track record
    C. tax laws
    B. technical knowledge
    D. capital equipment

5.____

6. What is the main DISADVANTAGE associated with the use of a behavioral model for decision–making in a company?

    A. Difficulty in perceiving existing problems
    B. The search for solutions is unlimited
    C. There is no assumption that decision makers evaluate their decisions against a set of organizational goals
    D. It is an abstraction that cannot fully describe actual decision–making behavior

6.____

7. If a matrix structure creates problems within an organization, they will *most likely* involve

    A. unity of command
    C. labor specialization
    B. direction
    D. morale

7.____

8. _____ power, if exercised by a manager, is most likely to result in the compliance of subordinates.

    A. Legitimate
    C. Coercive
    B. Expert
    D. Referent

8.____

9. An airline company decides to expand its route structure beyond its resource capability.   9.____
The company has ignored the _____ criterion for strategic planning.

    A. internal consistency   B. external consistency
    C. competitive advantage   D. contribution to society

10. For a process layout, the MOST important factor for success is   10.____

    A. automation   B. materials handling
    C. personnel training   D. materials availability

11. Which of the following is LEAST likely to be a way in which managerial controls might   11.____
create bureaucratic barriers to innovation?

    A. Focusing on short–term results
    B. Frequent, unpleasant surprises
    C. Use of accounting controls that assess all costs associated with a project in its
       early stage
    D. Excessive rationalism

12. Which of the following is a destructive force that is most likely to affect the initial problem–   12.____
solving phase of the development of a quality circle?

    A. Disagreement on problems
    B. Savings not realized
    C. Lack of operations knowledge
    D. Resistance by implementation groups

13. Each of the following factors should be considered by a manager before deciding to fire a   13.____
poorly performing employee EXCEPT

    A. family situation
    B. previous rewards
    C. satisfaction of job–related needs
    D. adequacy of job training

14. In an open job market,   14.____

    A. it is difficult for all candidates to find a job
    B. there are more jobs available than qualified candidates
    C. there are more qualified candidates than jobs available
    D. the number of jobs available and qualified candidates are roughly equal

15. The principle of _____ states that a job grouping arrangement can change at different   15.____
levels of an organization.

    A. mutation   B. effort
    C. alternation   D. dispersion

16. According to Fiedler's theory, an employee–oriented style of leadership is most appropri-   16.____
ate when there is _____ level of certainty.

    A. any   B. a high
    C. a moderate   D. a low

17. Corporate strategic plans should NOT be   17.____

    A. short–term   B. original
    C. enlivening   D. decisional

18. In order to effectively solve a technical problem facing a computer company that wants to   18.____
enter the network computer market, a manager sends a questionnaire to various hardware experts throughout the country, soliciting their ideas about how to solve the problem.
This is an example of

    A. outsourcing   B. the Delphi technique
    C. nominal group technique   D. linear programming

19. The use of a standard cost center is appropriate *only* if   19.____

    A. the unit has significant control over other expenses
    B. standards for costs involved in producing a product cannot be accurately estimated
    C. it is used to measure the direct profit impact of the unit's efforts
    D. the unit cannot be held directly responsible for profit levels

20. Which type of managerial power is NOT based on the control of important organizational   20.____
resources?

    A. Information   B. Reward
    C. Coercive   D. Legitimate

21. A company performs an internal social audit in which the company's social activities over   21.____
a given period of time are merely listed. What type of assessment has been made?

    A. Cost–benefit analysis
    B. Program management approach
    C. Cost approach
    D. Inventory approach

22. A stock of items that have been produced and are awaiting transit to a customer is a(n)   22.____
_____ inventory.

    A. input   B. work–in–process
    C. finished–goods   D. feedforward

23. For _____, formal rules and procedures would be MOST effective.   23.____

    A. a research company
    B. a manufacturing company
    C. executive management
    D. test–marketing new products

24. Each of the following is an order cost for raw materials EXCEPT   24.____

    A. spoilage costs   B. transportation expenses
    C. bid preparation expenses   D. clerical expenses

25. A company's financial planning process typically includes each of the following EXCEPT   25.____
     A. predicting revenues
     B. budgeting
     C. forming separate planning staffs
     D. predicting costs

———

KEY (CORRECT ANSWERS)

1.	B	11.	B
2.	C	12.	C
3.	C	13.	A
4.	B	14.	B
5.	C	15.	C
6.	D	16.	C
7.	A	17.	A
8.	A	18.	B
9.	A	19.	D
10.	B	20.	A

21.	D
22.	C
23.	B
24.	A
25.	C

———

TEST 3

DIRECTIONS: Each question or incomplete statement is followed by several suggested answers or completions. Select the one that BEST answers the question or completes the statement. *PRINT THE LETTER OF THE CORRECT ANSWER IN THE SPACE AT THE RIGHT.*

1. Which of the following factors favors centralization of computerized information system resources?   1._____

   A. Higher degree of user control
   B. Avoidance of project backlog
   C. Cost–effectiveness of smaller computers
   D. Enhanced staff professionalism

2. Nonprogrammed decisions are MOST likely made by   2._____

   A. workers   B. low–level management
   C. middle–level management   D. executives

3. Each of the following is a factor in human resource planning EXCEPT   3._____

   A. the actions of competitors
   B. organizational goals
   C. labor trends
   D. the legal environment

4. Moving from _____ is an example of a radial career path.   4._____

   A. finance to marketing
   B. a line position to a staff position
   C. sales to management
   D. production to marketing

5. _____ is a statistical technique that uses periodic random samples taken during pro-duction to determine whether acceptable quality levels are being met.   5._____

   A. AQL
   B. Statistical process control
   C. EOQ
   D. Acceptance sampling

6. A company's ability to meet its maturing financial obligations is known as its _____ ratio.   6._____

   A. profitability   B. liquidity
   C. leverage   D. operating

7. Which of the following is a DISADVANTAGE associated with the use of external recruit-ment in the management of human resources?   7._____

   A. Fewer new ideas introduced into the company
   B. Susceptibility of selection to office politics
   C. Frequent necessity for extensive training
   D. Higher costs than internal recruitment

8. A company's management sets a goal defined as decreasing customer complaints. What type of goal has been set for the company? 8.____

   A. Operational   B. Resource
   C. Developmental   D. Improvement

9. Each of the following is a type of inventory EXCEPT 9.____

   A. in–process   B. raw materials
   C. subassemblies   D. finished products

10. Which of the following was NOT involved in developing the scientific approach to management? 10.____

   A. Babbage   B. Gantt   C. Taylor   D. Gilbreth

11. The decision to introduce a new product line is a(n) _____ decision. 11.____

   A. programmed   B. nonprogrammed
   C. detail   D. under certainty

12. A statistical analysis of a company's present employees is termed 12.____

   A. replacement chart   B. human resources audit
   C. performance ratio   D. staffing analysis

13. Medium–range capacity planning 13.____

   A. is typically made only by top management
   B. is aimed at ensuring that the capacities of the current major facilities are being utilized effectively within the context of the master production schedule
   C. is more likely to make use of capacity requirements planning than other methods
   D. provides information on possible means of making limited adjustments in capacity

14. Which of the following is NOT an element of a company's internal environment? 14.____

   A. Competitors   B. Personnel
   C. Budgeting   D. Working capital

15. The degree to which individuals can plan and control the work involved in their jobs is known as 15.____

   A. task identity   B. job depth
   C. job enrichment   D. job scope

16. The bottom–up method of budgeting works particularly well when 16.____

   A. unit managers have limited knowledge of the current situation
   B. first–line management is excluded from the process
   C. competitive pressures require a quick response
   D. there is a considerable degree of interdependence among units

17. What type of control is illustrated by production quality control?   17.____

   A. Screening   B. Process   C. Input   D. Output

18. As they are widely practiced, what is the main DISADVANTAGE associated with inter-   18.____
views as a means of job selection?

   A. Does not allow preliminary consideration
   B. Formality
   C. Adverse impact
   D. Low validity of information

19. _____ technology involves the highest demands for communication.   19.____

   A. Long–linked   B. Intensive
   C. Long–term   D. Mediating

20. Typically, which of the following steps in the budgetary process would occur LAST?   20.____

   A. Unit manager formulates performance targets.
   B. Top management outlines resource restraints.
   C. Top management combines unit budgets.
   D. Unit managers plan activities in detail.

21. Each of the following is typically a feature of a collective bargaining agreement EXCEPT   21.____

   A. union security clause
   B. rules for selection of arbitrators
   C. grievance procedures
   D. employment–at–will provision

22. Managers at the lowest level of management who are directly responsible for the work of   22.____
operating employees are known as _____ managers.

   A. functional level   B. general
   C. first–line   D. operative

23. _____ is a condition in which individuals engage in behaviors that are encouraged by   23.____
controls and related reward systems, even though the behaviors are actually inconsistent
with organizational goals.

   A. Role conflict   B. Extinction
   C. Negative reinforcement   D. Behavioral displacement

24. _____ data is a characteristic of the preceptive style of information–gathering.   24.____

   A. Expanding   B. Filtering
   C. Anticipating   D. Processing all

25. Which of the following is a characteristic of a bureaucratic organization?   25.____

   A. Stability   B. Uncertainty
   C. Flexibility   D. Dynamic structure

KEY (CORRECT ANSWERS)

1.	D	11.	B
2.	D	12.	B
3.	A	13.	D
4.	B	14.	A
5.	B	15.	B
6.	B	16.	C
7.	D	17.	B
8.	D	18.	D
9.	C	19.	B
10.	A	20.	C

21.	D
22.	C
23.	D
24.	B
25.	A

EXAMINATION SECTION
TEST 1

DIRECTIONS: Each question or incomplete statement is followed by several suggested
answers or completions. Select the one that BEST answers the question or
completes the statement. *PRINT THE LETTER OF THE CORRECT ANSWER
IN THE SPACE AT THE RIGHT.*

1. What type of reinforcement schedule is illustrated by a sales commission?   1._____

    A. Variable interval   B. Variable ratio
    C. Fixed interval   D. Fixed ratio

2. Mathematical models of management grew out of the _____ school of management.   2._____

    A. behavioral   B. systems
    C. contingency   D. scientific

3. *Individual equity* is the term for the extent to which   3._____

    A. pay rates allocated to specific individuals within the organization reflect variations
        in individual merit
    B. pay rates for particular jobs correspond to rates paid for similar jobs on the entire
        job market
    C. pay rates for various jobs inside the organization reflect the relative worth of those
        jobs
    D. compensable factors will be used to rate the worth of particular jobs

4. External audits of a company are normally performed every   4._____

    A. month   B. quarter
    C. year   D. two years

5. Production design is primarily concerned with _____ controls.   5._____

    A. marginal   B. process   C. input   D. output

6. The use of profit centers is appropriate only when   6._____

    A. it is used to measure the direct profit impact of the unit's efforts
    B. the unit is responsible for revenues, but does not have control over costs of the
        products they handle
    C. the unit has significant control over both costs and revenues
    D. the unit has control over investment decisions

7. A human resource manager's attention should be focused *primarily* on _____ during   7._____
managerial selection.

    A. job behavior   B. education level
    C. interview results   D. test scores

8. Which of the following computer–based information systems would be used to handle   8._____
word processing?

    A. TPS   B. MIS   C. OAS   D. DSS

9. The technique most useful for solving inventory problems is 9.____

    A. the Delphi technique   B. EOQ
    C. queuing   D. linear programming

10. A commission formed by a company is responsible to 10.____

    A. the general public   B. top–level management
    C. union leaders   D. stockholders

11. Each of the following is typically considered an ordering cost EXCEPT 11.____

    A. time   B. paperwork
    C. pilferage   D. postage

12. The use of scenarios may help managers to 12.____

    A. tighten day–to–day control
    B. examine different possible outcomes
    C. lengthen their reaction times
    D. anticipate the unknowable

13. During the appraisal of an employee's performance, a human resources manager tends 13.____
to compare the employee with other coworkers, rather than with a performance standard.
What type of rating error is occurring?

    A. Severity error   B. Contrast error
    C. Halo effect   D. Recency error

14. A supervisor rates a subordinate's initiative in an evaluation. This is an example of a(n) 14.____
_____ measure.

    A. cognitive   B. emotional
    C. qualitative   D. quantitative

15. A _____ budget is NOT an operating budget. 15.____

    A. profit   B. cash   C. expense   D. sales

16. Which of the following is a characteristic of a dynamic, complex company environment? 16.____

    A. Predictability
    B. Minimal need of sophisticated knowledge
    C. Numerous products and services
    D. Stability

17. A management information system is capable of each of the following EXCEPT 17.____

    A. making unprogrammed decisions
    B. providing early warning signals
    C. aiding decision–making
    D. automating clerical functions

18. In reinforcement theory, a technique that involves withholding previously available posi-   18.____
    tive consequences associated with a behavior, in order to *decrease* that behavior, is
    known as

    A. negative reinforcement   B. shaping
    C. punishment   D. extinction

19. Which of the following is NOT a disadvantage associated with highly specialized, low–   19.____
    discretion jobs?

    A. Failing to utilize employee intelligence
    B. Can result in unproductive behaviors
    C. Requiring hiring highly trained, more expensive labor
    D. Is inconsistent with values and lifestyles of employees

20. Which of the following is an example of a line department?   20.____

    A. Production   B. Finance
    C. Accounting   D. Research and development

21. A computer–based OAS system is intended *primarily* to   21.____

    A. execute routine transactions
    B. allow access to historic information
    C. improve the decision–making process
    D. facilitate communication

22. The process of acquainting new employees with the policies and standards of the com-   22.____
    pany is known as

    A. recruitment   B. orientation
    C. staffing   D. development

23. What is the term for the process of planning how to match supply with product or service   23.____
    demand over a time horizon of approximately one year?

    A. Capacity planning
    B. Forecasting
    C. Aggregate production planning
    D. Capacity requirements planning

24. Authority is correctly defined as the   24.____

    A. right to command and allocate resources
    B. accountability for achievement of goals and the efficient use of resources
    C. ability to influence others and control resources
    D. tendency to delegate tasks

25. According to situational leadership theory, when subordinates are able and willing to take   25.____
    appropriate responsibility, the appropriate leadership action is

    A. telling   B. selling
    C. delegating   D. participating

KEY (CORRECT ANSWERS)

1.	D	11.	C
2.	D	12.	B
3.	A	13.	B
4.	C	14.	C
5.	C	15.	B
6.	C	16.	C
7.	A	17.	A
8.	C	18.	D
9.	B	19.	C
10.	A	20.	A

21.	D
22.	B
23.	C
24.	A
25.	C

TEST 2

DIRECTIONS: Each question or incomplete statement is followed by several suggested answers or completions. Select the one that BEST answers the question or completes the statement. *PRINT THE LETTER OF THE CORRECT ANSWER IN THE SPACE AT THE RIGHT.*

1. Formalized job rotation programs are an example of   1.____

   A. training   B. career pathing
   C. recruitment   D. career counseling

2. A(n) _____ is an example of a process layout pattern.   2.____

   A. automobile assembly line
   B. food processing plant
   C. department store
   D. hospital

3. Which of the following is MOST likely to be an output from a computerized decision sup-   3.____
   port system?

   A. Projections   B. Summary reports
   C. Special reports   D. Schedules

4. When a company's replacement ratio is too high,   4.____

   A. replacement costs are too high
   B. there has been blocking of lower–level personnel
   C. insufficient weeding out has taken place
   D. a shortage of capable managers exists

5. An advantage associated with functional job grouping is that it   5.____

   A. facilitates organizational growth
   B. allows for easier hiring
   C. makes allocation of expenses easier
   D. facilitates coordination of top managers

6. Which of the following is an advantage associated with group decision–making?   6.____

   A. Choice of best alternative
   B. Less time–consuming
   C. Encouragement of innovative thinking
   D. Lower cost

7. On an organization chart, a solid line represents a(n)   7.____

   A. vertically integrated distribution channel
   B. indirect authority relationship
   C. horizontally integrated distribution channel
   D. line authority relationship

8. Which type of power, if exercised by a manager, is most likely to secure the commitment   8.____
   of subordinates?

   A. Legitimate   B. Reward
   C. Information   D. Referent

9. Which functional area of a company involves employee relations?   9.____

    A. Finance   B. Marketing
    C. Operations   D. Development

10. In a restaurant, a manager tallies the number of meals that are served within 15 minutes   10.____
of the customer orders. Which type of statistical quality control measure is the manager
using?

    A. Input   B. Marginal   C. Attribute   D. Variable

11. Low–level analysis is most likely to be processed by which of the following kinds of com-   11.____
puter information systems?

    A. TPS   B. DSS   C. OAS   D. MIS

12. Of the following, bottom–up budgeting best incorporates   12.____

    A. information on markets
    B. company planning parameters
    C. corporate goals
    D. industry projections

13. A worker experiences role _____ when his/her role within the organization is   13.____
unclear.

    A. discord   B. confusion
    C. ambiguity   D. conflict

14. Which of the following is a DISADVANTAGE associated with the use of pay as an   14.____
enforcer of employee performance?

    A. Time lag
    B. Low employee value
    C. Unequal pay among employees
    D. Erosion of value due to inflation

15. A company forms a temporary task force to study a problem in the community, and the   15.____
company's relationship to that problem. In terms of forming responses to social issues,
the company is practicing

    A. implicit change   B. structural change
    C. tokenism   D. functional change

16. A manager cannot assign probabilities to outcomes because he lacks information. The   16.____
manager is said to be making a decision under the condition of

    A. peril   B. certainty
    C. uncertainty   D. risk

17. Using the resource dependence approach to controls, a manager determines that her   17.____
unit is highly dependent on another unit for a particular resource, and that the expected
resource flows are unacceptable. It is also determined, however, that the control process
is probably not feasible for her department.
The manager should

    A. do nothing
    B. research a way to lower costs
    C. develop alternatives to control
    D. initiate the control process and try to adjust as it progresses

18. In the path–goal theory of leadership, the monitoring and control aspects of a leader's   18.____
behavior are examples of _____ behavior.

    A. participative   B. supportive
    C. instrumental   D. goal–oriented

19. When a particular task is simple and morale is not an issue, _____ communication is   19.____
probably the best method.

    A. circle   B. chain
    C. wheel   D. all–channel

20. In production and operations control, establishing a wage and salary structure is a func-   20.____
tion of

    A. production planning   B. production design
    C. production evaluation   D. selection

21. Which of the following is a type of inventory that consists of raw materials, components,   21.____
and subassemblies that are used in the production of an end product or service?

    A. Dependent demand inventory
    B. Bill of materials
    C. Independent demand inventory
    D. Cost inventory

22. _____ job testing is a means of measuring mainly mental, mechanical, and clerical   22.____
capacities.

    A. Personality   B. Ability
    C. Performance   D. Replacement

23. Historically, the management theory that first emphasized the need for companies to   23.____
operate in a rational manner rather than according to the whims of owners and managers
was the theory of _____ management.

    A. behaviorist   B. quantitative
    C. administrative   D. bureaucratic

24. Which of the following is an example of *discretionary* costs?   24.____

    A. Raw materials   B. Mortgages
    C. Sales commissions   D. Accounting fees

25. According to the systems approach to management, a system that operates in continual   25.____
    interaction with its environment is a(n) _____ system.

    A. open   B. feedback   C. charged   D. looped

_____

KEY (CORRECT ANSWERS)

1.	A	11.	D
2.	C	12.	A
3.	C	13.	C
4.	B	14.	A
5.	B	15.	D
6.	A	16.	C
7.	D	17.	C
8.	D	18.	C
9.	C	19.	C
10.	C	20.	B

21.	A
22.	B
23.	D
24.	D
25.	A

_____

TEST 3

DIRECTIONS: Each question or incomplete statement is followed by several suggested answers or completions. Select the one that BEST answers the question or completes the statement. *PRINT THE LETTER OF THE CORRECT ANSWER IN THE SPACE AT THE RIGHT.*

1. In a complex organization, the process of differentiation is likely to create problems associated with   1.____

    A. controlling size   B. management training
    C. coordination   D. motivation

2. Before a company can determine whether a management information system can be developed, a(n) _____ must be performed.   2.____

    A. algorithm   B. organizational chart
    C. feasibility study   D. conversion

3. Job testing is considered to be reliable when   3.____

    A. a good test score is a clear predictor of job success
    B. the test measures what it professes to measure
    C. the test is clearly related to the job
    D. the candidate would earn roughly the same score if the test were repeated

4. A control system that is self–regulating is said to be   4.____

    A. formalized   B. feedback–looped
    C. cybernetic   D. centralized

5. A company with many rules and procedures is usually described as having a(n) _____ span of control.   5.____

    A. almost nonexistent   B. narrow
    C. moderate   D. wide

6. Altogether, the various types of financial statements are considered _____ control.   6.____

    A. input   B. output   C. process   D. steering

7. A human resources manager teaches a new employee what to do, where to go for help, and what the company's important rules and policies are. What stage of orientation is being transacted?   7.____

    A. Implementation   B. Socialization
    C. Induction   D. Evaluation

8. The factors necessary in order to estimate partial–factor productivity are _____ and goods/services produced.   8.____

    A. labor hours
    B. labor hours, capital,
    C. capital, energy, materials,
    D. labor hours, capital, energy, technology, materials,

9. A company's _____ policy will decide the channels of distribution for a given product.   9.____

    A. financial   B. personnel
    C. marketing   D. product

10. Which of the following factors favors decentralization of computerized information system resources?   10.____

    A. Increasing availability of user–friendly software
    B. Staff specialization
    C. Easier control of corporate databases
    D. Potential for economies of scale

11. Each of the following typically helps implement authority in an organization EXCEPT   11.____

    A. span of control   B. centralization
    C. chain of command   D. familiarity

12. A maintenance goal   12.____

    A. implies a specific level of activity over time
    B. expresses the hope for growth
    C. uses action verbs to indicate change
    D. implies an effort to reorganize

13. Each of the following is a potential pitfall associated with financial controls EXCEPT   13.____

    A. neglecting to link controls to strategic planning process
    B. stifling innovation and creativity
    C. not sophisticated enough for organizational needs
    D. mixed messages about desired behaviors

14. The term for a statement of the skills, abilities, education, and previous work experience required to perform a particular job is the   14.____

    A. replacement chart   B. job specification
    C. job description   D. job analysis

15. The most successful use of the practice of job rotation is   15.____

    A. to create maximum flexibility through cross–training
    B. as an employee development tool
    C. to alleviate boredom with simple jobs
    D. to improve departmental loyalty

16. A company vice president delegates the authority to make a decision to a product manager. This is an example of   16.____

    A. outsourcing
    B. horizontal decentralization
    C. vertical decentralization
    D. centralized decision–making

17. Time–and–motion studies were first carried out by the _____ school of management.   17.____

    A. scientific   B. human relations
    C. classical   D. contingency

18. What is the term for the dispersion of organizational power?   18.____

    A. Unity of command   B. Span of control
    C. Formalization   D. Decentralization

19. _____ is the term for a technique to enhance creativity that relies on analogies.   19.____

    A. Storming   B. Entropy
    C. Cybernetics   D. Synectics

20. Which of the following is NOT considered to be a limitation associated with organization   20.____
charts?

    A. May not indicate real power and influence of people on the chart
    B. Does not show a picture of the structure at a particular point in time
    C. Frequently outdated
    D. May not show actual formal relationships

21. Which of the following is considered to be a *snapshot* of an organization at a particular   21.____
point in time?

    A. Expense budget   B. Income statement
    C. Balance sheet   D. Cash flow statement

22. Each of the following would be considered a safety and security need for an employee   22.____
EXCEPT

    A. merit pay raises
    B. job security
    C. pay raises references to the cost of living
    D. benefits

23. The behavioral model of management contributed the idea of   23.____

    A. quantitative aids for decision–making
    B. organization members as active human resources
    C. the potential importance of the environment to organizational success
    D. the need for a scientific approach to management

24. According to the contingency perspective, which of the following would NOT be a major   24.____
contingency factor for a business?

    A. Strategy   B. Size
    C. External environment   D. Technology in use

25. Which of the following is NOT an example of a single–use plan?   25.____

    A. Standing plan   B. Budget
    C. Project   D. Program

KEY (CORRECT ANSWERS)

1.	B		11.	D
2.	C		12.	A
3.	D		13.	C
4.	C		14.	B
5.	D		15.	B
6.	B		16.	C
7.	C		17.	C
8.	A		18.	D
9.	C		19.	D
10.	A		20.	B

21.	C
22.	A
23.	B
24.	B
25.	A

EXAMINATION SECTION
TEST 1

DIRECTIONS: Each question or incomplete statement is followed by several suggested answers or completions. Select the one that BEST answers the question or completes the statement. *PRINT THE LETTER OF THE CORRECT ANSWER IN THE SPACE AT THE RIGHT.*

1. Which of the following is NOT generally considered to be one of the current strengths of the field of organizational behavior?

    A. Its widespread application among organizations of all types
    B. Its interdisciplinary nature
    C. Its emerging base of research knowledge and conceptual frameworks
    D. The increasing acceptance of theory and research by practicing managers

1.____

2. Informal group requirements for the behavior of group members are known as

    A. mores   B. ethics   C. norms   D. codes

2.____

3. In most organizations, the generally accepted view concerning conflict is that

    A. a moderate level of conflict should be maintained in order to stimulate creativity
    B. most conflicts are the result of political alliances
    C. conflict should be avoided at all costs in order to maintain harmony
    D. the only meaningful conflict exists between management and labor

3.____

4. As a science, the field of organizational behavior involves each of the following objectives EXCEPT

    A. controlling and developing some human activity at work
    B. predicting future employee behaviors
    C. comparing the behaviors of employees at work and at home
    D. describing how people behave under a variety of conditions

4.____

5. The conventional wisdom about group effectiveness states that, for most situations, the ideal number of group members is

    A. 4   B. 5   C. 9   D. 12

5.____

6. One principle of organizational behavior is that when people are observed, or believe someone is paying close attention, they behave differently. This phenomenon is known as

    A. role ambiguity   B. the Peter principle
    C. Kaizen   D. the Hawthorne effect

6.____

7. In organizational management, the dominant approach to job redesign is

    A. enrichment   B. enlargement
    C. simplification   D. rotation

7.____

8. A complex set of forces affects the nature and operation of organizations today. Which of the following is NOT a significant force?

    A. Internal structures
    B. People in the organization
    C. Theory
    D. Technology

8.____

9. Which of the following is TRUE of informal organizations?

    A. Rewards and penalties are the most common sources of control.
    B. Their primary focus is position.
    C. Within them, behavior is governed by norms.
    D. The source of the leader's power is delegated by management.

9.____

10. What is the term for an employee's belief that he or she has the necessary capabilities to perform a specific task?

    A. Self-efficacy
    B. Instrumentality
    C. Valence
    D. Self-serving bias

10.____

11. Which of the following is an example of a person using a social exchange in order to gain political power?

    A. Manager X arranges with the vice president for production to transfer part of manager Y's department to manager X.
    B. A chief engineer helps a line manager to acquire a new machine on the condition that the manager support an upcoming project.
    C. A young manager joins a country club.
    D. An executive's personal assistant makes minor decisions for her.

11.____

12. Which of the following is a psychological/emotional reason that an employee might resist change in an organization?

    A. The desire to retain existing friendships
    B. A dislike in management or other change agent
    C. The possibility of less desirable conditions
    D. Political coalitions

12.____

13. In the verbal communication process, meaning is most commonly provided by

    A. inference
    B. context
    C. words
    D. body language

13.____

14. What is the term for the process by which organizations bring new employees into the culture?

    A. Socialization
    B. Integration
    C. Accommodation
    D. Attachment

14.____

15. Which of the following statements about organizational structure is FALSE?

    A. Is purposeful and goal-oriented
    B. Partly consists of recurring activities
    C. Influences behavior
    D. Depends on the organization's functions

15.____

16. According to the expectancy theory of motivation, which of the following is NOT a factor in an individual's motivation to perform a specific behavior?   16.____

    A. Instrumentality   B. Valence
    C. Frequency   D. Expectancy

17. The *dimensions* of organizational structure include each of the following EXCEPT   17.____

    A. formalization   B. size
    C. centralization   D. complexity

18. Which of the following is not a benefit that is typically associated with systematic organization development (OD)?   18.____

    A. Increased productivity
    B. Better conflict resolution
    C. Simplified evaluation processes
    D. Greater motivation

19. When one type of organization is laid over another, so that there are two chains of command directing individual employees, a _____ is created.   19.____

    A. matrix organization   B. needs hierarchy
    C. nominal group   D. role conflict

20. Prior to a planned change in an organization, which of the following data collection methods offers a combination of both validity and flexibility?   20.____

    A. Questionnaires   B. Secondary data
    C. Observation   D. Interviewing

21. What is the term for people whose roles are to stimulate, facilitate, and coordinate change within a system while remaining independent of it?   21.____

    A. Consultants   B. Boundary spanners
    C. Stressors   D. Change agents

22. Which of the following is LEAST likely to be a symptom of stress?   22.____

    A. Emotional instability   B. Lethargy
    C. Sleep problems   D. Digestive problems

23. An attempt to improve a job by making it more novel and challenging is known as   23.____

    A. job analysis   B. job enlargement
    C. norming   D. job enrichment

24. Personality   24.____

    A. appears to be organized into patterns that are observable and measurable to some degree
    B. is a product solely of social and cultural environments, and has no basis in biology
    C. involves unique characteristics, none of which are shared with others
    D. refers to the deeper core of a person, rather than superficial aspects

25. Which of the following steps in the two-way communication process occurs FIRST?   25.____

    A. Decoding   B. Encoding
    C. Using   D. Transmitting

KEY (CORRECT ANSWERS)

1.	A		11.	B
2.	C		12.	B
3.	A		13.	B
4.	C		14.	A
5.	B		15.	D
6.	D		16.	C
7.	A		17.	B
8.	C		18.	C
9.	C		19.	A
10.	A		20.	C

21.	D
22.	B
23.	D
24.	A
25.	B

TEST 2

DIRECTIONS: Each question or incomplete statement is followed by several suggested answers or completions. Select the one that BEST answers the question or completes the statement. *PRINT THE LETTER OF THE CORRECT ANSWER IN THE SPACE AT THE RIGHT.*

1. Key concepts of an organization include each of the following EXCEPT they

    A. are social systems
    B. cannot operate effectively without placing people above profit
    C. are formed on the basis of mutual interest
    D. must treat employees ethically

    1.____

2. Which of the following is an advantage associated with the use of nominal groups for problem-solving in organizations?

    A. Flexibility in process and procedures
    B. Equal participation of all members
    C. A feeling of cohesiveness among group members
    D. The opportunity for cross-fertilization of ideas

    2.____

3. The amount of control that an individual has to alter or influence a job and the surrounding environment is known as

    A. self-efficacy
    C. instrumentality
    B. job context
    D. job depth

    3.____

4. Participative leaders in an organization

    A. depend on the work group to establish goals
    B. decentralize authority
    C. structure the entire work situation for their employees
    D. avoid power and responsibility

    4.____

5. Which of the following is NOT one of the alternative consequences used in a system of behavioral modification?

    A. Extinction
    C. Goal-setting
    B. Positive reinforcement
    D. Punishment

    5.____

6. According to Hertzberg's motivational model, which of the following is a motivational factor?

    A. Achievement
    C. Fringe benefits
    B. Working conditions
    D. Job security

    6.____

7. What is the term for a specific type of group in which members in their group role have to be delegated by the authority to handle a problem at hand?

    A. Team
    C. Committee
    B. Informal organization
    D. Select session

    7.____

8. It is NOT an objective of work simplification to   8._____

    A. minimize the steps needed to perform a particular job
    B. remove unnecessary tasks
    C. improve a job by making it more exciting and challenging
    D. make an employee more productive by eliminating duplication of effort

9. In the field of organizational behavior, the tendency of some people to bring their individual thoughts in line with a group's beliefs is known as   9._____

    A. consonance   B. harmony
    C. projection   D. groupthink

10. According to Likert's organization development approach, which of the following is a causal variable?   10._____

    A. Skilled behaviors   B. Lower costs
    C. Policies   D. Motivation

11. Which of the following is an example of upward communication in an organization?   11._____

    A. Performance feedback   B. Suggestion boxes
    C. Social support   D. Job instruction

12. Of the following elements that can affect a person's perception, which is associated with the perceiver?   12._____

    A. Proximity   B. Values and attitudes
    C. Cultural context   D. Intensity

13. A manufacturing plant has divided the work into two general units: fabricating and assembly. This method of work division is an example of   13._____

    A. vertical specialization
    B. horizontal specialization
    C. divisional organization
    D. personal specialization

14. Which of the following is NOT a commonly encountered limitation of the expectancy model of motivation and rewards?   14._____

    A. Measurement of its variables is not entirely reliable.
    B. It does not consider employees completely as thinking individuals.
    C. It is not yet complete enough in its explanations for employee behavior.
    D. It often does not include predicted effects of multiple outcomes.

15. According to Oldham's job characteristics model, the job dimension that promotes increased feelings of personal responsibility is   15._____

    A. task significance   B. task identity
    C. autonomy   D. feedback

16. The brainstorming approach to conducting group processes typically offers each of the following advantages EXCEPT   16._____

    A. broader than normal participation
    B. greater than normal group cohesion

C. maintenance of strong task orientation
D. generally more enthusiastic group members

17. Managers that are described as achievement-oriented will most likely have difficulty in   17.____

    A. directing work activities
    B. delegating responsibility to other employees
    C. supplying specific feedback to employees
    D. taking on tasks that have a moderate failure rate

18. A reason why management may want to centralize authority in an organization would be   18.____
to

    A. encourage managerial delegation
    B. avoid duplication of functions
    C. encourage managerial autonomy
    D. lower administrative costs

19. The attribution model of human behavior considers three basic factors in assessing an   19.____
employee's behavior. Which of the following is not one of these?

    A. Consensus
    B. Distinctiveness
    C. Desirability
    D. Consistency of the behavioz

20. Of the following well-known leadership models, which places the greatest emphasis on   20.____
relationships and task guidance?

    A. Hersey and Blanchard's situational model
    B. The path-goal model
    C. Blake and Mouton's managerial grid
    D. Vroom's decision-making model

21. Managers who seek good relationships with subordinates but are unable to express their   21.____
own feelings are described as type

    A. A   B. B   C. C   D. D

22. In terms of consideration and structure, it is generally accepted that the most successful   22.____
managers in organizations are those who

    A. combine relatively high consideration and structure, giving somewhat more
       emphasis to consideration
    B. emphasize structure and de-emphasize consideration, making for a strictly con-
       trolled work situation
    C. combine relatively high consideration and structure, giving somewhat less empha-
       sis to consideration
    D. emphasize consideration and downplay structure, encouraging employees to for-
       mulate schedules and solve problems

23. Which of the following approaches to organizational behavior places the greatest empha-   23.____
    sis on employee growth and development?

    A. Systems   B. Results-oriented
    C. Contingency   D. Human resources

24. What is the term for an employee's beliefs about whether her achievements are the prod-   24.____
    uct of her efforts or of outside forces?

    A. Perceived job content   B. Locus of control
    C. Situational attribution   D. Collegiality

25. Most stress-performance models reveal that   25.____

    A. employees work best in a stress-free environment
    B. though employees often feel pressured in a high-stress environment, it is usually
        true that the greater the pressures on them, the higher their productivity
    C. performance depends more on internal stressors than external stressors
    D. either too little or too much stress on an employee will result in the deterioration of
        performance

KEY (CORRECT ANSWERS)

1.	B		11.	B
2.	B		12.	B
3.	D		13.	B
4.	B		14.	B
5.	C		15.	C
6.	A		16.	B
7.	C		17.	B
8.	C		18.	C
9.	D		19.	C
10.	C		20.	A

21.	B
22.	A
23.	D
24.	B
25.	D

EXAMINATION SECTION
TEST 1

DIRECTIONS: Each question or incomplete statement is followed by several suggested answers or completions. Select the one that BEST answers the question or completes the statement. *PRINT THE LETTER OF THE CORRECT ANSWER IN THE SPACE AT THE RIGHT.*

1. In the terminology of power bases, which of the following terms does NOT mean the same as the others?
   _____ power.

   A. Charismatic   B. Legitimate
   C. Referent   D. Personal

   1.____

2. To resist change, organizations often seem to be equipped with a self–correcting mechanism by which energies are called up to restore balance. This characteristic is called

   A. equipoise   B. stagnancy
   C. lock–step   D. homeostasis

   2.____

3. In an organization, *boundary spanners* are employees who play a major role in _____ communication.

   A. upward   B. downward
   C. lateral   D. public relations

   3.____

4. According to the equity theory of motivation and reward, under–rewarded individuals are most likely to

   A. work harder
   B. encourage other employees to obtain more rewards
   C. lower productivity
   D. discount rewards as significant

   4.____

5. Each of the following is considered to be an important function of work attitudes EXCEPT

   A. ego–defense   B. motivation
   C. knowledge   D. value expression

   5.____

6. A higher goal that integrates the efforts of two or more team members is described as

   A. fundamental   B. superordinate
   C. contributive   D. superfluous

   6.____

7. Which of the following is a cause of organizational, rather than individual, effectiveness?

   A. Ability   B. Motivation
   C. Environment   D. Stress

   7.____

8. In conducting an organizational confrontation meeting, which of the following steps is typically performed FIRST?

   A. Information collection
   B. Organization action planning
   C. Progress review
   D. Priority setting

   8.____

9. Most of the current thinking about job satisfaction and performance holds that   9.____

    A. high job satisfaction leads to high employee performance
    B. satisfaction affects performance, but performance does not affect satisfaction
    C. high performance contributes to high job satisfaction
    D. there is little correlation between job satisfaction and performance

10. Which of the following is NOT a key design decision involved in organizational structure?   10.____

    A. Division of labor   B. Authority
    C. Departmentalization   D. Size

11. Which of the following is a situational attribution?   11.____

    A. Ability   B. Internal motivation
    C. Skill   D. Office environment

12. Managers who are described as affiliation–oriented are probably most effective at   12.____

    A. assigning challenging tasks
    B. establishing a cooperative work environment
    C. monitoring work effectiveness
    D. directing work activities

13. One's ability to think in terms of models, frameworks, and broad relationships is known as   13.____

    A. conceptual skill   B. thematic apperception
    C. collectivism   D. inference

14. Social desirability bias often causes employees to   14.____

    A. make appraisals of co–workers that are based on their social functioning rather than job performance
    B. attribute their successes to skill, while blaming external factors for failures
    C. modify their responses to surveys or interviews based on what they think are desirable responses
    D. strive for leadership positions within an organization

15. In a work system, which of the following *initiations of actions* is most likely to create interpersonal problems?   15.____

    A. Initiation from a slow worker to a fast one
    B. From an inexperienced worker to one with more experience
    C. From an older person to a younger one
    D. From a worker with high status to one with lower status

16. Which of the following statements about *resilient* employees is generally FALSE? They   16.____

    A. set realistic goals
    B. can endure high–intensity stress for long periods of time
    C. have achieved a balanced life away from work
    D. tend to keep minor irritations in perspective

17. The existence of informal organizations within a larger organization often   17._____

    A. weakens motivation and satisfaction
    B. discourages cooperation
    C. increases workload for managers
    D. forms a less effective total system

18. The process of organizational socialization involves the accommodation stage, which is   18._____
characterized by each of the following individual behaviors EXCEPT

    A. clarifying one's role in the organization, and within formal and informal groups
    B. establishing new interpersonal relationships with co–workers and supervisors
    C. adequately dividing time and energy between the job and one's role in a family
    D. learning the tasks required to perform the job

19. The principle that two people in a continuing relationship feel a strong obligation to repay   19._____
their social debts to one another is the

    A. Hawthorne effect   B. law of empathy
    C. norm of reciprocity   D. law of effect

20. Which of the following is an example of continuous reinforcement of correct behaviors?   20._____

    A. Sales employees are given a bonus after every seventh appliance sold.
    B. A paycheck arrives every month.
    C. A lottery is held for employees with good attendance during intervening periods of
       varying lengths.
    D. A piece rate of $100 per suggestion is paid for each suggestion that is integrated
       into management policies.

21. Of the following categories of human values, which reflect an orientation toward prag-   21._____
matic and useful things?

    A. Political   B. Social
    C. Economic   D. Esthetic

22. As a firm grows into a larger organization, it becomes increasingly likely that it will   22._____
develop a departmental structure that is based on

    A. product   B. territory   C. function   D. customers

23. Ideally, non–programmed decisions in an organization should be the concern of   23._____

    A. top management   B. mid–level managers
    C. supervisors   D. line workers

24. Which of the following is NOT a negative consequence of turnover within an organiza-   24._____
tion?

    A. Demoralization of remaining workers
    B. Damaged reputation in the community
    C. Decreased opportunities for internal promotion
    D. High costs of replacing workers

25. Of the following bases of power in an organization, which is most likely to produce the commitment of workers? _____ power.

25.____

   A. Referent   B. Legitimate
   C. Reward   D. Expert

KEY (CORRECT ANSWERS)

1.	B		11.	D
2.	D		12.	B
3.	C		13.	A
4.	C		14.	C
5.	B		15.	B
6.	B		16.	B
7.	C		17.	A
8.	A		18.	C
9.	C		19.	C
10.	D		20.	D

21.	C
22.	A
23.	A
24.	C
25.	A

TEST 2

DIRECTIONS: Each question or incomplete statement is followed by several suggested answers or completions. Select the one that BEST answers the question or completes the statement. *PRINT THE LETTER OF THE CORRECT ANSWER IN THE SPACE AT THE RIGHT.* .

1. The physical and mental actions by an individual that change the form or content of an object or idea are known as

   A. leadership
   B. self–efficacy
   C. mores
   D. technology

   1.____

2. In an organization, a custodial leadership style is based primarily on

   A. leadership
   B. partnership
   C. economic resources
   D. power

   2.____

3. The primary advantage of Hersey and Blanchard's situational leadership model is its

   A. emphasis on goals
   B. thoroughness in including elements that determine leadership style
   C. widely accepted research base
   D. simplicity

   3.____

4. Which of the following is a means of coping with stress on the job?

   A. Participating in a personal wellness program
   B. Taking early retirement
   C. Acquiring assertiveness skills that allow one to confront stressors
   D. Finding alternative employment

   4.____

5. Which of the following approaches to conflict can be truly viewed as a strategy for resolution?

   A. Compromising
   B. Smoothing
   C. Confronting
   D. Forcing

   5.____

6. In the motivational process of goal–setting, the manager's first step is typically to

   A. specify goals
   B. challenge employees
   C. build and reinforce employee self–efficacy
   D. establish goal acceptance

   6.____

7. In order to gain political power, a newly–hired controller arranges to increase the size of her office, richly decorate it, and hire a personal assistant. The tactic being used in this situation is

   A. power and status symbols
   B. building alliances
   C. power play
   D. identifying with a higher authority

   7.____

8. Which of the following is the proponent of the E–R–G model of motivation?

    A. McClelland   B. Alderfer
    C. Hertzberg   D. Maslow

8.____

9. In most multi–national corporations, the prevalent departmental basis is

    A. customer   B. product   C. territory   D. function

9.____

10. In terms of people and attitudes, an *affect* is

    A. a person's intention to act toward someone or something in a certain way
    B. the perception, opinion, or belief segment of an attitude
    C. a positive or negative feeling or state of readiness
    D. the emotional segment of an attitude

10.____

11. Which of the following is not a style of leadership that is identified by the path–goal model?

    A. Directive   B. Achievement–oriented
    C. Free–rein   D. Participative

11.____

12. The rise of organization development (OD) as a systematic process occurred in the 1950s and 1960s primarily because

    A. many managers failed to recognize that organizations were held together by dynamic interpersonal relationships
    B. market forces were too static to prompt much change
    C. the growing environmental movement placed additional demands on organizations
    D. most employees demonstrated a profound resistance to change

12.____

13. A disadvantage associated with product departmentalization in organizations is that it

    A. often limits the resources necessary for managers to carry out profit plans
    B. does not encourage autonomy
    C. contains a degree of redundancy
    D. tends to restrict initiative

13.____

14. The type of counseling that is most often used in organizations to help individuals adjust to stress is

    A. non–directive   B. directive
    C. psychoanalytical   D. participative

14.____

15. Which of the following is considered to be a task leadership role in groups?

    A. Reducing tension and reconciling disagreements
    B. Defining a problem or goal for the group
    C. Facilitating participation of all members
    D. Supporting the contributions of others

15.____

16. In behavioral modification, negative reinforcement occurs when a behavior is   16.____

    A. discouraged by the administration of an unfavorable consequence
    B. ignored
    C. accompanied by the removal of an unfavorable consequence
    D. rewarded with a favorable consequence

17. Which of the following is not a problem commonly associated with the job design process?   17.____

    A. Delay in production of tangible performance improvements
    B. Possible resistance by labor unions
    C. Tendency to reduce the perceived significance of work tasks
    D. Time consumption

18. Which of the following terms is used to describe a person in an organization who is a manipulator and abuser of power?   18.____

    A. Locus of control   B. Macchiavellian
    C. Delphic   D. Maverick

19. What is the commonly used term for the rewards and penalties that a group uses to persuade members to conform?   19.____

    A. Norms   B. Sanctions   C. Mores   D. Inhibitors

20. Which of the following does NOT accurately describe the process of organizational development (OD)?   20.____

    A. It is carefully planned in advance.
    B. It is organization wide.
    C. It is an intervention that uses the principles of behavioral science.
    D. Its management begins at many different levels.

21. According to the leadership approach proposed by Stephen Kerr, which of the following is a leadership neutralizer?   21.____

    A. Increased group status
    B. Employees with high ability or experience
    C. Gain–sharing reward systems
    D. Leader as the central source of information

22. Which of the following is a disadvantage associated with the practice of job rotation?   22.____
It

    A. can make work burdensome and repetitive
    B. doesn't provide substantive changes in job content
    C. can require extensive retraining
    D. involves a temporary decrease in productivity

23. Which of the following organizational decisions is in line with the idea of high complexity?   23.____

    A. Functional departments   B. Centralized authority
    C. Narrow spans of control   D. Low specialization

24. The law of effect states that   24._____

    A. a person tends to repeat behavior that is accompanied by favorable consequences and tends not to repeat behavior that is accompanied by unfavorable consequences

    B. the alteration of an individual's surroundings influences a person's feelings and behaviors

    C. the mere observation of a group tends to change the way it operates

    D. a person tends to pay attention to those features of the work environment which reinforce one's own expectations

25. When an organization achieves a unity of effort among its different units and individuals   25._____
through rules, planning, and leadership, _____ has been achieved.

    A. decentralization   B. integration

    C. mechanization   D. differentiation

KEY (CORRECT ANSWERS)

1.	D		11.	C
2.	C		12.	A
3.	D		13.	C
4.	A		14.	D
5.	C		15.	B
6.	C		16.	C
7.	A		17.	C
8.	B		18.	B
9.	C		19.	B
10.	D		20.	D

21.	B
22.	B
23.	C
24.	A
25.	B

EXAMINATION SECTION
TEST 1

DIRECTIONS: Each question or incomplete statement is followed by several suggested answers or completions. Select the one that BEST answers the question or completes the statement. *PRINT THE LETTER OF THE CORRECT ANSWER IN THE SPACE AT THE RIGHT.*

1. In terms of organizational behavior, *transformational* leaders can be described in each of the following ways EXCEPT they

   A. stimulate learning among employees
   B. create and communicate a vision for the organization
   C. help employees narrow their focus
   D. charismatically model desired behaviors

   1.____

2. When people work in teams, they often engage in a set of activities that help others focus on what is currently going on around them. Collectively, these activities are known a

   A. constructive reaction   B. polarization
   C. process consultation   D. rationalization

   2.____

3. Which of the following are typically considered to be necessary elements of self-leadership?
   I. Leading oneself to perform naturally motivating tasks
   II. Determining and obtaining rewards when none are offered from an external source
   III. Managing oneself to do work that is required but not naturally rewarding
   The CORRECT answer is:

   A. I *only*   B. I, III
   C. II, III   D. All of the above

   3.____

4. Managing conflict in organizations often requires assertive behavior. Which of the following stages in assertive behavior is generally performed LAST?

   A. Indicating consequences
   B. Empathizing
   C. Presenting problem-solving strategies
   D. Describing the behavior that is the source of the transaction

   4.____

5. The tendency for one to ascribe the achievements of others to good luck or easy tasks, while assuming their failures to be due to a lack of ability or experience, is known as

   A. fundamental attribution bias   B. the Hawthorne effect
   C. self-serving bias   D. kaizen

   5.____

6. Which of the following statements about groups and individuals in organizations is FALSE?

    A. Group decisions tend to dilute and thin out responsibility.
    B. Group members often escalate their commitment to bad ideas in order to save face.
    C. Group meetings are among the slowest and most costly ways of getting things done.
    D. In groups, people tend to be more conservative with an organization's resources.

6.____

7. Each of the following is usually a major challenge for a manager who is using the equity model of motivation and reward EXCEPT

    A. identifying employees' choice of references
    B. evaluating employee perceptions of inputs and outcomes
    C. developing greater awareness of their own attributional processes
    D. measuring employee assessments of their inputs and outcomes

7.____

8. A manager with a life position of *I'm not OK–you're OK* will most likely attempt to resolve conflict by

    A. forcing
    C. confronting
    B. smoothing
    D. avoiding

8.____

9. When employees respond to frustration in ways such as pouting or self-pity, they are said to be reacting by means of

    A. passive aggression
    C. withdrawal
    B. fixation
    D. regression

9.____

10. Which of the following does NOT describe an organization that is likely to use a matrix structure?
It

    A. Faces uncertainties that create high information processing requirements
    B. Requires responses to rapid change in more than one environment
    C. Must deal with financial and human resources restraints
    D. Requires staff to be highly generalized, rather than specialized

10.____

11. The practice of total quality management (TQM) is most likely to be an element in an approach to organizational behavior that is oriented to

    A. contingencies
    C. systems
    B. human resources
    D. results

11.____

12. Which of the following is/are characteristics of Delphi decision-making groups?
    I. Responses are typically given in oral presentations.
    II. A panel of experts is chosen to address an issue.
    III. Members meet face-to-face to discuss problems.
The CORRECT answer is:

    A. I *only*
    C. *I, III*
    B. II *only*
    D. All of the above

12.____

13. A drawback associated with the application of organizational behavior modification is that it

    A. overemphasizes the role of modeling and imitation in determining behavior
    B. tends to ignore cognitive processes
    C. does not encourage managers to become conscious motivators
    D. takes time away from monitoring employee behaviors

13.____

14. Among the following descriptions of an organizational structure, which does NOT mean the same as the others?

    A. Bureaucratic   B. System 4
    C. Classical   D. Mechanistic

14.____

15. According to Hertzberg's motivational model, which of the following would be the strongest motivator for an employee?

    A. Vacation
    B. A feeling of responsibility
    C. Health insurance
    D. A retirement plan

15.____

16. Which of the following is not typically a problem associated with upward communication in organizations?

    A. Overload   B. Delay
    C. Filtering   D. Distortion

16.____

17. Which of the following types of personality assessments is often avoided by managers because of its association with psychological problems?

    A. Behavioral measure
    B. Inkblot test
    C. Minnesota Multiphasic Personality Inventory (MMPI)
    D. Myers-Briggs Type Indicator (MBTI)

17.____

18. The credibility of interpersonal communication is often affected by each of the following factors EXCEPT

    A. dynamism   B. trustworthiness
    C. status   D. expertise

18.____

19. What is the term for a widespread belief that all people in an organization should constantly drive themselves to seek ways of improving everything around them?

    A. Transformational modeling   B. Kaizen
    C. Action planning   D. Achievement modeling

19.____

20. In the terminology of power bases, _____ power is delegated from higher established authorities to others.

    A. personal   B. reward
    C. legitimate   D. referent

20.____

21. The *impostor* phenomenon refers to 21.____

    A. an employee's perception that he or she is not really as capable as it may appear
    B. an employee's tendency to claim credit for success that has not been earned, while minimizing their responsibility for problems
    C. the belief that a manager is only pretending to represent the interests of employees
    D. an employee's varying desires for behavioral rewards over a given period of time

22. According to most research, approximately _____% of the information that is delivered 22.____
through the informal network, or *grapevine*, is accurate.

    A. 10   B. 35   C. 50   D. 75

23. If a major goal of an organization is to provide a training ground for managerial person- 23.____
nel, the most effective method of departmentalization for this goal would be

    A. product-based   B. territorial
    C. customer-based   D. functional

24. Which of the following is NOT typically a recommended guideline for making changes 24.____
within an organization?

    A. If long periods pass between needed changes, make minor changes to keep employees accustomed to the process.
    B. Involve employees throughout the change process.
    C. Teach employees to expect continual change.
    D. Change gradually rather than dramatically.

25. An organizational culture in which people tend to interpret cues literally, rely on written 25.____
rules and legal documents, and value expertise and performance is described as

    A. micromotivated   B. low context
    C. mechanistic   D. high functioning

KEY (CORRECT ANSWERS)

1.	C		11.	D
2.	C		12.	B
3.	B		13.	B
4.	A		14.	B
5.	A		15.	B
6.	D		16.	A
7.	C		17.	C
8.	B		18.	C
9.	D		19.	B
10.	D		20.	C

21.	A
22.	D
23.	B
24.	A
25.	B

TEST 2

DIRECTIONS: Each question or incomplete statement is followed by several suggested answers or completions. Select the one that BEST answers the question or completes the statement. *PRINT THE LETTER OF THE CORRECT ANSWER IN THE SPACE AT THE RIGHT.*

1. An important function of stress counseling in an organization is to allow for _____, which is another term for the release of emotional tension.　　　　1.____

   A. reassurance
   C. spillover
   B. catharsis
   D. flushing

2. According to the transactional analysis model, each of the following describes the adult ego state EXCEPT　　　　2.____

   A. calculating
   C. unemotional
   B. instructive
   D. rational

3. Content theories of motivation argue that　　　　3.____

   A. most people dislike work
   B. external consequences determine behavior
   C. most people are affiliation-oriented
   D. internal needs lead to behavior

4. The degree to which an organization can be described as *centralized* is made difficult by a number of factors.
   Which of the following is NOT one of these?　　　　4.____

   A. Not all decisions are of equal importance in organizations.
   B. Spans of control tend to fluctuate in accordance with the turnover rate.
   C. People at the same level in an organization often have different decision-making authority.
   D. Individuals may not perceive that they have authority, though their job descriptions include it.

5. In expectancy theory, *valence* refers to　　　　5.____

   A. how much a person wants a particular reward
   B. the belief that one has the necessary capabilities to perform a task
   C. a person's estimate of whether effort will result in success
   D. one's estimate of how much a performance will be rewarded

6. Which of the following is not considered to be a component dimension of self-efficacy?　　　　6.____

   A. Generality
   C. Strength
   B. Magnitude
   D. Performance

7. Managers who are more interested in their own opinions than those of others are described as type

    A. A   B. B   C. C   D. D

7.____

8. Which of the following steps in a typical organization development (OD) process typically is performed FIRST?

    A. Problem solving   B. Action planning
    C. Data collection   D. Confrontation

8.____

9. Which of the following is most likely to be a supervisory role within the self-managing team structure?

    A. Coach   B. Expert
    C. Problem solver   D. Teacher

9.____

10. Which of the following has developed a theory about the human body's response to stress?

    A. Maslow   B. Piaget   C. Skinner   D. Selye

10.____

11. *Face-saving* becomes a powerful individual driving force when interpersonal conflict

    A. threatens an individual's status
    B. results from different sets of values
    C. is caused by a lack of trust
    D. is moderate in response to organizational change

11.____

12. In behavioral modification theory, what is the term for the gradual diminishment of a behavior that is not met with positive reinforcement?

    A. Punishment   B. Extinction
    C. Negative scheduling   D. Atrophy

12.____

13. Mechanistic organizations tend to be more effective than organic ones in situations where

    A. environmental forces such as the market and technology are rapidly changing
    B. tasks are flexible and fluid
    C. workers are capable of directing their own work
    D. employees are threatened by ambiguity and insecurity

13.____

14. The primary purpose of directive counseling in an organization is to

    A. clarify thinking   B. reorient
    C. advise   D. reassure

14.____

15. Each of the following is a condition that is ideal for conducting a job satisfaction survey EXCEPT   15._____

    A.   both results and action plans are revealed to employees
    B.   management is capable of taking follow-up action
    C.   employees are involved in planning the survey
    D.   top management's involvement in the survey is downplayed to workers

16. When one group in an organization must complete its task before another can begin, a situation of_____ has arisen.   16._____

    A.   sequential interdependence
    B.   boundary spanning
    C.   role ambiguity
    D.   horizontal integration

17. Which of the following is an example of a person using selective service in order to gain political power?
A(n)   17._____

    A.   mail room clerk makes several key routing decisions
    B.   salesman intentionally neglects the most unproductive accounts in his territory
    C.   information manager and a financial vice president working together on a proposal for a new information system
    D.   purchasing manager giving more attention to cooperative associates in processing orders

18. In spite of their complexity, matrix organizations are used for a number of reasons. Which of the following is NOT one of these?
They   18._____

    A.   have a more flexible structure
    B.   lend more authority to position power
    C.   develop a strong team identity
    D.   focus on individual projects rather than the status quo

19. Which of the following models of organizational behavior is most likely to meet the needs of status and recognition in employees?   19._____

    A.   Autocratic   B.   Collegial
    C.   Custodial   D.   Supportive

20. Which of the following is considered to be a disadvantage associated with the dialectic decision method (DDM)?   20._____

    A.   Restrictive technology requirements
    B.   Confidence among members about choices made
    C.   Generally poorer understanding of the proposals under consideration
    D.   A tendency to focus more on who were better debaters rather than the quality of the decision

21. Fiedler's contingency model of leadership emphasizes

    A. employee orientation and task orientation
    B. people and production
    C. employee acceptance and decision quality
    D. relationships and task guidance

21.____

22. Which of the following is a conclusion of Fiedler's contingency model of leadership?

    A. In situations where tasks are highly routine and the leader has good relations with employees, employees may perceive a task orientation as not supportive to their job performance.
    B. The considerate leader is most likely to be effective when task structure is poor.
    C. The structured leader is most likely to be effective when task structure is good.
    D. In highly unstructured situations, the leader's structure and control are seen as removing undesirable ambiguity and the resulting anxiety.

22.____

23. Which of the following statements about Hertzberg's motivational model is FALSE?

    A. It demonstrates the powerful influence in intrinsic rewards.
    B. It tends to overemphasize the importance of pay and status as motivators.
    C. The classification of its motivators is not universal.
    D. It does not apply well to line workers.

23.____

24. Which of the following are symptoms of groupthink?
    I.   Tendency toward high-risk group decisions
    II. Self-censorship
    III. Stereotyping
    IV. Infighting
The CORRECT answer is:

    A. I, III   B. II, III
    C. III, IV   D. All of the above

24.____

25. Which of the following is most likely to be a benefit associated with the existence of informal organizations within a larger organization?

    A. Reduces interpersonal and intergroup conflicts
    B. Discourages undesirable rumors
    C. Improves communication
    D. Discourages conformity

25.____

KEY (CORRECT ANSWERS)

1.	B		11.	A
2.	B		12.	B
3.	D		13.	D
4.	B		14.	C
5.	A		15.	D
6.	D		16.	A
7.	C		17.	D
8.	C		18.	B
9.	A		19.	D
10.	D		20.	D

21.	A
22.	D
23.	B
24.	B
25.	C

EXAMINATION SECTION
TEST 1

DIRECTIONS: Each question or incomplete statement is followed by several suggested answers or completions. Select the one that BEST answers the question or completes the statement. *PRINT THE LETTER OF THE CORRECT ANSWER IN THE SPACE AT THE RIGHT.*

1. The conventional wisdom about group effectiveness states that once a group's member-ship rises above _____, communication tends to become focused within a few members.

    A. 3   B. 5   C. 7   D. 9

1.____

2. Which of the following is a reason why management may want to centralize authority in an organization?

    A. Encouraging the development of professional managers
    B. Avoiding duplication of functions
    C. Encouraging competitiveness in the organization
    D. Discouraging managerial delegation

2.____

3. Which of the following is a process theory of motivation?

    A. E-R-G model
    B. Two-factor model
    C. Organizational behavior modification
    D. Maslow's hierarchy of needs

3.____

4. Which of the following organizational decisions is in line with the idea of centralization?

    A. Product departments   B. Delegated authority
    C. Wide spans of control   D. Low specialization

4.____

5. Committees within an organization often create special human problems, most likely because

    A. people are unable to get along with outsiders
    B. people are unable to make adjustments from their normal work roles and relation-ships
    C. lines of authority are not clearly drawn
    D. it is difficult to agree on the nature of problems

5.____

6. Which of the following is considered to be a direct cause of group productivity?

    A. Member motivation   B. Norms
    C. Group size   D. Group cohesiveness

6.____

7. In general, people tend to pay attention to those features of their work environment which are consistent with or which reinforce their own expectations. This phenomena is known as

    A. adverse selection   B. ethnocentrism
    C. individualization   D. selective perception

7.____

8. Within an organization, a supervisor's span of control is LEAST likely to depend on the   8.____

    A.   rate of change in the organization
    B.   ability of the supervisor to delegate work to others
    C.   number of potential relationships
    D.   amount of personal contact between employees

9. What is the term for a mental state of anxiety that occurs when there's a conflict among a   9.____
   person's attitudes and beliefs after a decision has been made?

    A.   Paradox   B.   Cognitive dissonance
    C.   Situational assonance   D.   Paranoia

10. In the non–verbal communication process, meaning is most commonly provided by   10.____

    A.   body language   B.   symbols
    C.   words   D.   context

11. The general consensus about quality circles is that when they are used, the ideal size is   11.____
    _____ members.

    A.   4   B.   8   C.   11   D.   15

12. The safety department of an organization makes three safety checks a year in each   12.____
   department, on a random basis. According to the theory of organizational behavior
   modification, the department is practicing a _____ schedule of behavioral reinforcement.

    A.   variable interval   B.   fixed interval
    C.   variable ratio   D.   fixed ratio

13. In organizational decision-making, the alternative outcome relationship is based on each   13.____
   of the following possible conditions EXCEPT

    A.   risk   B.   certainty
    C.   feasibility   D.   uncertainty

14. In job design, which of the following is a way for management to increase an employee's   14.____
   core job dimensions?

    A.   Separating task elements
    B.   Opening feedback channels
    C.   Assigning smaller fragments of work
    D.   Clearly delineating work methods to be used

15. In order to achieve the maximum benefits of bureaucratic design in an organization,   15.____

    A.   employment should be based on technical qualifications
    B.   tasks should be divided along generalized lines
    C.   employees should relate in an informal, personal manner
    D.   members or offices should report to more than one manager

16. During planned change in an organization, the *unfreezing* situation is characterized by each of the following EXCEPT

    A. the linking of rewards with a willingness to change
    B. the strengthening of social supports
    C. experiences designed to help individuals see a current routine as less attractive
    D. the physical removal of the individual or group being changed from accustomed routines

16.____

17. *Theory X* of human behavior can be described as a(n)

    A. model that adapts the elements of Japanese management systems to the U.S. organizational culture
    B. humanistic and supportive set of assumptions
    C. approach to management that emphasizes cooperation and interdependence
    D. autocratic and traditional set of assumptions

17.____

18. In the theory and practice of contingency design, environmental factors are divided into subenvironments which influence the structure of an organization. Which of the following is not a type of subenvironment?

    A. Technical
    B. Market
    C. Strategic
    D. Production

18.____

19. The practice of allowing employees to perform a complete piece of work is commonly referred to as

    A. job enlargement
    B. modulation
    C. task identity
    D. positive reinforcement

19.____

20. Which of the following is considered to be a social leadership role in groups?

    A. Evaluating the group's effectiveness
    B. Summarizing the discussion
    C. Determining whether agreement has been reached
    D. Requesting facts, ideas, or opinions from members

20.____

21. Which of the following is described as a *primary* individual need?

    A. Sense of duty
    B. Competitiveness
    C. Safety
    D. Self-esteem

21.____

22. Which of the following is TRUE of an organization with an organic structure?

    A. Motivation taps physical, security, and economic motives
    B. Performance goals are low and passively sought
    C. Information flows upward, downward, and laterally
    D. Interaction is closed and restricted

22.____

23. Which of the following is NOT generally considered to be a necessary prerequisite for the job redesign process?

    A. Securing the involvement of unions
    B. Determining the exact size of the necessary workforce
    C. Making changes in the work itself
    D. Using monetary rewards

23._____

24. In Fiedler's contingency model of leadership, a structured leader is most likely to be effective in a position of _____ power, _____ task structure, and _____ leader member relations.

    A. weak; high; moderately good
    B. high; high; good
    C. weak; low; poor
    D. high; low; good

24._____

25. Each of the following is generally considered to be a logical, rational reason for an employee who resists change in the organization EXCEPT the .

    A. economical costs of change
    B. need for security
    C. extra effort required to relearn
    D. technical feasibility of change

25._____

KEY (CORRECT ANSWERS)

1.	C		11.	B
2.	B		12.	A
3.	C		13.	C
4.	C		14.	B
5.	B		15.	A
6.	A		16.	B
7.	D		17.	D
8.	C		18.	C
9.	B		19.	C
10.	A		20.	A

21.	C
22.	C
23.	B
24.	C
25.	B

TEST 2

DIRECTIONS: Each question or incomplete statement is followed by several suggested answers or completions. Select the one that BEST answers the question or completes the statement. *PRINT THE LETTER OF THE CORRECT ANSWER IN THE SPACE AT THE RIGHT.*

1. Which of the following is TRUE of formal organizations?   1.____

    A. Within them, behavior is governed by sanctions.
    B. Their leaders' power is granted by the group.
    C. Their primary focus is on people, rather than positions.
    D. Their major concepts are authority and responsibility.

2. Which of the following steps in the two-way communication process occurs LAST?   2.____

    A. Using   B. Decoding
    C. Accepting   D. Providing feedback

3. Which of the following is considered to be a potential disadvantage associated with the Delphi decision-making process?   3.____

    A. Inadequate time for reflection
    B. Few opportunities for interaction between panelists
    C. Inefficient uses of experts' time
    D. Interpersonal problems among panelists

4. A person's attitudes are considered to be composed of each of the following EXCEPT   4.____

    A. experiences   B. intentions to act
    C. feelings   D. thoughts

5. Which of the following is another term for product departmentalization?   5.____

    A. Horizontal specialization
    B. Divisional organization
    C. Categorical compartmentalization
    D. Vertical integration

6. Oldham's job characteristics model suggests that there are critical psychological states which are crucial in determining a person's motivation and job satisfaction. Which of the following is NOT one of these?   6.____

    A. Knowledge   B. Responsibility
    C. Meaningfulness   D. Satisfaction

7. The principal advantage of using functional departmentalization within an organization is   7._____

    A. provision of an ideal training ground for new workers
    B. clear priority of organizational goals over departmental goals
    C. easier expansion into new geographic areas
    D. efficiency

8. Which of the following reports or statistics relating to stress in U.S. organizations is inac-   8._____
    curate or false?

    A. 70 percent of workers report that stress-related health problems have made them
        less productive.
    B. 30 percent of executives believe their work has adversely affected their health.
    C. The annual cost of stress-related absenteeism, lower productivity, rising health
        insurance costs, and other medical expenses is now somewhere near $100 million.
    D. Stress-related workers' compensation claims have tripled in the last decade, jump-
        ing from 5 percent to 15 percent of all claims.

9. What is the term for the cyclical process of identifying system problems, gathering data,   9._____
    taking corrective action, and making ongoing adjustments?

    A. Consultative management   B. Affirmative action
    C. Double-loop learning   D. Action research

10. Symptoms of *burnout* on the job do NOT typically include   10._____

    A. a feeling of inability to accomplish goals
    B. emotional exhaustion
    C. chronic worry
    D. a feeling of detachment from clients and work

11. What is the term for the process of reducing a communication to a few basic details that   11._____
    can be remembered and passed on to others?

    A. Filtering   B. Seep
    C. Distorting   D. Distilling

12. _____ personality theories are based on the premise that predispositions direct the   12._____
    behavior of an individual in a consistent pattern.

    A. Psychodynamic   B. Behavioral
    C. Trait   D. Humanistic

13. Each of the following is a commonly used method for encouraging upward communica-   13._____
    tion within organizations EXCEPT

    A. employee meetings   B. open-door policies
    C. grievance systems   D. suggestion screening

14. According to Likert's organization development approach, which of the following is/are   14._____
    intervening variables?

    A. Attitudes   B. Leadership behavior
    C. Organizational structure   D. Customer loyalty

15. Of the following, which is NOT a type of barrier to effective communication?　　15.____

    A. Personal　　　B. Semantic　　　C. Syntactic　　　D. Physical

16. Which of the following is the proponent of the two-factor model of motivation?　　16.____

    A. Vroom　　　　　　　　B. Alderfer
    C. Hertzberg　　　　　　D. Maslow

17. Which of the following is a perceptual defect which causes a person to attribute his or her　　17.____
own characteristics and feelings to others?

    A. Projection
    B. Self-serving bias
    C. Fundamental attribution bias
    D. Stereotyping

18. Each of the following behaviors is considered to be a part of a leader's *coaching* role in　　18.____
an organization EXCEPT

    A. listening to employee input
    B. personally participating in work tasks
    C. selecting the appropriate personnel for tasks
    D. reviewing resource needs

19. Which of the following is a procedure that is generally observed by nominal groups?　　19.____

    A. Group members individually designate their preferences for alternatives by secret
       ballot.
    B. Ideas are shared with others in an open, non-structured format.
    C. Group members develop solutions cooperatively, in discussion.
    D. Several periods of time are allotted for questioning.

20. Which of the following is LEAST likely to be a cause of stress on the job?　　20.____

    A. Differences in company values and employee values
    B. Time pressures
    C. Narrowly-defined roles
    D. Work overload

21. Most often, the rationale for grouping jobs in an organization rests on　　21.____

    A. the necessity for coordinating them
    B. the existing formal hierarchy
    C. the need for lines of communication
    D. industry standards

22. According to the performance model, potential performance is a product of　　22.____

    A. motivation and experience
    B. ability and motivation
    C. satisfaction and ability
    D. ability and experience

23. In terms of organizational structure, it has become standard practice to use the term _____ to refer to the number of different units at the same level.   23.____

    A. boundary division
    B. formalization
    C. horizontal differentiation
    D. vertical differentiation

24. In nondirective counseling that occurs in the workplace, an emphasis is generally placed on   24.____

    A. psychological adjustment
    B. social integration
    C. solution of current problems
    D. individual performance

25. In the path-goal model of leadership, which of the following steps is typically performed FIRST?   25.____

    A. Appropriate goals are established.
    B. Leader connects rewards with goals.
    C. Leader provides assistance.
    D. Leader identifies employee needs.

KEY (CORRECT ANSWERS)

1. D		11. A	
2. D		12. C	
3. B		13. D	
4. A		14. A	
5. B		15. C	
6. D		16. C	
7. D		17. A	
8. C		18. B	
9. D		19. A	
10. C		20. C	

21.	A
22.	B
23.	C
24.	A
25.	D

EXAMINATION SECTION
TEST 1

DIRECTIONS: Each question or incomplete statement is followed by several suggested answers or completions. Select the one that BEST answers the question or completes the statement. *PRINT THE LETTER OF THE CORRECT ANSWER IN THE SPACE AT THE RIGHT.*

1. Which of the following is another term for social learning?　　　　　　1.____

   A. Behavior modification
   B. Organizational development
   C. Vicarious learning
   D. Positive reinforcement

2. _____ power is derived not from one's position in an organization but from within oneself.　　2.____

   A. Coercive　　　　　　　　　B. Expert
   C. Reward　　　　　　　　　　D. Legitimate

3. Which of the following statements, comparing achievement-motivated employees to affil-iation-motivated workers, is generally FALSE?　　3.____

   A. Achievement-oriented people select assistants with whom they can have meaning-ful relationships, regardless of past performance.
   B. Achievement-oriented people work harder when supervisors provide detailed eval-uations of their work behavior.
   C. Affiliation-motivated people work better when they are complimented for their favor-able attitudes and cooperation.
   D. Affiliation-oriented people function better in a cooperative work environment.

4. Programmed decisions　　　　　　　　　　4.____

   A. have a high tolerance for ambiguity
   B. depend on creativity and intuition
   C. are frequent and repetitive
   D. are novel and unstructured

5. The desire of an employee to be understood and accepted is described as a(n) _____ need.　　5.____

   A. functional　　　　　　　　B. relatedness
   C. security　　　　　　　　　D. attributive

6. The use of transactional analysis in an organization tends to be most useful in　　6.____

   A. executive relations　　　　B. sales
   C. finance　　　　　　　　　D. line production work

7. Which of the following is NOT a common assumption underlying the application of orga-nization development (OD)?　　7.____

   A. Employees have much to offer that is not currently being utilized at work.
   B. Groups have a powerful influence on individual behavior.
   C. The more rules, controls, and policies in place at an organization, the better.
   D. Conflict in an organization can serve a useful function.

8. According to the leadership approach proposed by Stephen Kerr, which of the following is a leadership enhancer?

    A. Use of crises to demonstrate leader's abilities
    B. Peer appraisal
    C. Cohesive work groups
    D. Jobs redesigned for more feedback

8.____

9. In conducting a job satisfaction survey at an organization, which of the following would typically be done FIRST?

    A. Obtaining the commitment of management
    B. Administering the survey
    C. Identifying the reason for the survey
    D. Developing the surveying instrument

9.____

10. A manager views herself as both the manager of a team responsible for protecting and enlarging its resources, and a member of the executive staff charged with the task of reducing operating costs. This situation is an example of

    A. role ambiguity
    B. the Hawthorne effect
    C. cognitive dissonance
    D. intrapersonal conflict

10.____

11. Viewing an organization as having many variables that affect each other and interact in a complex relationship is a key element in the _____ approach to organizational behavior.

    A. human resources
    B. systems
    C. results-oriented
    D. contingency

11.____

12. According to Blake and Mouton's managerial grid, a 1,9 leader is

    A. so concerned with both people and production that minutiae and details consume most work time
    B. a free-rein leader who does not place adequate emphasis on either people or production
    C. overly concerned with production, to the exclusion of employees' needs
    D. high in concern for people, but so low in concern for production that output is typically low

12.____

13. The tendency of people to perceive what they expect to perceive is known as

    A. self-serving bias
    B. perceptual set
    C. filtration
    D. fundamental attribution bias

13.____

14. The optimal design for an organization is determined by an interaction of size, environmental, and managerial factors. Matching the appropriate structure to these factors is the essence of

    A. contingency design
    B. horizontal integration
    C. functional departmentalization
    D. total quality management (TQM)

14.____

15. Of the following ego defense mechanisms, which is applied in an organization by means of covering up weaknesses through an emphasis on desirable traits?   15.____

   A. Identification   B. Compensation
   C. Denial   D. Rationalization

16. The capacity to control and administer items that are valued by another is known as _____ power.   16.____

   A. reward   B. coercive   C. personal   D. expert

17. Which of the following management principles has arisen from the interpretation of Maslow's needs hierarchy?   17.____
    Employees are motivated

   A. most strongly by their lower-order needs
   B. by the desire to protect what they already have
   C. most strongly by external factors
   D. by what they are currently seeking

18. Which of the following organizational decisions is in line with the idea of formalization?   18.____

   A. Functional departments   B. Centralized authority
   C. Narrow spans of control   D. Low specialization

19. According to the equity theory of motivation and reward, over-rewarded individuals are most likely to   19.____

   A. inflate the value of rewards
   B. bargain for greater rewards
   C. decrease productivity
   D. discount the importance of reward

20. A manager becomes aware of the development of informal groups within the organization. Which of the following would NOT be an effective tactic for dealing with the situation?   20.____

   A. Accept the informal groups as unavoidable
   B. Reorganize periodically, to keep groups from becoming stagnant or cliquish
   C. Integrate, as far as possible, the interests of the informal group with those of the formal organization
   D. Consider the possible effects on informal systems when taking any kind of action

21. Deficiencies in the way an organization operates are often referred to as   21.____

   A. output restrictions   B. functional effects
   C. performance gaps   D. task faults

22. An individual's secondary needs are characterized by each of the following EXCEPT they   22.____

   A. tend to remain fixed for an individual across time
   B. vary in type and intensity among people
   C. are often hidden from conscious perception
   D. tend to work in combination with each other:

23. Which of the following is/are considered to be effective ways for organizations to prevent groupthink? 23.____
    I. Inviting attendance by outsiders
    II. Announcing temporary delays before final decision making
    III. Putting pressure on dissidents
    IV. Periodically rotating in new group members
    The CORRECT answer is

    A. III *only*
    C. I, II, IV
    B. I, II
    D. None of the above

24. Managers who are the most effective interpersonal communicators are classified as type 24.____

    A. A   B. B   C. C   D. D

25. Government-mandated worker representation on the board of directors of an organiza- 25.____
    tion is commonly referred to as

    A. affirmative action
    C. codetermination
    B. consensus building
    D. industrial democracy

KEY (CORRECT ANSWER)

1.	C		11.	B
2.	B		12.	D
3.	A		13.	B
4.	C		14.	A
5.	B		15.	B
6.	B		16.	A
7.	C		17.	D
8.	A		18.	A
9.	C		19.	D
10.	D		20.	B

21. C
22. A
23. C
24. D
25. C

TEST 2

DIRECTIONS: Each question or incomplete statement is followed by several suggested answers or completions. Select the one that BEST answers the question or completes the statement. *PRINT THE LETTER OF THE CORRECT ANSWER IN THE SPACE AT THE RIGHT.*

1. In the job design process, a position analysis questionnaire is used to analyze the following job aspects EXCEPT   1.____

    A. reactions of individuals to working conditions
    B. group effectiveness resulting from job performance
    C. physical activity and dexterity required by the job
    D. interpersonal relationships required of the job

2. Which of the following is a problem or limitation that is often associated with the organization development (OD) process?   2.____

    A. Decreased willingness to change
    B. Major time requirements
    C. Lowered job satisfaction
    D. Better work quality

3. Which of the following is NOT a general guideline to be used for applying behavior modification in an organization?   3.____

    A. Use punishment only in unusual circumstances
    B. Use positive reinforcement rarely, so as not to inflate the sense of accomplishment
    C. Identify the exact behaviors to be modified
    D. Ignore minor undesirable behavior

4. Which of the following is an example of an unprogrammed decision?   4.____

    A. A merit system for the promotion of government employees
    B. The diversification into new products and markets
    C. The maintenance of a necessary grade point average at a university for good academic standing
    D. A business firm's periodic reorders of inventory

5. Which of the following types of stressors are most likely to be experienced by supervisory employees at an organization?   5.____

    A. Pressure for short-term financial results
    B. Lack of perceived control
    C. Pressures to increase quality and customer service
    D. Fear of a hostile takeover attempt

6. Most matrix organizations superimpose   6.____

    A. function-based design over an existing territorial design
    B. function-based design over an existing product-based design
    C. territorial design over an existing product- or project-based design
    D. product- or project-based design over an existing function-based design

7. An assessment of job *scope* depends on the two dimensions of job _____ and _____.   7.____

    A. content; context
    B. satisfaction; depth
    C. duration; skills
    D. depth; breadth

8. A key principle of organizational behavior is that the way a change is handled in an organization should not only reflect the current information gathered, but also prepare the participants to manage future changes even more effectively. This process is called   8.____

    A. double-loop learning
    B. unfreezing
    C. single-loop learning
    D. transformational learning

9. Which of the following is a *lower-order* human need, as identified in Maslow's hierarchy?   9.____

    A. Belonging
    B. Status
    C. Fulfillment
    D. Security

10. What is the term for the degree to which people are comfortable with ambiguous situations and with the inability to accurately predict future events?   10.____

    A. Thematic apperception
    B. Sequential interdependence
    C. Uncertainty avoidance
    D. Cognitive dissonance

11. In organizations, frameworks of possible explanations of how things work are often referred to as   11.____

    A. parochialism
    B. paradigms
    C. prototypes
    D. perceptions

12. What is the term for the systematic and progressive application of positive reinforcement?   12.____

    A. Molding
    B. Mentoring
    C. Focusing
    D. Shaping

13. Which of the following is not a characteristic of perceived job content?   13.____

    A. Uniqueness
    B. Variety
    C. Feedback
    D. Autonomy

14. Which of the following is NOT a guideline for resolving conflict through confrontation?   14.____

    A. Commit oneself to fixed positions on the matter
    B. Be candid and do not withhold key information
    C. Agree on a common goal
    D. Clarify strengths and weaknesses of both parties' positions

15. Which of the following types of employees tend to be LEAST satisfied with their jobs?   15.____

    A. Entry-level line workers
    B. Workers in small organizational units
    C. Executives
    D. Older workers

16. According to most research, job enrichment will probably lead to improvements in each   16.____
    of the following areas EXCEPT

    A. absenteeism   B. job attitudes
    C. productivity   D. turnover

17. Under the model of *Confucian dynamism,* people are likely to believe in the importance   17.____
    of

    A. feeling shame
    B. respect for tradition
    C. personal stability
    D. reciprocation of favors and gifts

18. Which of the following statements comparing group to individual decision-making is   18.____
    FALSE?

    A. Implementing a decision is usually accomplished by individual managers.
    B. In choosing an alternative, groups tend to accept greater risks than individuals.
    C. In evaluating different alternatives, groups tend to be superior than individuals
        because of a wider range of viewpoints.
    D. In establishing objectives, individuals are probably superior to groups because of
        their ability to focus.

19. Which of the following models of organizational behavior is most likely to encourage self-   19.____
    discipline among employees?

    A. Collegial   B. Custodial
    C. Autocratic   D. Supportive

20. Among the following descriptions of an organizational structure, which does NOT mean   20.____
    the same as the others?

    A. System 1   B. Organic
    C. Neoclassical   D. Informalistic

21. Of the following categories of human values, which reflect an interest in abstract truths   21.____
    which unify knowledge?

    A. Metaphysical   B. Religious
    C. Theoretical   D. Esthetic

22. Organic organizations tend to be more effective than mechanistic ones in situations   22.____
    where

    A. changes in the market are minimal
    B. employeess seek autonomy and opportunity
    C. workers prefer routine tasks and direction from others
    D. tasks are well-defined

23. As a method of data collection within an organization, interviewing offers each of the fol-   23.____
    lowing advantages EXCEPT it

    A. is one of the most efficient methods in terms of time
    B. can be used to convey real empathy for employees
    C. offers flexibility in its methods
    D. is a rich source of data

24. Which of the following is TRUE of an organization with a mechanistic structure?   24.____

    A. Motivation taps a number of motives through participatory methods.
    B. Performance goals are high and actively sought by superiors.
    C. Leadership includes no perceived confidence and trust.
    D. Control is dispersed throughout the organization.

25. When a job is _____, responsibilities and controls that were formerly reserved for man-   25.____
    agement are given to employees as part of the job.

    A. vertically loaded   B. rotated
    C. horizontally loaded   D. looped

KEY (CORRECT ANSWERS)

1.	B		11.	B
2.	B		12.	D
3.	B		13.	A
4.	B		14.	A
5.	C		15.	A
6.	D		16.	B
7.	D		17.	A
8.	A		18.	D
9.	D		19.	A
10.	C		20.	A

21.	C
22.	B
23.	A
24.	C
25.	A

EXAMINATION SECTION
TEST 1

DIRECTIONS: Each question or incomplete statement is followed by several suggested answers or completions. Select the one that BEST answers the question or completes the statement. *PRINT THE LETTER OF THE CORRECT ANSWER IN THE SPACE AT THE RIGHT.*

1. During the maturity period of a product's life cycle, a company's strategic marketing objective will generally be to

    A. improve competitive position
    B. maintain position
    C. accelerate market growth
    D. harvest

1.____

2. A franchiser can MOST effectively minimize the risks of product liability by

    A. carefully preparing the trademark licensing agreement
    B. using an agent or broker to determine distribution
    C. constructing a multi-channel distribution system
    D. avoiding entanglement in claims against licensees

2.____

3. Which of the following is not an advantage associated with product management organizations?

    A. Improved coordination of functional activities within and across product-market entries
    B. Long-term orientation on the part of product managers
    C. Ability to identify and react more quickly to threats and opportunities faced by individual product-market entries

3.____

4. The retailing of service products differs from that of physical goods in each of the following ways EXCEPT

    A. more difficult consumer choice
    B. tendency toward localization
    C. easier quality control
    D. heterogeneous delivery process

4.____

5. A _____ is a name, term, or symbol which is intended to identify the goods or services of one seller or group of sellers and to differentiate them from those of competitors.

    A. patent   B. brand
    C. copyright   D. trademark

5.____

6. According to the categories established by the VALS psychographic segments, the smallest psychographic segment of Americans is the_____ category.

    A. achievers   B. experiential
    C. integrated   D. societally conscious

6.____

7. _____ is NOT typically a characteristic of department store retailers.   7.____

    A. Large sales volume
    B. Wide product mix
    C. Self-service outlets
    D. Achieve most sales through apparel and cosmetics

8. Face-to-face selling is likely to be of great importance under each of the following condi-   8.____
tions EXCEPT

    A. a small target market consisting of relatively few customers
    B. a technically complex product or service
    C. the use of an extensive distribution network
    D. a marketing strategy aimed at wresting market share away from established com-
       petitors

9. A company wants to target a market that is highly competitive, but the company's com-   9.____
petitive position is estimated to be only moderate by marketing advisers. Typically, which
of the following should be part of the company's strategy?

    A. Invest to grow at maximum digestible rate
    B. Invest to improve position only in areas where risk is low
    C. Reinforce vulnerable areas
    D. Defend strengths

10. Which of the following is not a major INTERNAL variable that affects a company's ability   10.____
to implement particular marketing strategies?

    A. Fit between individual product marketing strategies and the company's higher-level
       corporate and business strategies
    B. Administrative relationships between strategic business units and other members
       of the distribution channel
    C. Mechanisms used to coordinate and resolve conflicts among departments
    D. Contents of the detailed marketing action plan for each product-market entry

11. Each of the following is a projective technique for analyzing consumers' motives   11.____
EXCEPT

    A. depth interviews
    B. sentence completion tests
    C. balloon tests
    D. word-association tests

12. As a selling objective, the gathering of information is especially useful in the   12.____

    A. maturity phase of consumer durables
    B. marketing of most shopping goods
    C. shakeout period of specialty markets
    D. introductory or growth stage of industrial products

13. A new lower-priced brand of shampoo is introduced into a highly competitive market by a   13.____
competitor with limited resources. Companies with strong existing brands are likely to
respond in each of the following ways EXCEPT

A.   hold prices the same
B.   offer coupons, discounts, or larger sizes at the same price
C.   lower prices dramatically to drive the competitors out
D.   lower prices to the level of the new brand

14.   When marketing managers attempt to control marketing activities, they frequently
      encounter several problems. Which of the following is NOT typically one of these prob-
      lems?   14.____

      A.   Information required to control marketing activities is unavailable
      B.   Internal cost analysis is unavailable
      C.   Frequent and unpredictable changes in environmental factors
      D.   Time lag between marketing activities and their effects

15.   Each of the following is a typical characteristic of one-level marketing channels EXCEPT   15.____

      A.   retail sales personnel must often exert pressure on shoppers
      B.   extensive postsale servicing demand
      C.   usually involve companies with limited distribution allocation
      D.   retail sales personnel must be more knowledgeable about the product

16.   Which of the following is NOT a limitation associated with the use of profitability analysis   16.____
      as a means of organizational control?

      A.   Many objectives can best be measured in non-financial terms.
      B.   Costs associated with specific marketing activities need to be analyzed in different
           market segments and distribution channels.
      C.   Profits can be affected by factors over which management has no control.
      D.   Profit is a short-term measure and can be manipulated by actions that may prove
           dysfunctional in the longer term.

17.   A market aggregation strategy is appropriate where the total market   17.____

      A.   uses limited distribution channels
      B.   has few differences in customer needs or desires
      C.   is organizational in nature
      D.   is concentrated in one particular geographic location

18.   A company produces a food seasoning that is widely used in restaurants. If the company   18.____
      decides to introduce this seasoning into supermarkets for home use, it is likely that the

      A.   company has discovered a new market segment
      B.   product has experienced a decline in restaurant sales
      C.   product has been slightly modified
      D.   product line has been widened

19.   Which of the following is NOT usually a type of organizational purchase?   19.____

      A.   Discretionary purchase   B.   Straight rebuy
      C.   Modified rebuy   D.   New-task purchase

20. In a growth market situation, a company defines its primary marketing objective as attracting a smaller share of new customers in a variety of smaller, specialized segments where customers' needs or preferences differ from those of early adopters in the mass market.
    The company's marketing strategy could best be described as   20._____

    A. encirclement   B. guerrilla attack
    C. leapfrog   D. frontal attack

21. Contractual systems sponsored by wholesalers, which independent retailers can join, are known as   21._____

    A. manufacturer-sponsored franchises
    B. cooperative chains
    C. administered systems
    D. voluntary chains

22. The practice of skimming pricing is MOST likely to be used in the marketing of   22._____

    A. high-technology products
    B. clothing
    C. franchised restaurants
    D. low-margin household products

23. The institution with the authority to deal with trademark infringements is the   23._____

    A. Federal Trade Commission
    B. municipal, county, or state court
    C. Department of Commerce
    D. Patent and Trademark Office

24. In the relationship between a business unit and the company within which it operates, *centralization* refers to the   24._____

    A. location of decision authority and control within an organization's hierarchy
    B. degree to which decisions and working relationships are governed by formal rules and standard policies
    C. geographic location of the business unit in relation to the administrative center of the company
    D. division of tasks and activities across positions within the organizational unit

25. A leading stationery manufacturer, due to the large demand for its product, was able to force less desirable lines upon retailers, who had to accept these lines in order to receive the fast-moving items. Eventually, the manufacturer experienced an off-year, and the retailers struck back by refusing to take any items they did not want, even buying only minimal amounts of the faster-moving items. This situation is an example of   25._____

    A. trust-busting   B. an administered system
    C. the natural retail cycle   D. channel conflict

_____

KEY (CORRECT ANSWERS)

1.	B	11.	A
2.	A	12.	D
3.	C	13.	C
4.	C	14.	B
5.	B	15.	C
6.	C	16.	B
7.	C	17.	B
8.	A	18.	A
9.	C	19.	A
10.	B	20.	A

21.	D
22.	A
23.	B
24.	A
25.	D

TEST 2

DIRECTIONS: Each question or incomplete statement is followed by several suggested answers or completions. Select the one that BEST answers the question or completes the statement. *PRINT THE LETTER OF THE CORRECT ANSWER IN THE SPACE AT THE RIGHT.*

1. A company might decide to engage in the practice of penetration pricing in order to   1.____

    A. increase market share and gain greater visibility and market power
    B. create a high-quality image for the product
    C. clear out inventories of older models
    D. discourage potential competitors from entering the market at all

2. When a buyer questions whether he or she should have purchased a product at all, or would have been better off purchasing another brand, this is an example of   2.____

    A. demarketing   B. cognitive dissonance
    C. consumerism   D. evoked set

3. The primary responsibility of a company's sales force is to gain and maintain support for the company's products within the distribution channel by providing merchandising and promotional services to the channel members. The company's sales force is MOST likely composed of _____ sellers.   3.____

    A. new business   B. missionary
    C. technical   D. trade

4. Under the Uniform Commercial Code, certain remedies are available to a party in a sales contract who claim a breach of the contract. The code sets forth each of the following specific measures for ascertaining the amount of damages to goods named in such a contract EXCEPT the _____ standard.   4.____

    A. resale   B. actual cash value
    C. market value   D. profit

5. A company has adopted a prospector strategy for entrance into a certain market. Typically, a business unit in the company will perform best when one of its functional strengths is   5.____

    A. production   B. distribution
    C. financial management and control   D. marketing

6. _____ is the specific term for the entity that permits .
the identification of goods as the product of a particular maker, seller, or sponsor.   6.____

    A. patent   B. trademark
    C. copyright   D. brand

7. A group of smaller hotel chains finds that they can make a reasonable profit by following the prices of the price leader – a large, nationwide chain as long as they can keep their hotels reasonably well-filled. To do this, the smaller chains advertise heavily and try to book as many meetings, conventions, and tours as possible.
This is an example of   7.____

    A. imitation   B. market saturation
    C. nonprice competition   D. leader pricing

8. Which of the following consumer selections is likely to be nost strongly influenced by a reference group?   8.____

     A. Radio   B. Coffee
     C. Automobile   D. Magazine or book

9. Generally, the practice of offering seasonal discounts to a consumer is beneficial in each of the following ways EXCEPT   9.____

     A. lower inventory carrying costs for the seller
     B. less overload on distribution facilities
     C. encourages buyer to pay as soon as possible
     D. less overtime pay for employees

10. The first introduction of a graphite golf club into the market was an example of   10.____

     A. adaptive replacement   B. product innovation
     C. imitation   D. line simplification

11. According to market research conventions, which of the following qualities or behaviors would be displayed by members of the lower-middle class?   11.____

     A. Tend to be brand loyal
     B. Buy relatively expensive homes to indicate social position
     C. Avoid mass merchandisers
     D. Common joint shopping of husband and wife

12. In a marketing audit, a company focuses on whether the company has adequate and timely information about consumers' satisfaction with its products. Which area of the company's marketing activities is being audited?   12.____

     A. Planning and control system   B. Organization
     C. Objectives and strategy   D. Marketing environment

13. A credit-card company decides to segment its market using a product-related approach. Most likely, the users will be segmented according to   13.____

     A. their level of disposable income
     B. the types of goods and services they use their cards for
     C. the frequency with which they use their cards
     D. the pattern of credit services they utilize

14. A personal characteristic considered to be important for missionary sellers is   14.____

     A. knowledge of customers   B. maturity
     C. verbal skill   D. empathy

15. Under the Uniform Commercial Code, the parties in a sales contract can conclude a contract for sale even if the price has not been settled. In such a case, the price will be considered to be a reasonable price at the time of delivery under any of the following conditions EXCEPT   15.____

     A. the price is to be fixed in good faith by the buyer or seller
     B. nothing at all has been said as to price
     C. the price is definitively scheduled for consideration by an impartial arbitrator
     D. the price is yet to be agreed upon by the parties and they fail to agree

16. A strategic business unit within a company desires a high level of autonomy within the organization. Which type of business strategy would be most conducive to this?

16.____

    A. Prospector
    B. Analyzer
    C. Differentiated defender
    D. Low-cost defender

17. In a certain marketing channel network, a wholesaler's markup on a certain product is 20%, and the retailer's markup is 50%. An end-use customer pays $300 for the product. What was the price at which the wholesaler purchased the product from the producer?

17.____

    A. $150   B. $166.67   C. $200   D. $233.34

18. Under the Uniform Commercial Code, certain remedies are available to a party in a sales contract who claim a breach of the contract. Generally, which of the following remedies is NOT available to the buyer in such a contract?

18.____

    A. Purchase of substitute goods, holding seller liable for any reasonable losses the buyer might have incurred in the cover operation
    B. Cancel the contract entirely, and recover moneys which might have been paid, as well as recovering damages
    C. Sue for possession of the goods
    D. Acceptance of nonconforming goods and suing for compensatory damages as well as punitive damages

19. A _____ is most likely to extend credit to customers.

19.____

    A. selling agent
    B. manufacturer's agent
    C. commission merchant
    D. broker

20. In exercising control over inventory, it is important to remember that individual reorders depend on

20.____

    A. the probability of obsolescence
    B. the trade-off between the cost of carrying larger inventories and the cost of processing small orders
    C. the total amount of capital tied up in inventory
    D. overall demand

21. The PRIMARY difference between a facilitating agency and a marketing channel member is that a facilitating agency

21.____

    A. does not perform negotiating functions
    B. is less specialized
    C. is not involved with physical distribution of a product
    D. has no influence over pricing

22. Most business firms judge their effectiveness in terms of

22.____

    A. total revenue
    B. profits as a percentage of sales
    C. segments controlled
    D. return on investment (ROI)

23. A market segmentation study describes a certain population as *typical light users* of the   23.____
product under investigation. In this example, the study is using a _____ descriptor.

    A.   customer needs
    B.   person-related behavioral
    C.   product-related behavioral
    D.   demographic

24. Under which of the following conditions is a personal selling strategy targeted toward the   24.____
development of new customers most appropriate?

    A.   The product is in the introductory stage
    B.   Business is pursuing a differentiated defender strategy
    C.   Firm intentions to increase market share of a mature market
    D.   Lengthy purchase decision process

25. Generally, the more conspicuous a product is, the more likely it is that a consumer's   25.____
brand decision will be influenced by

    A.   reference groups   B.   family roles
    C.   situational factors   D.   demographics

KEY (CORRECT ANSWERS)

1.	D		11.	D
2.	B		12.	A
3.	D		13.	B
4.	B		14.	C
5.	D		15.	C
6.	B		16.	A
7.	C		17.	B
8.	C		18.	D
9.	C		19.	A
10.	A		20.	B

21.	A
22.	D
23.	C
24.	C
25.	A

———

TEST 3

DIRECTIONS: Each question or incomplete statement is followed by several suggested answers or completions. Select the one that BEST answers the question or completes the statement. *PRINT THE LETTER OF THE CORRECT ANSWER IN THE SPACE AT THE RIGHT.*

1. Each of the following is a reason why marketing channels in a distribution system might change EXCEPT   1.____

    A. one or more middlemen find a way to increase their own profits or strength in the channel
    B. new technology
    C. one or more companies discover a less expensive way to distribute their goods
    D. greater customer service provisions offered by a company

2. A blended *Scotch* whiskey, made in the United States, is priced at a low margin, and sells poorly. After the manufacturer raises the price of the product by $2 a bottle, without any change in the product or its packaging, sales increase dramatically.
This can be best explained by asserting that customers   2.____

    A. believe the product offers greater prestige
    B. mistakenly believe the product is a single-malt Scotch
    C. believe the quality of the product to be comparable to that of higher-priced whiskeys
    D. are more likely to believe the product was imported from Scotland

3. A well-established personal computer manufacturer with several product lines introduces a new line of computers at a very low price, and receives an estimated $10 billion in orders before the machines are available at retail outlets. The introduction of this product line will most likely result in a *decrease* in the company's sales by   3.____

    A. discouraging competition that will supply long-term technological growth to the market
    B. starting a price war with competitors
    C. encouraging the proliferation of a horizontal marketing channel structure
    D. drawing customer attention away from other, higher-margin product lines

4. In establishing physical distribution objectives, the distribution-center concept has a few distinct advantages. Which of the following is NOT one of these advantages?   4.____

    A. Greater control over shipments
    B. Justified expenditures on automated equipment for more efficient handling
    C. Lower total cost
    D. Goods can be shipped directly from producer in the form or number ordered by customers

5. A company may want to use a salesforce compensation plan combining both salary and commission when   5.____

    A. company cannot closely control salesforce activities
    B. sales territories have relatively similar sales potentials
    C. when salespersons need to perform many non-selling activities
    D. highly aggressive selling is required

6. Which of the following goods are characterized by limited availability, an emphasis on personal selling, and availability in a limited number of stores?

    A. Specialty   B. Convenience
    C. Shopping   D. Unsought

6.____

7. A company's pricing practice interacts with promotion expenditures in many ways. Which of the following statements is NOT true in the case of advertising for consumer products?

    A. Higher prices for a new type of consumer product can provide the funds necessary to advertise heavily, in order to inform people of the improved benefits offered by the new product.
    B. Advertising often has a greater effect on the sales of high-priced than low-priced products.
    C. Higher advertising expenditures can reduce the total cost of selling by preselling the buyer.
    D. Companies that want to support a high price for their product often spend a great deal on advertising.

7.____

8. When making purchase decisions, resellers typically consider each of the following factors EXCEPT

    A. amount of space required to handle a product
    B. lowest acceptable bid for products or services
    C. supplier's ability to provide adequate quantities when needed
    D. product demand

8.____

9. Generally, due to potential changes in cash flow and production practices, which department in a company would have the EASIEST time accepting a decision to simplify a product line?

    A. Higher-level management   B. Sales
    C. Production   D. Finance

9.____

10. In pinpointing the essential tasks of distribution, the producer must keep in mind the basic trade-relations mix. Which of the following is NOT an element of the trade-relations mix?

    A. Conditions of sale   B. Price policy
    C. Trademark status   D. Territorial rights

10.____

11. During the shakeout period of a product's life cycle, a company's investments in the product (R&D, working capital, and marketing) will generally be

    A. negative   B. low   C. moderate   D. high

11.____

12. A registered trademark can be made incontestable as soon as it has been in use, subsequent to the date of the certificate, for

    A. 6 months   B. 1 year   C. 5 years   D. 10 years

12.____

13. A large snack-food company periodically experiences declines in the sales of its products. In the long term, the company can probably BEST counteract the decrease in profits by

   A. spending more on promotion and advertising
   B. shifting its promotion and advertising to other market segments
   C. periodically introducing new product lines
   D. periodically changing the packaging of its products

13.____

14. According to the categories established by the VALS psychographic segments, most Americans fall into the category

   A. achievers
   B. belongers
   C. societally conscious
   D. emulators

14.____

15. In a single year, company X sold $800,000 worth of its product. The entire industry sold a total of $9 million. What was the approximate market share of company X for this product in this year?

   A. .09%   B. 8.9%   C. 11.1%   D. 17.8%

15.____

16. Each of the following is a reason why a retailer might practice scrambled merchandising EXCEPT

   A. generation of more traffic
   B. generating brand loyalty
   C. increasing impulse purchases
   D. realizing higher profit margins

16.____

17. When a business faces an extremely complex and uncertain environment, which form of organization is MOST likely to be appropriate?

   A. Matrix
   B. Product management
   C. Market management
   D. Functional

17.____

18. The exemption of dedicated export-trade associations from existing antitrust legislation is the major provision of the_____ Act.

   A. Webb-Pomerene
   B. Clayton
   C. Robinson-Patman
   D. Federal Trade Commission

18.____

19. For a business that has adopted a differentiated defender strategy with respect to a certain market, which of the following policies would be LEAST appropriate?

   A. High salesforce expenditure as a percent of sales
   B. Relatively high prices
   C. Broad, technically sophisticated product lines
   D. Low trade promotion expenses as a percent of sales

19.____

20. Which of the following is categorized as a social influence on the consumer buying decision process?

   A. Personality
   B. Reference group
   C. Attitude
   D. Job status (promotion, firing, etc.)

20.____

21. A company's marketing department adopts the communication of product information as one of its primary selling objectives.
Which of the following is LEAST likely to be true? The

    A. product is technically complex
    B. purchase decision is typically a lengthy process
    C. product is in the maturity stage of its life cycle
    D. purchase decision is influenced by multiple factors

21.____

22. In terms of trademark law, most foreign countries differ from the United States *primarily* in the

    A. means by which infringement is litigated
    B. legal definition of a trademark
    C. requirement of use as a prerequisite to registration
    D. distinction between a trademark and a service mark

22.____

23. Which of the following is an example of an indirect cost?

    A. Materials   B. General management
    C. Advertising   D. Labor

23.____

24. The tendency to remain loyal to a company rather than a particular brand or product is known as

    A. evoked set   B. discrimination
    C. mental set   D. generalization

24.____

25. The purpose of *push money* is to

    A. provide an incentive to retail sales personnel
    B. encourage transport agents to pay freight costs
    C. encourage customer trade-ins
    D. provide a buying incentive to customers

25.____

KEY (CORRECT ANSWERS)

1.	D	11.	C
2.	C	12.	C
3.	D	13.	C
4.	D	14.	B
5.	B	15.	B
6.	C	16.	B
7.	B	17.	A
8.	B	18.	A
9.	A	19.	C
10.	C	20.	B

21.	C
22.	C
23.	B
24.	D
25.	A

TEST 4

DIRECTIONS: Each question or incomplete statement is followed by several suggested answers or completions. Select the one that BEST answers the question or completes the statement. *PRINT THE LETTER OF THE CORRECT ANSWER IN THE SPACE AT THE RIGHT.*

1. The total costs of producing an additional quantity of a product, less the total costs of producing the current quantity, will yield the _____ costs.

    A. total
    C. marginal

    B. average total
    D. total variable

    1.____

2. Each of the following is a consideration associated with the profitability factor of a business analysis EXCEPT

    A. time to recoup initial costs
    B. risk
    C. control over price
    D. potential sales at different prices

    2.____

3. A strategy in which one name is used for several products is known as _____ branding.

    A. family   B. net   C. line   D. wide

    3.____

4. Which of the following is NOT a common means of preventing or resolving channel conflict?

    A. Proper channel design
    B. Selective distribution
    C. Employment of cooperation techniques
    D. Exertion of power

    4.____

5. Which of the following is a disadvantage associated with the sales force survey as a means of sales forecasting?

    A. Assumption that areas will behave similarly in the future
    B. Does not reveal traits of heavy users
    C. Lack of awareness of competitor's intentions
    D. Regions nor representative

    5.____

6. Which of the following is typically controlled by a company's top management, rather than by the marketing department?

    A. Role of marketing decisions
    B. Selection of target markets
    C. Profit objectives
    D. Type of marketing organization

    6.____

7. A disadvantage associated with independent ownership of a retail outlet is

    A. inflexibility
    B. much competition
    C. limited decision-making ability
    D. high investment costs

    7.____

8. Advertising will dominate in a company's promotional mix when　　8.____

    A. products are simple and inexpensive, and differential advantages are clear
    B. the market is small and concentrated, and organized consumers are involved
    C. customers expect assistance and service in retail stores
    D. the budget is limited or tailored to the needs of specific customers

9. Which of the following factors is NOT used to calculate the, target price of a product?　　9.____

    A. Standard volume   B. Variable per unit costs
    C. Investment costs   D. Target ROI percentage

10. A manufacturer's brand　　10.____

    A. is not widely advertised
    B. is targeted to price-conscious consumers
    C. has a price usually controlled by the dealer
    D. is usually part of a deep product line

11. Which of the following steps in a segmentation strategy would typically be performed FIRST?　　11.____

    A. Establishing an appropriate marketing plan
    B. Selecting consumer segments
    C. Analyzing consumer similarities and differences
    D. Developing consumer group profiles

12. A company's retail merchandise manager　　12.____

    A. supervises several buyers
    B. supervises the day-to-day activities of the store
    C. is responsible for purchasing items for resale
    D. is a buyer for a manufacturer, wholesaler, or retailer

13. Which of the following market research techniques would typically be best for discovering consumer attitudes?　　13.____

    A. Simulation   B. Survey
    C. Experimentation   D. Observation

14. The MOST significant in number and volume of those engaged in the wholesaling business are　　14.____

    A. merchant wholesalers
    B. assemblers
    C. manufacturer's sales branches
    D. merchandise agents and brokers

15. Which of the following types of organizational consumer decision processes involves the greatest amount of perceived risk?　　15.____

    A. Impulse buy   B. New task purchase
    C. Modified rebuy   D. Straight rebuy

16. Each of the following is a consideration associated with the demand projection factor of a business analysis EXCEPT   16.____

    A. speed of consumer acceptance   B. channel intensity
    C. per unit fixed costs   D. seasonally of sales

17. Which of the following questions would appear on a disguised market research survey?   17.____

    A. At what time of day do you usually eat dinner?
    B. Which of the following is most important to you?
    C. What factors do you consider in the purchase of home furnishings?
    D. Are people who purchase sports cars status conscious;

18. Most franchisors require each of the following of a franchisee EXCEPT   18.____

    A. college education
    B. age 26-60
    C. owning one's own home
    D. able to finance leasehold improvements

19. A company conducts its sales analysis by gathering small, separate market segments and then aggregating them. This approach is known as   19.____

    A. consumer survey   B. market buildup method
    C. simple trend analysis   D. chain-ratio method

20. $\dfrac{\text{Cost of goods sold}}{\text{Net sales}}$ is a formula for which performance ratio?   20.____

    A. Stock turnover ratio   B. Cost of goods sold ratio
    C. Return on investment   D. Sales efficiency ratio

21. What is the term for the number of product items within each of the product lines offered by a company?   21.____

    A. Width   B. Depth   C. Scope   D. Consistency

22. In organizational purchasing for middlemen, the search for sources can have a large number of influences. Which of the following is NOT typically one of these influences?   22.____

    A. Past dates of sales for similar products
    B. Consumer surveys
    C. Shopping competitors' offerings
    D. Market research studies

23. What is the term for a form of price adjustment in which across-the-board price increases are published to supplement list prices?   23.____

    A. Bundling   B. Surcharge   C. Stimulus   D. Tariff

24. Which of the following promotional activities has the LOWEST overall cost per potential customer?   24.____

    A. Sales promotion   B. Publicity
    C. Advertising   D. Personal selling

25. In the multiple segmentation method for developing a target market,

      25.____

    A. there is one product or service brand tailored to one consumer group
    B. there is a distinct price range for each consumer group
    C. a mass media promotion is used
    D. the object is a broad range of consumers

KEY (CORRECT ANSWERS)

1.	C		11.	C
2.	D		12.	A
3.	A		13.	B
4.	B		14.	A
5.	C		15.	B
6.	A		16.	C
7.	B		17.	D
8.	A		18.	A
9.	B		19.	B
10.	D		20.	B

21.	B
22.	B
23.	B
24.	C
25.	B

EXAMINATION SECTION
TEST 1

DIRECTIONS: Each question or incomplete statement is followed by several suggested answers or completions. Select the one that BEST answers the question or completes the statement. *PRINT THE LETTER OF THE CORRECT ANSWER IN THE SPACE AT THE RIGHT.*

1. The term of a federal trademark registration is   1._____

   A. 10 years
   B. 20 years
   C. until the company stops using the trademark for any purpose
   D. indefinite

2. Generally, the most significant basis for product liability is the potential liability for   2._____

   A. design defects
   B. manner of complaint handling
   C. misrepresentation
   D. distribution decisions

3. _____ goods are not an example of convenience products.   3._____

   A. Impulse   B. Unsought
   C. Staple   D. All of the above

4. The marketing channel *produoer→ retailer→ consumer* is MOST comnonly used in the   4._____
   distribution of

   A. agricultural produce   B. automobiles
   C. refrigerators   D. candy

5. Market segmentation CANNOT   5._____

   A. identify opportunities for new-product development
   B. reflect the realities faced by companies in most markets
   C. help in the design of products and marketing programs that are most effective for
      reaching heterogeneous groups of customers
   D. improve the strategic allocation of marketing resources

6. According to market research conventions, which of the following qualities or behaviors   6._____
   would be displayed by members of the lower-lower class?

   A. Spend a relatively larger proportion of income on household items
   B. Prefers to shop at nonexclusive department stores
   C. Spend a relatively larger proportion of income on products to improve personal
      appearance
   D. Respectability a major objective

7. Which of the following strategic marketing objectives is used during the shakeout period   7._____
   of a product's life cycle?

   A. Hold share   B. Harvest
   C. Stimulate primary demand   D. Build share

8. Mass merchandisers, as compared to department stores,   8._____

   A. are more service-oriented
   B. have a shallower product mix
   C. appeal to homogeneous target markets
   D. have a narrower product mix

9. Each of the following is an example of process goods EXCEPT   9._____

   A. thermostats for refrigerators
   B. truck tires
   C. portable drills
   D. sheet steel

10. A *dealer loader* is   10._____

   A. an advertisement that promotes a product and identifies the names of participating retailers who sell the product
   B. a gift given to a retailer who purchases a specified quantity of merchandise
   C. used to promote a line of goods by providing additional compensation to salespeople
   D. a manufacturer's agreement to pay resellers certain amounts of money for providing special promotional efforts such as advertising or displays

11. Which of the following is NOT a kind of full-service wholesaler?   11._____

   A. General merchandise   B. Mail order
   C. Specialty-line   D. Limited-line

12. From a marketing planning standpoint, there are three major strategic options most companies have under conditions of a kinked demand curve. Which of the following is NOT one of these options?   12._____

   A. Change both price and one or more other elements of the marketing mix
   B. Stay at the market price, but change one or more element of the marketing mix
   C. Lower production costs for a particular product and stay at the market price
   D. Raise or lower prices to maximize short-term profits on the basis of the kinked curve

13. A manufacturer experiences high transportation costs, but low storage costs in the physical distribution of its product. Which of the following transport modes is probably being used by the company?   13._____

   A. Rail   B. Truck   C. Air   D. Water

14. Which of the following is an example of a producer market?   14._____

   A. A hospital buying tongue depressors
   B. A wholesaler buying lumber for resale to a hardware franchise
   C. The Postal Service buying wood pulp for stamp production
   D. A grocery store buying paper bags for customer purchases

15. A _____ set is the term used to denote a group of brands that a buyer views as possible   15.____
    alternatives after a successful information search.

    A. mental   B. inert   C. inept   D. evoked

16. Five buyers consistently purchase the products of five producers. If an intermediary   16.____
    serves both producers and buyers, the number of transactions necessary to provide buy-
    ers with their products can be reduced to

    A. 2   B. 5   C. 10   D. 25

17. A marketing department groups customers according to the characteristics of the individ-   17.____
    uals who influence purchasing decisions. This is an example of

    A. psychographics   B. focus grouping
    C. macrosegmentation   D. microsegmentation

18. In an automobile showroom, a salesperson informs a customer of a car's highly success-   18.____
    ful EPA mileage rating. The customer does not believe the salesperson, and soon forgets
    all about the car's rating.
    This is an example of

    A. selective retention   B. self-fulfilling prophecy
    C. selective distortion   D. cognitive dissonance

19. In an organizational buying center, the final authority over buying decisions is held by   19.____

    A. deciders   B. gatekeepers
    C. users   D. buyers

20. Which of the following personal characteristics is MOST likely to be useful to a trade   20.____
    seller?

    A. Product knowledge   B. Aggressiveness
    C. Technical ability   D. Knowledge of customers

21. A marketing department determines that a certain product is in the declining phase. The   21.____
    company should probably

    A. narrow the product line
    B. rationalize the line or eliminate weaker items
    C. reduce the length of the line
    D. hold the length of the line

22. Each of the following are examples of specialty goods EXCEPT   22.____

    A. office furniture   B. automobiles
    C. designer clothing   D. personal computers

23. If an industrial buyer is offered a cash discount of *2/10 net 30* after purchasing a product, 23.____
    the

    A. buyer will receive a 20% discount if the bill is paid within 30 days
    B. buyer agrees to pay in 2 cash installments of $10 within 30 days
    C. bill must be paid in full within 30 days
    D. buyer must pay in cash

24. A consumer sees an advertisement by a toothpaste producer claiming that one-third of the people using their product have fewer cavities. The consumer takes this claim to mean that two-thirds of the people who use the product have more cavities.
This is an example of

    24.____

    A. selective retention   B. cognitive dissonance
    C. selective distortion   D. mental set

25. Each of the following is a way in which a private warehouse facility differs from a public warehouse EXCEPT

    25.____

    A. private warehouses are usually leased
    B. private warehouses involve fixed costs
    C. public warehouses do not establish field warehouses
    D. public warehouses provide bonded storage

KEY (CORRECT ANSWERS)

1.	B		11.	B
2.	A		12.	C
3.	B		13.	C
4.	B		14.	D
5.	C		15.	D
6.	C		16.	C
7.	D		17.	D
8.	B		18.	A
9.	C		19.	A
10.	B		20.	D

21.	C
22.	A
23.	C
24.	C
25.	C

TEST 2

DIRECTIONS: Each question or incomplete statement is followed by several suggested answers or completions. Select the one that BEST answers the question or completes the statement. *PRINT THE LETTER OF THE CORRECT ANSWER IN THE SPACE AT THE RIGHT.*

1. Generally, the MOST significant problem associated with unreliable transport services is   1._____

    A. high inventory
    B. lack of security
    C. longer delivery lead times
    D. lower margin

2. Each of the following is a sales promotion aimed primarily at resellers EXCEPT   2._____

    A. dealer loaders
    B. push money
    C. point-of-purchase displays
    D. buying allowances

3. Which of the following is NOT a characteristic of the growth stage of a product's life cycle?   3._____

    A. Large profitability
    B. Moderate technical change in product
    C. Few to many market segments
    D. Limited competition

4. Which of the following types of wholesalers will NOT take physical possession of a producer's merchandise?   4._____

    A. Mail order   B. Rack jobber
    C. Drop shipper   D. Cash and carry

5. A company wants to target a market that is moderately competitive, and the company's competitive position is estimated to be very strong by marketing advisers. Typically, which of the following should be part of the company's strategy?   5._____

    A. Build up ability to counter competition
    B. Specialize around limited strengths
    C. Minimize investments and focus operations
    D. Invest to grow at maximum digestible rate

6. A company producing relatively low-priced watches decides to seek widespread distribution through drugstores and discount stores, because many jewelers will not accept the lower relative markup of the company's watches, and because most other watches are being sold through jewelry stores.
In this case, the company's distribution strategy was decided primarily by   6._____

    A. the nature of the product
    B. company resources
    C. competitors' distribution strategies
    D. the nature of the market

7. A marketing department decides to conduct marketing research using the exploratory   7.____
design. Which of the following will probably NOT be used as a source for this research?

    A.   Interviews with knowledgeable people
    B.   Secondary data
    C.   Experimental research studies
    D.   Case studies

8. Which of the following is generally considered to be the personal characteristic that   8.____
would be LEAST important for a salesperson practicing new business selling?

    A.   Empathy   B.   Experience
    C.   Age   D.   Aggressiveness

9. Motives that influence where a person purchases products on a regular basis are com-   9.____
monly called _____ motives.

    A.   projected   B.   patronage
    C.   learning   D.   circadian

10. A company decides to conduct an audit of its marketing environment. Which of the fol-   10.____
lowing questions is it likely to ask?

    A.   Which opportunities or threats emerge from within the company?
    B.   Does the organizational structure fit the evolving needs of the marketplace?
    C.   How effective are each of the major marketing activities?
    D.   How well do the products/brands meet the needs of the target markets?

11. Which of the following is the federal legislation governing the establishment and use of   11.____
trademarks?

    A.   Lanham Act
    B.   Celler-Kefauver Act
    C.   Clayton Act
    D.   Fair Packaging and Labeling Law

12. Which of the following is a person-specific influence on the consumer buying decision   12.____
process?

    A.   Perception   B.   Learning
    C.   Social class   D.   Marital status

13. Market segmentation has become increasingly important in developing business and   13.____
marketing strategies for each of the following reasons EXCEPT

    A.   a decreasing trend in population growth
    B.   increasingly diverse customer needs
    C.   decreasing trend in disposable incomes
    D.   increasing consumer awareness through media advancements

14. A company might decide to engage in the practice of skimming pricing in order to   14.____

    A.   clear out excess inventories of older models
    B.   keep demand low enough to be filled by a company's productive capacity
    C.   drive some of the smaller competitors out of the market
    D.   enter a market already dominated by other companies

15. Each of the following is a typical provision of a trademark licensing agreement EXCEPT   15.____

    A. assurance not to sue the user if conditions of the agreement are met
    B. geographical or other limitations or requirements of the use of the mark
    C. requirement of royalty payments to licensor for use of the mark
    D. licensee control over the nature and quality of licensed product or services

16. Agents are appropriate in industrial channels for each of the following conditions EXCEPT when   16.____

    A. selling functions are important
    B. the buyer is extremely large
    C. products are standardized
    D. information gathering is important

17. Within a company that has adopted a low-cost defender business strategy,   17.____

    A. there is relatively little synergy
    B. performance is likely to be best when marketing, R&D, and manufacturing facilities are shared with other business units in the company
    C. individual business units operate with a relatively high degree of autonomy
    D. a business unit manager's compensation is typically based on share growth

18. A _____ is most likely to take physical possession of a producer's merchandise.   18.____

    A. commission merchant   B. selling agent
    C. manufacturer's agent   D. broker

19. Under the terms of federal regulations, it is NOT a justifiable reason for offering different prices to different wholesalers for the same product when   19.____

    A. it can be proven that the cost of selling to one customer were the same or less than the difference in price
    B. goods are deteriorating or obsolete
    C. a lower price was offered to markedly undercut a competitive offer from another seller
    D. the goods are of different grade and quality

20. Which of the following is NOT a typical way in which organizational transactions differ from consumer sales?   20.____

    A. More reciprocity
    B. Less frequent negotiation
    C. Involve more buyers
    D. Longer negotiation periods needed to complete sales

21. The main difference between the full-cost and direct-cost methods for determining marketing costs is that the   21.____

    A. direct-cost method does not use non-traceable common costs
    B. direct-cost method uses costs attributable to the performance of marketing functions
    C. full-cost method does not use direct costs
    D. full-cost method uses marketing function accounts

22. One of the highest priorities for a producer in transporting its goods is traceability. If possible, which mode of transport should be selected?   22.____

    A. Air   B. Water   C. Rail   D. Truck

23. The abandonment of a given product line is a strategy that should be considered by a company   23.____

    A. during the introductory stage in the product life cycle
    B. during the maturity stage
    C. during the shakeout stage
    D. at every stage in the product life cycle

24. A company has adopted a prospector strategy for entrance into a certain market. For a business unit within the company, it would NOT be true that the unit will   24.____

    A. perform best when formalization is high
    B. perform best when controller, financial, and production managers have a substantial influence on business and marketing strategy decisions
    C. experience high levels of interfunctional conflict
    D. perform best when its functional strengths include sales, product R&D, and engineering

25. A company experiences a rapidly decreasing growth rate in sales of a certain product that results in strong price competition, after which many firms are forced to exit the market. In terms of the product life cycle concept, this situation illustrates the _____ stage or period.   25.____

    A. growth   B. decline   C. mature   D. shakeout

KEY (CORRECT ANSWERS)

1.	A	11.	A
2.	C	12.	D
3.	D	13.	C
4.	C	14.	B
5.	A	15.	D
6.	C	16.	B
7.	C	17.	B
8.	A	18.	A
9.	B	19.	C
10.	A	20.	C

21.	A
22.	A
23.	D
24.	A
25.	D

TEST 3

DIRECTIONS: Each question or incomplete statement is followed by several suggested answers or completions. Select the one that BEST answers the question or completes the statement. *PRINT THE LETTER OF THE CORRECT ANSWER IN THE SPACE AT THE RIGHT.*

1. The primary responsibility of a company's sales force is to build and maintain volume from current customers by giving purchase decision makers product information and service assistance.
   The sales force is MOST likely composed of _____ sellers.

   A. new business   B. missionary
   C. technical   D. trade

   1.____

2. Which of the following sectors is most likely to achieve sales through a franchising arrangement?

   A. Gasoline service stations
   B. Fast-food restaurants
   C. Soft-drink bottlers
   D. Automotive products and services

   2.____

3. Each of the following is an advantage of compensating sales employees with straight commissions EXCEPT:

   A. Selling expenses are directly related to sales resources
   B. It permits sales managers to push certain items
   C. It gives sales manager large amount of control over sales staff
   D. There is maximum incentive for sales

   3.____

4. The strategy of selective distribution would MOST likely be successful with

   A. specialty goods   B. convenience goods
   C. low-margin services   D. durable goods

   4.____

5. Each of the following is a clear sign that inventory is not in control EXCEPT

   A. consistently long delivery lead times
   B. large inventory write-offs
   C. inventory growing at a slower rate than sales
   D. surplus inventory

   5.____

6. Which of the following is categorized as a situational influence on the consumer buying decision process?

   A. Marital status   B. Health status
   C. Social class   D. Roles and family influences

   6.____

7. A retailer sets very low prices on one or more items in its store to attract as many shoppers as possible, figuring that the lost revenue from these items will be offset by additional purchases of regular-priced merchandise .
   This is an example of

   A. leader pricing   B. odd-even pricing
   C. price leadership   D. bait pricing

   7.____

8. An example of *line extension* is when a   8._____

    A. clockmaker changes the second hand movement from a ticking to a sweeping motion
    B. company that produces baking soda begins to promote the product as a deodorizer
    C. paper towel producer tries to acquire new customers by targeting organizational markets
    D. cola company develops a new lemon-lime flavored soft drink

9. An effective and useful market segmentation scheme should define segments that meet each of the following criteria EXCEPT   9._____

    A. undifferentiated response to marketing variables
    B. measurability
    C. size
    D. accessibility

10. Each of the following is a practice specifically forbidden by the provisions of the Robinson-Patman Act EXCEPT   10._____

    A. indefensible quantity discounts
    B. exclusive dealings and tying contracts
    C. fictitious brokerage
    D. disproportional supplementary services and allowances

11. Typically, which of the following elements would appear FIRST within an annual marketing plan?   11._____

    A. Current situation   B. Executive summary
    C. Objectives   D. Marketing strategy

12. Marketing efforts that are based on the information-search phase of the consumer decision-making process typically take each of the following factors into account EXCEPT   12._____

    A. total amount of information available to consumers
    B. relative importance of information sources
    C. percentage of the target market using specific information sources
    D. relative influence of family members

13. A consumer displays the following patterns of buying behavior: She purchases products such as insurance to achieve financial security, consumes consciously but cautiously, and typically purchases high-quality products in pursuit of gracious living.
According to market conventions, this consumer most likely
occupies the _____ class.   13._____

    A. upper   B. upper-middle
    C. lower-middle   D. upper-lower

14. In terms of security and defensibility, which of the following trademarks is ranked highest in the trademark hierarchy?   14._____

    A. Pacific Bell (telephone service)   B. Kodak (film)
    C. Marion (laboratories)   D. Escalator

15. Typically, most of a company's product lines are in the _____ stage of their respective   15.____
    life cycles at any given point in time.

    A. introductory or growth   B. growth or shakeout
    C. growth or maturity   D. maturity or decline

16. Legal protection for utility and design inventions is provided by a   16.____

    A. patent   B. trademark
    C. copyright   D. brand

17. Which of the following is NOT a step involved in the workload approach to establishing   17.____
    the size of a sales force?

    A. Determining how many customers are in each of a set of established categories
    B. Multiplying the number of potential customers in each category by the number of
       categories
    C. Estimating the number of calls a salesperson can make in one year
    D. Dividing the total number of calls that need to be made by the average number of
       calls a salesperson can make in a year

18. Which of the following factors, used to determine the buying power index (BPI) of a cer-   18.____
    tain geographic area, is nost highly weighted?

    A. Retail sales   B. Distribution
    C. Income   D. Population

19. Each of the following is an example of supporting goods EXCEPT   19.____

    A. lubricants
    B. flour sold to bakeries
    C. cash register tape
    D. cleaning materials

20. Generally, one who manufactures, produces, or packages products may be held respon-   20.____
    sible to a person who suffers harn from the use of the product upon each of the following
    grounds EXCEPT

    A. assault
    B. breach of implied warranty of fitness
    C. negligence
    D. breach of express warranty

21. Which of the following marketing strategies is probably LEAST useful for a company that   21.____
    has adopted an *analyzes* position in a certain market?

    A. Encirclement   B. Flanker strategy
    C. Leapfrog strategy   D. Frontal attack

22. What is the term for market-research tests in which subjects are asked to perform tasks   22.____
    for specific purposes while they are in fact being evaluated for other purposes?

    A. Patronage motives   B. Attitude scales
    C. Projective techniques   D. Covert interviews

23. The practice of penetration pricing is likely to be used in the marketing of   23.____

    A. an older line of children's clothing
    B. food and beverage products
    C. a frequently stocked-out line of home appliances
    D. a new line of personal computers

24. The easiest, but still generally effective, method for determining absolute market poten-   24.____
tial is to base the potential on

    A. the buying power index
    B. estimates prepared and aggregated from information on the use opportunities pre-
        sented by various segments
    C. current industry sales
    D. the competitive structure of the market

25. A company produces a liniment as a remedy for muscle pain due to bruises or overexer-   25.____
tion, and distributes the product to retail supermarkets. If the company discovers a new
use for the product, it would MOST likely

    A. promote the liniment as a means of warming up muscles before exercise
    B. simplify the product line
    C. begin to withdraw from the retail market and target professional sports teams
    D. modify the product slightly to widen its appeal

KEY (CORRECT ANSWERS)

1.	B		11.	B
2.	A		12.	A
3.	C		13.	B
4.	D		14.	B
5.	C		15.	D
6.	B		16.	A
7.	A		17.	B
8.	D		18.	C
9.	A		19.	B
10.	B		20.	A

21.	D
22.	C
23.	B
24.	C
25.	A

TEST 4

DIRECTIONS: Each question or incomplete statement is followed by several suggested answers or completions. Select the one that BEST answers the question or completes the statement. *PRINT THE LETTER OF THE CORRECT ANSWER IN THE SPACE AT THE RIGHT.*

1. In setting physical distribution objectives, which of the following strategies is MOST likely to be adopted by a marketing-oriented company?

    A. Do everything possible to minimize physical distribution costs, and then establish a multi-channel system in which intermediaries can assume a large portion of service costs
    B. Establish a reasonable level of service that will keep customers happy, and do everything possible to minimize physical distribution costs of providing this level of service
    C. View service costs as variable, doing everything possible to ensure customer satisfaction, and look upon the increased costs of physical distribution as an investment in future expansion
    D. Focus entirely on the minimum total cost

1.____

2. As a promotional tool, personal selling is MOST significant in the marketing of _____ goods.

    A. durable   B. convenience
    C. industrial   D. specialty

2.____

3. A company that decides to produce a pocket calculator that is much like the calculator produced by a competitor will probably encounter each of the following EXCEPT

    A. relatively low R&D costs
    B. a relatively high market share
    C. a lowered risk
    D. an easier introductory period

3.____

4. In marketing a certain product, a business is pursuing a differentiated defender strategy, and competition for distribution support is strong.
   Most likely, what is the company's most important personal selling objective?

    A. Maintaining customer loyalty
    B. Developing new customers
    C. Communicating product information
    D. Technical service to facilitate sales

4.____

5. Which of the following is NOT considered to be a benefit associated with the practice of target-return pricing? It

    A. can assist in estimations of market demand
    B. can be set at a rate that is considered both fair from a public policy standpoint and attainable from a company standpoint
    C. is relatively clear for internal company purposes
    D. can assure a company of meeting its financial objectives

5.____

6. Each of the following is a typical advantage associated with a retailer's use of a whole-saler's services EXCEPT

   A. wider product line
   B. efficient handling of customer service claims
   C. more efficient physical distribution activities
   D. coordination of supply sources

6.____

7. Which of the following is NOT a type of factor that appears to influence organizational buying decisions?

   A. Psychological   B. Environmental
   C. Interpersonal   D. Individual

7.____

8. Each of the following is a typical risk assumed by a franchisee EXCEPT

   A. overexpansion
   B. unproven track record of product
   C. scant marketing research
   D. poor management

8.____

9. A snack-food company wants to enter the market with a cookie featuring white chocolate chips and macadamia nuts. Marketing research has revealed that most customers wanted the maximum amount of white chocolate in their cookies, with only a small amount of nuts. The research department labels this group as segment Y. There were two other distinct segments revealed in the study: segment X (people who wanted a lot of nuts, and very little white chocolate) and segment Z (people who wanted small amounts of each). Segment X was the smallest segment.
   After this study, the company decides to target segment Z. The most likely reason for this is

   A. the company already produces a product that will satisfy segment Y
   B. unreliable research staff
   C. strong competition for the largest market segment
   D. high cost of ingredients

9.____

10. The authorization of the FTC and the Secretary of Health, Education, and Welfare to issue regulations to ensure truthful disclosure of producer identity and other relevant packaging practices was the major provision of the

    A. Federal Trade Commission Act
    B. Magnuson-Moss Warranty--Federal Trade Commission Improvements Act
    C. Fair Packaging and Labeling Law
    D. Food, Drug, and Cosmetics Act

10.____

11. The purpose of offering trade discounts is to

    A. permit low-income end-use customers to obtain necessary goods through the offer of unique services
    B. discourage the extension of credit to end-use customers
    C. provide an agent with a commission that does not come from the sales budget
    D. pay a wholesaler or retailer for the functions they form for a manufacturer

11.____

12. Which of the following types of sales promotion usually has the smallest impact on sales?   12.____

    A. Coupons   B. Premiums
    C. Trading stamps   D. Money refunds

13. Which of the following are examples of shopping goods?   13.____

    A. Stereo equipment   B. Furniture
    C. Umbrellas   D. Cameras

14. Which of the following market characteristics is MOST favorable for a frontal attack strategy on the part of a company entering the market?   14.____

    A. A relatively homogeneous market with respect to customer needs and purchase criteria; relatively little preference or loyalty for existing brands
    B. Two or more major segments with distinct needs and purchase criteria; the needs of customers in at least one segment not being met by existing brands
    C. Relatively heterogeneous market with a number of larger segments; needs and preferences of customers in most segments currently satisfied by competing brands
    D. Relatively homogeneous market, but some needs of criteria not currently met by existing brands

15. _____ marketing research questioning will offer a marketer the greatest control over the sample used.   15.____

    A. Personal at home
    B. Mail
    C. Personal at shopping center
    D. Telephone

16. _____ goods are characterized by maximum distribution, consumer advertising, and merchandising.   16.____

    A. Convenience   B. Durable
    C. Shopping   D. Novelty

17. Which of the following types of wholesalers is concerned mainly with facilitating exchange through selling activities?   17.____

    A. Specialty-line   B. Truck wholesaler
    C. Drop shipper   D. Limited-line

Questions 18-19.

DIRECTIONS: Questions 18 and 19 refer to the following information.

In a certain marketing channel network, a wholesaler's markup on a certain product is 20%, and the retailer's markup is 50%. The producer sells the product to a wholesaler for a price of $14.50.

18. For what price would the wholesaler sell the product to the retailer?   18.____

    A. $14.50   B. $17.40   C. $17.98   D. $21.75

19. What would the end-use customer end up paying for the product? 19.____

    A. $17.98   B. $21.75   C. $23.20   D. $26.10

20. An example of an institutional market is a(n) 20.____

    A. church purchasing hymnals
    B. employee of the Federal government buying household goods for her own home
    C. wholesaler buying syringes for resale to individual medical practitioners
    D. municipal government purchasing a water treatment system

21. The MOST important factor in an organizational user's selection of equipment is typically 21.____

    A. technical simplicity   B. price
    C. prestige   D. customer service

22. Which of the following is NOT a *disadvantage* associated with horizontal channel integration? 22.____

    A. Difficulty coordinating large number of units
    B. Increase in planning and research
    C. Purchasing inefficiency
    D. Decrease in flexibility

23. Which of the following is LEAST likely to function as a separate facilitating agency? 23.____

    A. Transportation
    B. Marketing research agency
    C. Buying center
    D. Insurance company

24. Generally, the most commonly experienced *exit barrier* to a company's disengagement from a business that is unprofitable is that 24.____

    A. the fixed assets involved have little liquidation value or high conversion costs
    B. management has an emotional tie to the business because of history or tradition
    C. national economic policy prevents some firms from exiting an industry
    D. higher management's sense of loyalty to employees

25. According to the marketing concept, which of the following characteristics does NOT describe a retail institution that has recently entered a market? 25.____

    A. Low-inventory   B. Low-status
    C. Low-margin   D. Low-price

KEY (CORRECT ANSWERS)

1.	B		11.	D
2.	C		12.	D
3.	B		13.	B
4.	A		14.	A
5.	A		15.	D
6.	B		16.	A
7.	A		17.	C
8.	B		18.	B
9.	C		19.	D
10.	C		20.	A

21.	D
22.	C
23.	C
24.	A
25.	A

———

EXAMINATION SECTION
TEST 1

DIRECTIONS: Each question or incomplete statement is followed by several suggested answers or completions. Select the one that BEST answers the question or completes the statement. *PRINT THE LETTER OF THE CORRECT ANSWER IN THE SPACE AT THE RIGHT.*

1.____

1.

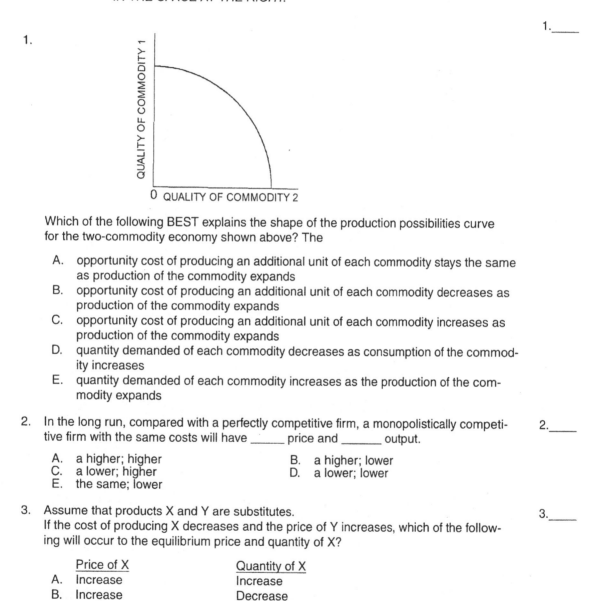

Which of the following BEST explains the shape of the production possibilities curve for the two-commodity economy shown above? The

    A. opportunity cost of producing an additional unit of each commodity stays the same as production of the commodity expands

    B. opportunity cost of producing an additional unit of each commodity decreases as production of the commodity expands

    C. opportunity cost of producing an additional unit of each commodity increases as production of the commodity expands

    D. quantity demanded of each commodity decreases as consumption of the commodity increases

    E. quantity demanded of each commodity increases as the production of the commodity expands

2. In the long run, compared with a perfectly competitive firm, a monopolistically competitive firm with the same costs will have _____ price and _____ output.

2.____

    A. a higher; higher   B. a higher; lower
    C. a lower; higher   D. a lower; lower
    E. the same; lower

3. Assume that products X and Y are substitutes.
If the cost of producing X decreases and the price of Y increases, which of the following will occur to the equilibrium price and quantity of X?

3.____

	Price of X	Quantity of X
A.	Increase	Increase
B.	Increase	Decrease
C.	Increase	Increase or decrease
D.	Increase or decrease	Increase
E.	Decrease	Decrease

4. Suppose that an effective minimum wage is imposed in a certain labor market above the equilibrium wage.
   If labor supply in that market subsequently increases, which of the following will occur?   4.____

   A. Unemployment in that market will increase.
   B. Quantity of labor supplied will decrease.
   C. Quantity of labor demanded will increase.
   D. Market demand will increase.
   E. The market wage will increase.

5. Imperfectly competitive firms may be allocatively inefficient because they produce at a level of output such that   5.____

   A. average cost is at a minimum
   B. price equals marginal revenue
   C. marginal revenue is greater than marginal cost
   D. price equals marginal cost
   E. price is greater than marginal cost

Questions 6-8.

DIRECTIONS: Questions 6 through 8 are to be answered on the basis of the table below, which shows a firm's total cost for different levels of output.

Output	Total Cost
0	$24
1	33
2	41
3	48
4	54
5	61
6	69

6. Which of the following is the firm's marginal cost of producing the fourth unit of output?   6.____

   A. $54.00   B. $13.50   C. $7.50   D. $6.00   E. $1.50

7. Which of the following is the firm's average total cost of producing 3 units of output?   7.____

   A. $48.00   B. $16.00   C. $14.00   D. $13.50   E. $7.00

8. Which of the following is the firm's average fixed cost of producing 2 units of output?   8.____

   A. $24.00   B. $20.50   C. $12.00   D. D, $8.00   E. $7.50

9. In the short run, if the product price of a perfectly competitive firm is less than the minimum average variable cost, the firm will   9.____

   A. raise its price
   B. increase its output
   C. decrease its output slightly but increase its profit margin
   D. lose more by continuing to produce than by shutting down
   E. lose less by continuing to produce than by shutting down

10. Which of the following statements is TRUE of perfectly competitive firms in long-run equilibrium?   10.____

    A. Firm revenues will decrease if production is increased.
    B. Total firm revenues are at a maximum.
    C. Average fixed cost equals marginal cost.
    D. Average total cost is at a minimum.
    E. Average variable cost is greater than marginal cost.

11. Assume that both input and product markets are competitive. If the product price rises, in   11.____
the short run firms will increase production by increasing

    A. the stock of fixed capital until marginal revenue equals the product price
    B. the stock of fixed capital until the average product of capital equals the price of capital
    C. labor input until the marginal revenue product of labor equals the wage rate
    D. labor input until the marginal product of labor equals the wage rate
    E. labor input until the ratio of product price to the marginal product of labor equals the wage rate

12. Half of the inhabitants of an island oppose building a new bridge to the mainland, since   12.____
they say it will destroy the island's quaint atmosphere.
The economic concept that is MOST relevant to the decision of whether or not to build
the bridge is

    A. externalities   B. natural monopoly
    C. economic rent   D. imperfect competition
    E. perfect competition

13. Which of the following BEST states the thesis of the law of comparative advantage?   13.____

    A. Differences in relative costs of production are the key to determining patterns of trade.
    B. Differences in absolute costs of production determine which goods should be traded between nations.
    C. Tariffs and quotas are beneficial in increasing international competitiveness.
    D. Nations should not specialize in the production of goods and services.
    E. Two nations will not trade if one is more efficient than the other in the production of all goods.

14. A student who attends college would pay $10,000 annually for tuition, books, and fees.   14.____
If the student's next best alternative is to work and earn $15,000 a year, the opportunity cost of a year in college would be equal to

    A. zero, since the lost opportunity to earn income is offset by the opportunity to attend college
    B. $5,000, representing the difference between forgone income and college costs
    C. $10,000, since opportunity costs include only actual cash outlays
    D. $15,000, representing forgone income, since the costs of tuition, books, and fees will be more than offset by additional income earned after graduation
    E. $25,000, representing the sum of tuition, books, fees, and forgone income

15. If an increase in the price of good X causes a drop in demand for good Y, good Y is a (n)   15.____

    A. inferior good   B. luxury good
    C. necessary good   D. substitute for good X
    E. complement to good X

16. An improvement in production technology for a certain good leads to a (n) _____ the   16.____
    good.

    A. increase in demand for
    B. increase in the supply of
    C. increase in the price of
    D. shortage of
    E. surplus of

17. A firm doubles all of its inputs and finds that it has more than doubled its output.   17.____
    This situation is an example of

    A. increasing marginal returns
    B. diminishing marginal returns
    C. constant returns to scale
    D. increasing returns to scale
    E. decreasing returns to scale

18. Reducing the tariff on Canadian beer sold in the United States will MOST likely have   18.____
    which of the following effects on the market for beer produced and sold in the United
    States?

    A. The quantity of United States beer purchased will increase.
    B. Total expenditure on United States beer will increase.
    C. The supply of United States beer will increase.
    D. The price of United States beer will decrease.
    E. More workers will be employed in the production of United States beer.

19. Suppose that the license paid by each business to operate in a city increases from $400   19.____
    per year to $500 per year.
    What effect will this increase have on a firm's short-run costs?

	Marginal Cost	Average Total Cost	Average Variable Cost
A.	Increase	Increase	Increase
B.	Increase	Increase	No effect
C.	No effect	No effect	No effect
D.	No effect	Increase	Increase
E.	No effect	Increase	No effect

20. In a perfectly competitive market, an individual farmer intending to increase her revenue   20.____
    decides to increase the price of her crop by 20 percent.
    As a result, her total revenue will

    A. decrease
    B. stay the same
    C. increase by less than 20 percent
    D. increase by 20 percent
    E. increase by more than 20 percent

21. If the supply of a factor of production is fixed, which of the following will be TRUE of its price?   21.____

    A. Supply is irrelevant to the determination of factor price.
    B. A positive factor price cannot be justified on economic grounds.
    C. Factor price will be determined by the demand for the fixed amount of the factor.
    D. Factor price will not be determined by supply and demand analysis.
    E. Factor price will be zero, since no payment is necessary to secure the services of the factor.

22. Which of the following is TRUE if a perfectly competitive industry is earning zero economic profits in the long run?   22.____

    A. The level of investment in long-run equilibrium is greater than the efficient level.
    B. Relatively few firms are able to survive the competitive pressures in the long run.
    C. Some firms will be forced to transfer their resources to more lucrative uses.
    D. The resources invested in this industry are earning at least as high a return as they would in any alternative use.
    E. Firms will exit until economic profits become positive.

23.   23.____

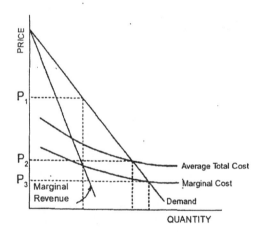

QUANTITY

The figure above shows cost and revenue curves for a public regulated power company and three possible prices for its output.
Which of the following statements about those prices is MOST accurate?

    A. If P_1 were approved, regulation would not be needed and the company would have every incentive to lower rates to P_2.
    B. P_1 is inefficient; it is better to have several utilities serve the area than to approve P_1.
    C. P_2 is ideal; it gives stockholders the maximum rate of return and protects consumers from exploitation.
    D. P_3 would maximize consumer welfare; greater electric use at this low rate would guarantee stockholders a fair rate of return.
    E. P_3 would maximize consumer welfare, but a public subsidy would be needed to keep the company in business.

24. If a competitive firm is faced with an increase in the ad valorem sales tax on its product, it is MOST likely to _____ the entire increase _____ if the elasticity of demand is _____.   24.____

    A. shift; to the consumer; infinite
    B. shift; to the consumer; zero
    C. bear; itself; zero
    D. bear; itself; one
    E. shift; to the consumer; one

25. In a market economy, public goods such as community police protection are unlikely to be provided in sufficient quantity by the private sector because   25.____

    A. private firms are less efficient at producing public goods than is the government
    B. the use of public goods cannot be withheld from those who do not pay for them
    C. consumers lack information about the benefits of public goods
    D. consumers do not value public goods highly enough for firms to produce them profitably
    E. public goods are inherently too important to be left to private firms to produce

---

KEY (CORRECT ANSWERS)

1.	C		11.	C
2.	B		12.	A
3.	D		13.	A
4.	A		14.	E
5.	E		15.	E
6.	D		16.	B
7.	B		17.	D
8.	C		18.	D
9.	D		19.	E
10.	D		20.	A

21.	C
22.	D
23.	E
24.	A
25.	B

TEST 2

DIRECTIONS: Each question or incomplete statement is followed by several suggested answers or completions. Select the one that BEST answers the question or completes the statement. *PRINT THE LETTER OF THE CORRECT ANSWER IN THE SPACE AT THE RIGHT.*

1. Problems faced by all economic systems include which of the following?   1.____
   How to
   I.   allocate scarce resources among unlimited wants
   II. decentralize markets
   III. decide what to produce, how to produce, and for whom to produce
   IV. set government production quotas
   The CORRECT answer is:

   A. I *only*   B. I, III   C. II, III
   D. I, II, III   E. I, II, III, IV

2. Of the following, a fall in the price of a product would be caused by a(n)   2.____

   A. increase in population and a decrease in the price of an input
   B. increase in population and a decrease in the number of firms producing the product
   C. increase in average income and an improvement in production technology
   D. decrease in the price of a substitute product and an improvement in production technology
   E. decrease in the price of a substitute product and an increase in the price of an input

3. The market equilibrium price of home heating oil is $1.50 per gallon.   3.____
   If a price ceiling of $1.00 per gallon is imposed, which of the following will occur in the market for home heating oil? Quantity
   I.   supplied will increase
   II. demanded will increase
   III. supplied will decrease
   IV. demanded will decrease
   The CORRECT answer is:

   A. II *only*   B. I, II   C. I, IV
   D. II, III   E. III, IV

4. Suppose that a family buys all its clothing from a discount store and treats these items as   4.____
   inferior goods. Under such circumstances, this family's consumption of discount store clothing will necessarily

   A. increase when a family member wins the state lottery
   B. increase when a family member gets a raise in pay at work
   C. remain unchanged when its income rises or falls due to events beyond the family's control
   D. decrease when a family member becomes unemployed
   E. decrease when a family member experiences an increase in income

5. Which of the following describes what will happen to market price and quantity if firms in   5.____
a perfectly competitive market form a cartel and act as a profit-maximizing monopoly?

	Price	Quantity
A.	Decrease	Decrease
B.	Decrease	Increase
C.	Increase	Increase
D.	Increase	Decrease
E.	Increase	No change

6.

Quantity Produced	Total Cost
0	$ 5
1	17
2	28
3	41
4	61
5	91

6.____

Barney's Bait Company can sell all the lures it produces at the market price of $14.
On the basis of the cost information in the table above, how many lures should the bait
company make?

A. 1   B. 2   C. 3   D. 4   E. 5

7. A natural monopoly occurs in an industry if   7.____

A.   economies of scale allow at most one firm of efficient size to exist in that market
B.   a single firm has control over a scarce and essential resource
C.   a single firm produces inputs for use by other firms
D.   a single firm has the technology to produce the product sold in that market
E.   above-normal profits persist in the industry

8. The typical firm in a monopolistically competitive industry earns zero profit in long-run   8.____
equilibrium because

A.   advertising costs make monopolistic competition a high-cost market structure
rather than a low-cost market structure
B.   the firms in the industry do not operate at the minimum point on their long-run aver-
age cost curves
C.   there are no restrictions on entering or exiting from the industry
D.   the firms in the industry are unable to engage in product differentiation
E.   there are close substitutes for each firm's product

9. Of the following, a shift in the market demand for workers with a certain skill is inevitably   9.____
caused by a (n) _____ workers.

A.   increase in the demand for goods produced by these
B.   decrease in tax rates on the income of these
C.   increase in the equilibrium wages received by these
D.   increase in the supply of these
E.   federally subsidized program created to train new

10. If hiring an additional worker would increase a firm's total cost by less than it would   10.____
increase its total revenue, the firm should

   A. not hire the worker
   B. hire the worker
   C. hire the worker only if another worker leaves or is fired
   D. hire the worker only if the worker can raise the firm's productivity
   E. reduce the number of workers employed by the firm

11. If a firm wants to produce a given amount of output at the lowest possible cost, it should   11.____
use each resource in such a manner that

   A. it uses more of the less expensive resource
   B. it uses more of the resource with the highest marginal product
   C. each resource has just reached the point of diminishing marginal returns
   D. the marginal products of each resource are equal
   E. the marginal products per dollar spent on each resource are equal

12. In which of the following ways does the United States government currently intervene in   12.____
the working of the market economy?
It
   I.   produces certain goods and services
   II.   regulates the private sector to achieve a more efficient allocation of
         resources
   III. redistributes income through taxation and public expenditures
The CORRECT answer is:

   A. I *only*   B. II *only*   C. III *only*
   D. II, III   E. I, II, III

13. If it were possible to increase the output of military goods and simultaneously to increase   13.____
the output of the private sector of an economy, which of the following statements about
the economy and its current position relative to its production possibilities curve would be
TRUE?
The economy is _____ and _____ the curve.

   A. inefficient; inside   B. inefficient; on
   C. efficient; on   D. efficient; inside
   E. efficient; outside

14. An effective price floor introduced in the market for rice will result in a (n) _____ in the   14.____
price of rice and a (n) _____ .

   A. decrease; increase in the quantity of rice sold
   B. decrease; decrease in the quantity of rice sold
   C. decrease; excess demand for rice
   D. increase; excess supply of rice
   E. increase; excess demand for rice

15. Marginal revenue is the change in revenue that results from a one-unit increase in the   15.____

   A. variable input   B. variable input price
   C. output level   D. output price
   E. fixed cost

16. A leftward shift in the supply curve of corn would result from a (n)   16.____

    A. decrease in the price of corn
    B. decrease in the price of farm machinery
    C. increase in the demand for corn bread
    D. increase in the labor costs of producing corn
    E. increase in consumers' incomes

17.   17.____

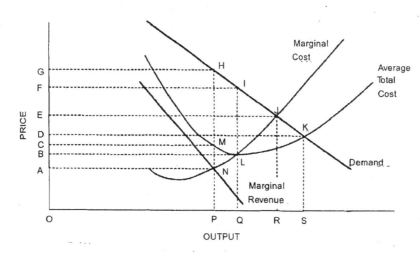

The diagram above depicts cost and revenue curves for a firm.
What are the firm's profit-maximizing output and price?

	Output	Price
A.	OS	OD
B.	OR	OE
C.	OQ	OF
D.	OQ	OB
E.	OP	OG

18. The government is considering imposing a 3 percent tax on either good A or good B.   18.____
In order to generate the LARGEST revenue, the tax should be imposed on the good for which

    A. demand is perfectly elastic
    B. demand is perfectly inelastic
    C. demand is unit elastic
    D. supply is perfectly elastic
    E. supply is unit elastic

19. Which of the following statements has to be TRUE in a perfectly competitive market?   19.____

    A. A firm's marginal revenue equals price.
    B. A firm's average total cost is above price in the long run.
    C. A firm's average fixed cost rises in the short run.
    D. A firm's average variable cost is higher than price in the long run.
    E. Large firms have lower costs than small firms.

20. Assume that an electric power company owns two plants and that, on a particular day, 10,000 kilowatts of electricity are demanded by the public.
In order to MINIMIZE the total cost of providing the 10,000 kilowatts, the company should allocate production so that

    A. marginal costs are the same for both plants
    B. average total costs are the same for both plants
    C. total variable costs are the same for both plants
    D. the sum of total variable cost and total fixed cost is the same for both plants
    E. only the plant with the lower average cost is used to produce the 10,000 kilowatts of electricity

20.____

21. Suppose that the consumption of a certain product results in benefits to others besides the consumers of the product.
Which of the following statements is MOST likely to be true?

    A. The demand for the product is price inelastic.
    B. A perfectly competitive industry will not produce the optimal quantity of the product.
    C. A perfectly competitive industry will not produce the product.
    D. Optimality requires that consumers of this product be taxed.
    E. Producers of this product earn an economic profit.

21.____

Questions 22-23.

DIRECTIONS: Questions 22 and 23 are to be answered on the basis of the table below, which lists the total output of workers in Greta's Jacket Shop.

Number of Workers	Total Output
2	12
3	22
4	28
5	32

22. Which of the following is the marginal product of the fourth worker?

    A. 4   B. 5   C. 6   D. 28   E. 112

22.____

23. Greta already employs 3 workers.
If the price of jackets is $5 and the wage rate is $25, she should

    A. go out of business altogether
    B. lay off the third worker
    C. keep the third worker but not employ more workers
    D. hire two more workers
    E. hire one more worker

23.____

24. A city council is deciding what price to set for a trip on the city's commuter train line. If the council wants to maximize profits, it will set a price so that

    A. price equals marginal cost
    B. price equals average cost
    C. price equals marginal revenue

24.____

D. marginal revenue equals marginal cost
E. marginal revenue equals average total cost

25. The demand curve for cars is downward sloping because an increase in the price of cars   25._____
    leads to a (n)

    A. increased use of other modes of transportation
    B. fall in the expected future price of cars
    C. decrease in the number of cars available for purchase
    D. rise in the prices of gasoline and other oil-based products
    E. change in consumers' tastes in cars

KEY (CORRECT ANSWERS)

1.	B	11.	E
2.	D	12.	E
3.	D	13.	A
4.	E	14.	D
5.	D	15.	C
6.	C	16.	D
7.	A	17.	E
8.	C	18.	B
9.	A	19.	A
10.	B	20.	A

21.	B
22.	C
23.	E
24.	D
25.	A

EXAMINATION SECTION
TEST 1

DIRECTIONS: Each question or incomplete statement is followed by several suggested answers or completions. Select the one that BEST answers the question or completes the statement. *PRINT THE LETTER OF THE CORRECT ANSWER IN THE SPACE AT THE RIGHT.*

1.   The simple circular flow model shows that

   A.   households are on the demand side of both product and resource markets
   B.   businesses are on the supply side of both product and resource markets
   C.   households are on the supply side of the resource market and on the demand side of the product market
   D.   businesses are on the demand side of the product market and on the supply side of the resource market

1.____

2.   The two basic markets shown by the simple circular flow model are

   A.   capital goods and consumer goods
   B.   free and controlled
   C.   product and resource
   D.   household and business
   E.   competitive and monopolistic

2.____

3.   In the resource market

   A.   businesses borrow money capital from households
   B.   businesses sell services to households
   C.   households sell resources to businesses
   D.   firms sell raw materials to households

3.____

4.   Which of the following is a limitation of the simple circular flow model?

   A.   Intrabusiness and intrahousehold transactions are ignored.
   B.   The economic activities of government are omitted.
   C.   The determination of product and resource prices is not explained.
   D.   All of the above

4.____

5.   In the simple circular flow model

   A.   households are suppliers of resources
   B.   businesses are suppliers of final products
   C.   households are demanders of final products
   D.   all of the above

5.____

Questions 6-9.

DIRECTIONS: Questions 6 through 9 are to be answered on the basis of the following circular flow model of the economy.

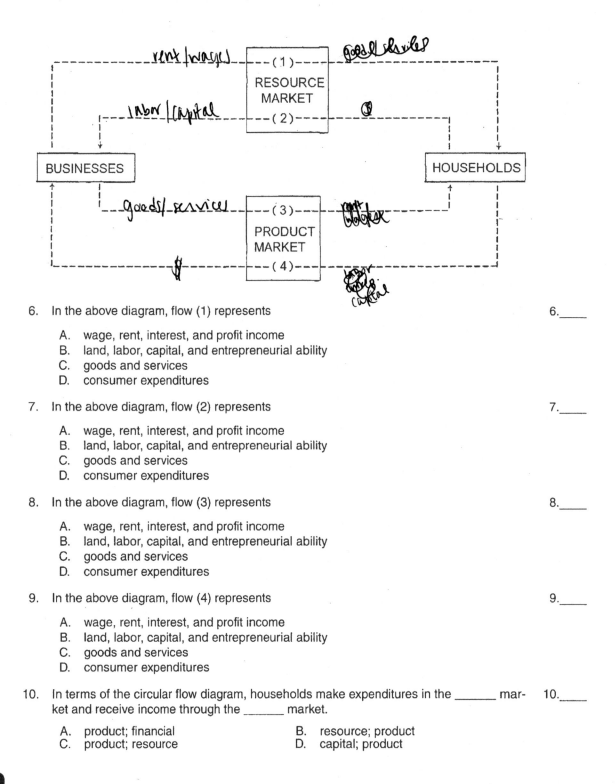

6. In the above diagram, flow (1) represents   6.____

    A. wage, rent, interest, and profit income
    B. land, labor, capital, and entrepreneurial ability
    C. goods and services
    D. consumer expenditures

7. In the above diagram, flow (2) represents   7.____

    A. wage, rent, interest, and profit income
    B. land, labor, capital, and entrepreneurial ability
    C. goods and services
    D. consumer expenditures

8. In the above diagram, flow (3) represents   8.____

    A. wage, rent, interest, and profit income
    B. land, labor, capital, and entrepreneurial ability
    C. goods and services
    D. consumer expenditures

9. In the above diagram, flow (4) represents   9.____

    A. wage, rent, interest, and profit income
    B. land, labor, capital, and entrepreneurial ability
    C. goods and services
    D. consumer expenditures

10. In terms of the circular flow diagram, households make expenditures in the _____ mar-   10.____
    ket and receive income through the _____ market.

    A. product; financial   B. resource; product
    C. product; resource   D. capital; product

11. In terms of the circular flow diagram, businesses obtain revenue through the _____ market and make expenditures in the _____ market.

    A. product; financial   B. resource; product
    C. product; resource   D. capital; product

11.____

12. Households and businesses are

    A. both buyers in the resource market
    B. both suppliers in the product market
    C. suppliers in the resource and product markets, respectively
    D. suppliers in the product and resource markets, respectively

12.____

13. In the circular flow model,

    A. households supply resources to firms
    B. households receive income through the resource market
    C. households spend income in the product market
    D. all of the above

13.____

Questions 14-15.

DIRECTIONS: Questions 14 and 15 are to be answered on the basis of the following diagram.

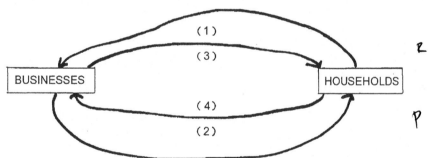

14. In the above diagram, arrows (1) and (2) represent

    A. goods and resources, respectively
    B. money incomes and output, respectively
    C. output and money incomes, respectively
    D. resources and goods, respectively

14.____

15. In the above diagram, arrows (3) and (4) represent

    A. goods and services, respectively
    B. money incomes and consumer expenditures, respectively
    C. resources and goods, respectively
    D. consumer expenditures and money income, respectively

15.____

16. When the price of a product rises, consumers shift their purchases to other products whose prices are now relatively lower.
This statement describes the

16.____

143

A. rationing function of prices
B. substitution effect
C. law of supply
D. income effect

17. When the price of a product falls, the purchasing power of our money income rises and thus permits us to purchase more of the product.
This statement describes the

   17.____

A. rationing function of prices
B. substitution effect
C. law of supply
D. income effect

18. During the 1970s, the price of oil rose dramatically, which in turn caused the price of coal to increase. This can best be explained by saying that oil and coal are

   18.____

A. complementary goods and the higher price for oil increased the demand for coal
B. substitute goods and the higher price for oil increased the demand for coal
C. complementary goods and the higher price for oil decreased the supply of coal
D. substitute goods and the higher price for oil decreased the supply of coal

19. An economist for a bicycle company predicts that, other things equal, a rise in consumer incomes will increase the demand for bicycles. This prediction is based upon the assumption that

   19.____

A. there are many goods which are substitutes for bicycles
B. there are many goods which are complementary to bicycles
C. there are few goods which are substitutes for bicycles
D. bicycles are normal goods

20. A rightward shift in the demand curve for product C might be caused by a(n)

   20.____

A. increase in income if C is a normal good
B. decrease in income if C is an inferior good
C. increase in the price of a product which is a close substitute for C
D. all of the above

21. If the price of product L increases, the demand curve for close-substitute product J will

   21.____

A. shift downward toward the horizontal axis
B. shift to the left
C. shift to the right
D. remain unchanged

22. A shift to the right in the demand curve for product A can be most reasonably explained by saying that

   22.____

A. consumer incomes have declined and they now want to buy less of A at each possible price
B. the price of A has increased and, as a result, consumers want to purchase less of it
C. consumer preferences have changed in favor of A so that they now want to buy more at each possible price

D. the price of A has declined and, as a result, consumers want to purchase more of it
E. the supply of A has increased because production costs have declined

23. Which of the following will cause the demand curve for product A to shift to the left?   23._____

   A. Population growth which causes an expansion in the number of persons consuming A
   B. An increase in money income if A is a normal good
   C. A decrease in the price of complementary product C
   D. An increase in money income if A is an inferior good
   E. An increase in the price of substitute product B

24. If X is a normal good, a rise in money income will shift the _____ curve for X to the   24._____
   _____.

   A. supply; left   B. supply; right
   C. demand; left   D. demand; right

25. If Z is an inferior good, a decrease in money income will shift the _____ curve for Z to   25._____
   the _____.

   A. supply; left   B. supply; right
   C. demand; left   D. demand; right

KEY (CORRECT ANSWERS)

1.	C		11.	C
2.	C		12.	C
3.	C		13.	D
4.	D		14.	D
5.	D		15.	B
6.	A		16.	B
7.	B		17.	D
8.	C		18.	B
9.	D		19.	D
10.	C		20.	D

21.	C
22.	C
23.	D
24.	D
25.	D

TEST 2

DIRECTIONS: Each question or incomplete statement is followed by several suggested answers or completions. Select the one that BEST answers the question or completes the statement. *PRINT THE LETTER OF THE CORRECT ANSWER IN THE SPACE AT THE RIGHT.*

1. Normal profits are   1.____

   A. a cost because any excess of total receipts over total costs will accrue to the businessperson
   B. a cost because they represent payments made for the resources which the businessperson owns and supplies in his or her own enterprise
   C. not a cost because a firm can avoid these payments by temporarily closing down
   D. not a cost of production because they need not be realized in order for a firm to retain entrepreneurial ability

2. Economic profits are   2.____

   A. a cost because they are really a part of wage costs
   B. a cost because they accrue to the entrepreneur
   C. not a cost because they cannot be calculated
   D. not an economic cost because they need not be realized in order for a business to acquire and retain entrepreneurial ability

3. If competitive industry Z is realizing substantial economic profits, we can expect that output will   3.____

   A. fall, product price will fall, and economic profits will tend to disappear
   B. fall, product price will rise, and economic profits will tend to disappear
   C. expand, product price will fall, and economic profits will tend to disappear
   D. expand, product price will fall, and economic profits will tend to rise

4. When a competitive industry is in equilibrium,   4.____

   A. economic profits will be zero
   B. product demand and derived demand are equal
   C. the economizing problem will have been solved for that industry
   D. normal profits will not be realized

5. From society's point of view, the economic function of profits and losses is to   5.____

   A. promote the equal distribution of real assets and wealth
   B. perpetuate full employment and price level stability
   C. contribute to a more equal distribution of income
   D. reallocate resources from less desired to more desired uses

6. In 1994 Ford sold 500,000 Escorts at an average price of $7,200 per car; in 1995, 600,000 Escorts were sold at an average price of $7,500 per car.
   These statements   6.____

A. suggest that the demand for Escorts decreased between 1994 and 1995
B. imply that Escorts are an inferior good
C. suggest that the demand for Escorts increased between 1994 and 1995
D. illustrate that the supply curve for Escorts is down-sloping

7. Other things equal, which of the following might shift the demand curve for gasoline to the left?   7.____

A. The discovery of vast new oil reserves in Montana
B. The development of a low-cost electric automobile
C. An increase in the price of train and air transportation
D. A large decline in the price of automobiles

8. A decrease in the price of cameras will   8.____

A. cause the demand curve for film to become vertical
B. shift the demand curve for film to the right
C. shift the demand curve for film to the left
D. not affect the demand for film

9. If products C and D are close substitutes, an increase in the price of C will shift the demand curve of   9.____

A. C to the left and the demand curve of D to the right
B. D to the right
C. both products to the right
D. both products to the left

10. In constructing a stable demand curve for product X,   10.____

A. consumer preferences are assumed constant
B. the prices of other goods are assumed given
C. money incomes are assumed constant
D. all of the above assumptions are made

11. The demand curve for a product might shift as the result of a change in   11.____

A. consumer incomes
B. the prices of related goods
C. the number of buyers in the market
D. all of the above

12. Suppose an excise tax is imposed on product X. We would expect this tax to   12.____

A. increase the demand for complementary good Y and decrease the demand for substitute product Z
B. decrease the demand for complementary good Y and increase the demand for substitute product Z
C. increase the demands for both complementary good Y and substitute product Z
D. decrease the demands for both complementary good Y and substitute product Z

13. When an economist says that the demand for a product has increased, this means that   13.____

    A. consumers are now willing to purchase more of this product at each possible price
    B. the product has become particularly scarce for some reason
    C. product price has fallen and as a consequence consumers are buying a larger quantity of the product
    D. the demand curve has shifted to the left

14. The term *quantity demanded* refers to   14.____

    A. the entire series of prices and quantities which comprise the demand schedule
    B. a situation where the income and substitution effects do not apply
    C. the amount of a product which will be purchased at some specific price
    D. none of the above

15. Assume that the demand schedule for product C is down-sloping. If the price of C falls from $2.00 to $1.75,   15.____

    A. a smaller quantity of C will be demanded
    B. a larger quantity of C will be demanded
    C. the demand for C will increase
    D. the demand for C will decrease

16. The law of supply   16.____

    A. reflects the amounts which producers will want to offer at each price in a series of prices
    B. is reflected in an upsloping supply curve
    C. shows that the relationship between price and quantity supplied is positive
    D. is reflected in all of the above

17. A firm"s supply curve is upsloping because   17.____

    A. the expansion of production necessitates the use of qualitatively inferior inputs
    B. mass production economies are associated with larger levels of output
    C. consumers envision a positive relationship between price and quality
    D. beyond some point the production costs of additional units of output will rise

18. A leftward shift of a product supply curve might be caused by   18.____

    A. an improvement in the relevant technique of production
    B. a decline in the prices of needed inputs
    C. an increase in consumer incomes
    D. some firms leaving an industry

19. The location of the product supply curve depends upon   19.____

    A. production technology
    B. the number of sellers in the market
    C. costs of required resources
    D. all of the above

20. An improvement in production technology will   20.____

    A. tend to increase equilibrium price
    B. shift the supply curve to the left
    C. shift the supply curve to the right
    D. shift the demand curve to the left

21. Because of unseasonably cold weather, the supply of oranges has substantially   21.____
    decreased.
    This statement indicates that

    A. consumers will be willing and able to buy fewer oranges at each possible price
    B. the demand for oranges will necessarily rise
    C. the equilibrium quantity of oranges will rise
    D. the amount of oranges that will be available at various prices has declined
    E. the price of oranges will fall

22. If producers must obtain higher prices than previously in order to produce various levels   22.____
    of output, one can say that there has occurred a (n)

    A. decrease in demand   B. increase in demand
    C. decrease in supply   D. increase in supply

23. Other things the same, we can expect the imposition of an excise tax on a product to   23.____

    A. decrease its supply
    B. increase its price
    C. decrease the quantity sold
    D. all of the above

24. In a market economy, a significant change in the demand for product X will   24.____

    A. alter the profits or losses received by certain firms
    B. cause a reallocation of scarce resources
    C. cause some industries to expand and others to contract
    D. all of the above

25. If competitive industry Y is incurring substantial losses, we can expect that output will   25.____

    A. expand, product price will rise, and losses will tend to disappear
    B. contract, product price will fall, and losses will increase
    C. contract, product price will rise, and losses will tend to disappear
    D. expand, product price will fall, and losses will tend to disappear

———————

KEY (CORRECT ANSWERS)

1.	B	11.	D
2.	D	12.	B
3.	C	13.	A
4.	A	14.	C
5.	D	15.	B
6.	C	16.	D
7.	B	17.	B
8.	B	18.	D
9.	B	19.	D
10.	D	20.	C

21.	D
22.	C
23.	D
24.	D
25.	B

———

TEST 3

DIRECTIONS: Each question or incomplete statement is followed by several suggested answers or completions. Select the one that BEST answers the question or completes the statement. *PRINT THE LETTER OF THE CORRECT ANSWER IN THE SPACE AT THE RIGHT.*

1. If an increase occurs in the demand for product X, we would expect all of the following to occur EXCEPT a(n)

    A. increase in the profits of industry X
    B. increase in the demand for resources employed by industry X
    C. increase in the output of industry X
    D. decrease in the prices of resources employed in industry X

1.____

2. The economic function of profits and losses is to

    A. bring about a more equal distribution of income
    B. signal that resources should be reallocated
    C. eliminate small firms and reduce competition
    D. tell government which industries need to be subsidized

2.____

3. In a competitive economy, prices influence

    A. consumers in their purchases of goods and services
    B. businesses in their purchases of economic resources
    C. workers in making occupational choices
    D. all of the above

3.____

4. If a competitive industry is neither expanding nor contracting, we would expect

    A. normal profits to be zero
    B. economic profits to be zero
    C. consumer demand and derived demand to be equal
    D. external costs or benefits to be large

4.____

5. Suppose a firm's total economic cost in producing 1,000 aluminum baseball bats is $10,000. These bats are then sold by the firm for $12,000. We can conclude that

    A. the firm is necessarily using the least-cost production technique because it is realizing an economic profit
    B. the firm's normal profit is $2,000
    C. the firm's pure or economic profit is $2,000
    D. there is no economic reason for the aluminum bat industry to either expand or contract

5.____

6. Suppose industry A is realizing substantial economic profits. Which of the following best describes the adjustment process which would bring about a new equilibrium?
Firms will _____ the industry, output will _____, and product price will _____.

    A. leave; fall; rise   B. enter; rise; rise
    C. leave; rise; fall   D. enter; rise; fall

6.____

7. An industry is in equilibrium when 7.____

    A. normal profits are zero
    B. total revenue exceeds total economic costs
    C. total economic costs exceed total revenue
    D. economic profits are zero

8. When economists say that the demand for a resource is a *derived demand,* they mean that 8.____

    A. producers tend to substitute low-priced for high-priced resources
    B. the demand for resources depends upon the demand for the product which those resources produce
    C. government demand complements private demand for most goods and services
    D. resource demand curves are often upsloping

9. The competitive market system 9.____

    A. encourages innovation because government provides tax breaks and subsidies to those who develop new products or new productive techniques
    B. discourages innovation because it is difficult to acquire additional capital in the form of new machinery and equipment
    C. discourages innovation because firms want to get all the profits possible from existing machinery and equipment
    D. encourages innovation because successful innovators are rewarded with economic profits

10. The most efficient combination of resources in producing any output is that combination which 10.____

    A. comes closest to using the same quantities of land, labor, capital, and entrepreneurial ability
    B. can be obtained for the smallest money outlay
    C. uses the smallest total quantity of all resources
    D. conserves most on the use of labor

Questions 11-14.

DIRECTIONS: Questions 11 through 14 are to be answered on the basis of the following data which show all available techniques by which 20 units of a given commodity can be produced.

Resource	Resource Prices	Possible Production Techniques				
		#1	#2	#3	#4	#5
Land	$4	2	4	2	4	4
Labor	3	1	2	4	1	3
Capital	3	5	2	3	1	2
Entrepreneurial ability	2	3	1	1	4	1

11. Given the indicated resource prices, the economically most efficient production technique(s) will be technique(s) 11.____

    A. #1   B. #2 and #4   C. #3
    D. #1 and #3   E. #5

12. Assuming that the firm is motivated by self-interest and that the 20 units which can be produced with each technique can be sold for $2 per unit, the firm will

    12._____

    A. realize an economic profit of $10
    B. realize an economic profit of $4
    C. only make a normal profit
    D. just manage to cover all of its costs
    E. close down rather than incur a loss by producing

13. Which of the following statements concerning this industry is CORRECT?

    13._____

    A. Firms in this industry will find that firms in other industries are able to outbid them for resources.
    B. The industry will contract as firms are forced out of business.
    C. The industry will expand as new firms enter.
    D. The industry is in equilibrium in that there is no reason for it to expand or contract.

14. If a new production technique is developed which enables a firm to produce 20 units of output with 3 units of land, 3 of labor, 1 of capital, and 2 of entrepreneurial ability, this technique would

    14._____

    A. not be adopted because although it reduces production costs, it does not increase profits
    B. be adopted because it would lower production costs and increase economic profits
    C. not be adopted because it entails higher production costs than other available techniques
    D. be adopted, even though economic profits would be reduced slightly

Questions 15-16.

DIRECTIONS: Questions 15 and 16 are to be answered on the basis of the following information: Suppose 30 units of product A can be produced by employing just labor and capital in the four ways shown below. Assume the prices of labor and capital are $2 and $3, respectively.

	Production		Techniques	
	I	II	III	IV
Labor	4	3	2	5
Capital	2	3	5	1

15. Which technique is economically most efficient in producing A?

    15._____

    A. I   B. II   C. III   D. IV

16. If the price of product A is $.50, the firm will realize a (n)

    16._____

    A. economic profit of $4   B. economic profit of $2
    C. economic profit of $6   D. loss of $3

17. In a competitive market economy, firms will select the least-cost production technique because

    17._____

A. such choices will result in the full employment of available resources
B. to do so will maximize firm profits
C. this will prevent new firms from entering the industry
D. *dollar voting* by consumers mandates such a choice

18. The *invisible hand* refers to the   18.____

A. fact that our tax system redistributes income from rich to poor
B. notion that, under competition, decisions motivated by self-interest promote the social interest
C. tendency of monopolistic sellers to raise prices above competitive levels
D. fact that government controls the functioning of the market system

19. Two major virtues of the competitive market system are that it   19.____

A. allocates resources efficiently and allows economic freedom
B. results in an equitable personal distribution of income and always maintains full employment
C. results in price level stability and a fair personal distribution of income
D. eliminates discrimination and minimizes environmental pollution

20. Supporters of the market system   20.____

A. contend that it is conducive to the efficient use of scarce resources
B. argue that it effectively harnesses the incentives of workers and entrepreneurs
C. believe it is consistent with freedom of choice
D. all of the above

21. The price elasticity of demand coefficient indicates   21.____

A. buyer responsiveness to price changes
B. the extent to which a demand curve shifts as incomes change
C. the slope of the demand curve
D. how far business executives can stretch their fixed costs

22. The basic formula for the price elasticity of demand coefficient is   22.____

A. absolute decline in quantity demanded/absolute increase in price
B. percentage change in quantity demanded/percentage change in price
C. absolute decline in price/absolute increase in quantity demanded
D. percentage change in price/percentage change in quantity demanded

23. The demand for a product is said to be inelastic with respect to price if   23.____

A. consumers are largely unresponsive to a per unit price change
B. the elasticity coefficient is greater than 1
C. a drop in price is accompanied by a decrease in the quantity demanded
D. a drop in price is accompanied by an increase in the quantity demanded

24. If the price elasticity of demand for a product is 2.5, then a price cut from $2.00 to $1.80   24.____
will _____ the quantity demanded by about _____ percent.

A. increase; 2.5   B. decrease; 2.5
C. increase; 25   D. increase; 250

154

25. Suppose that as the price of Y falls from $2.00 to $1.90, the quantity of Y demanded increases from 110 to 118.
It can be concluded that the price elasticity of demand is

    A. 4.00   B. 2.09   C. 1.37   D. 3.94

25.____

KEY (CORRECT ANSWERS)

1.	D	11.	B
2.	B	12.	A
3.	D	13.	C
4.	B	14.	B
5.	C	15.	D
6.	D	16.	B
7.	D	17.	B
8.	B	18.	B
9.	D	19.	A
10.	B	20.	D

21.	A
22.	B
23.	A
24.	C
25.	C

TEST 4

DIRECTIONS: Each question or incomplete statement is followed by several suggested answers or completions. Select the one that BEST answers the question or completes the statement. *PRINT THE LETTER OF THE CORRECT ANSWER IN THE SPACE AT THE RIGHT.*

1. If the demand for product X is inelastic, a 4 percent increase in the price of X will _____ the quantity of X demanded by _____ than 4 percent.   1.____

   A. decrease; more   B. decrease; less
   C. increase; more   D. increase; less

2. A perfectly inelastic demand schedule   2.____

   A. rises upward and to the right, but has a constant slope
   B. can be represented by a line parallel to the vertical axis
   C. cannot be shown on a two-dimensional graph
   D. can be represented by a line parallel to the horizontal axis

3. A given leftward shift in the supply curve of product X will increase equilibrium price to a greater extent the   3.____

   A. more elastic the supply curve
   B. larger the elasticity of demand coefficient
   C. more elastic the demand for the product
   D. more inelastic the demand for the product

4. The price of product X is reduced from \$100 to \$90 and, as a result, the quantity demanded increases from 50 to 60 units. From this we can conclude that the demand for X in this price range   4.____

   A. has declined   B. is of unit elasticity
   C. is inelastic   D. is elastic

5. The diagram shown at the right shows two product demand curves. On the basis of this diagram, we can say that   5.____

   A. over range P_1 P_2 price elasticity of demand is greater for D1 than for D_2
   B. over range P_1 P_2 price elasticity of demand is greater for D_2 than for D_1
   C. over range P_1P_2 price elasticity is the same for the two demand curves
   D. not enough information is given to compare price elasticities

6. The concept of price elasticity of demand measures the   6._____

    A. slope of the demand curve
    B. number of buyers in a market
    C. extent to which the demand curve shifts as the result of a price decline
    D. sensitivity of consumers to price changes

7. If the price elasticity of demand for gasoline is 0.20, this indicates that   7._____

    A. the demand for gasoline is linear
    B. a rise in the price of gasoline will reduce the total revenue going to sellers
    C. a 10 percent rise in the price of gasoline will decrease the amount purchased by 2 percent
    D. a 10 percent fall in the price of gasoline will increase the amount purchased by 20 percent

8. The demands for such products as salt, bread, and electricity tend to be   8._____

    A. perfectly price inelastic
    B. perfectly price elastic
    C. relatively price inelastic
    D. relatively price elastic

9. The demand for mass transit by commuters is likely to be   9._____

    A. more price elastic in the short run than in the long run
    B. more price elastic in the long run than in the short run
    C. of unitary elasticity
    D. nearly perfectly inelastic because there are no close substitutes

10. The demand for beer is likely to be   10._____

    A. less elastic than the demand for Budweiser
    B. more elastic than the demand for Budweiser
    C. of the same elasticity as the demand for Budweiser
    D. perfectly inelastic

11. An antidrug policy which reduces the supply of heroin will tend to _____ street crime   11._____
because the addict's demand for heroin is highly _____.

    A. increase; inelastic   B. reduce; elastic
    C. reduce; inelastic   D. increase; elastic

12. Other things the same, the shortage associated with a price ceiling will be greater the   12._____

    A. smaller the elasticity of both demand and supply
    B. greater the elasticity of both demand and supply
    C. greater the elasticity of supply and the smaller the elasticity of demand
    D. greater the elasticity of demand and the smaller the elasticity of supply

13. Price ceilings and price floors   13.____

    A. cause surpluses and shortages, respectively
    B. make the rationing function of free markets more efficient
    C. interfere with the rationing function of prices
    D. shift demand and supply curves and, therefore, have no effect upon the rationing function of prices

14. Students at Twin Peaks State University pay $40 per year for a parking permit but many   14.____
complain that they are unable to find a parking place in University lots. This suggests that

    A. student incomes are too low
    B. parking permits are underpriced
    C. parking permits are overpriced
    D. the University should make parking free

15. An effective minimum wage law can be expected to   15.____

    A. clear the market for blue-collar workers
    B. increase the number of firms in those industries wherein the law is effective
    C. increase employment for some affected workers
    D. cause unemployment for some affected workers

16. At the current price, there is a shortage of a product.   16.____
We would expect price to _____, quantity demanded to _____, and quantity supplied to _____.

    A. decrease; decrease; increase
    B. decrease; decrease; decrease
    C. decrease; increase; decrease
    D. increase; decrease; increase

17. A surplus of a product will arise when price is _____ equilibrium with the result that   17.____
quantity _____ exceeds quantity _____.

    A. above; demanded; supplied
    B. above; supplied; demanded
    C. below; demanded; supplied
    D. below; supplied; demanded

18. If we say that a price is *too high to clear the market,* we mean that   18.____

    A. quantity demanded exceeds quantity supplied
    B. the equilibrium price is above the current price
    C. quantity supplied exceeds quantity demanded
    D. the price of the good is likely to rise

19. Assume in a competitive market that price is initially above the equilibrium level. We can   19.____
predict that price will _____, quantity demanded will _____, and quantity supplied will
_____.

    A. decrease; decrease; increase
    B. decrease; decrease; decrease

C. decrease; increase; decrease
D. increase; decrease; increase

20. Assume in a competitive market that price is initially below the equilibrium level. We can predict that price will _____, quantity demanded will _____, and quantity supplied will _____.   20._____

    A. decrease; decrease; increase
    B. decrease; decrease; decrease
    C. decrease; increase; decrease
    D. increase; decrease; increase

21. In which of the following instances will the effect upon equilibrium price be indeterminant, that is, dependent upon the magnitude of the given shifts in supply and demand?   21._____

    A. Demand rises and supply rises.
    B. Supply falls and demand remains constant.
    C. Demand rises and supply falls.
    D. Supply rises and demand falls.

22. An unusually bountiful crop of coffee beans might be expected to   22._____

    A. increase the supply of coffee
    B. reduce the price of coffee
    C. increase the quantity of coffee consumed
    D. lower the price of tea

23. Data from the registrar's office at Michigan State University indicate that over the past twenty years tuition and enrollment have both increased. From this information we can conclude that   23._____

    A. higher education is an exception to the law of demand
    B. the supply of education provided by MSU has also increased over the twenty-year period
    C. school-age population, incomes, and preferences for education have changed over the twenty-year period
    D. MSU's supply curve of education is downsloping

24. The rationing function of prices refers to the   24._____

    A. tendency of supply and demand to shift in opposite directions
    B. fact that ration coupons are needed to alleviate wartime shortages of goods
    C. capacity of a competitive market to equate the quantity demanded and the quantity supplied
    D. ability of the market system to generate an equitable distribution of income

25. Depreciation of the dollar will tend to

                                                    25.____

    A.   decrease the prices of both American imports and exports
    B.   increase the prices of both American imports and exports
    C.   decrease the prices of the goods Americans import, but increase the prices to foreigners of the goods Americans export
    D.   increase the prices of the goods Americans import, but decrease the prices to foreigners of the goods Americans export

---

KEY (CORRECT ANSWERS)

1.	B		11.	A
2.	B		12.	B
3.	D		13.	C
4.	B		14.	B
5.	D		15.	C
6.	D		16.	B
7.	C		17.	B
8.	C		18.	C
9.	B		19.	C
10.	A		20.	D

21.	A
22.	A
23.	C
24.	C
25.	D

EXAMINATION SECTION
TEST 1

DIRECTIONS: Each question or incomplete statement is followed by several suggested answers or completions. Select the one that BEST answers the question or completes the statement. *PRINT THE LETTER OF THE CORRECT ANSWER IN THE SPACE AT THE RIGHT.*

Questions 1-4.

DIRECTIONS: Questions 1 through 4 are to be answered on the basis of the diagram below.

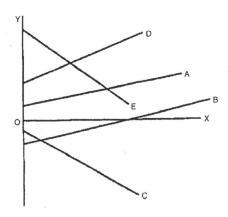

1. Which line(s) show(s) a positive relationship between x and y?   1.____

    A. A *only*   B. Both A and D
    C. A, B, and D   D. Both C and E

2. Which line(s) show(s) a negative relationship between x and y?   2.____

    A. A *only*   B. Both A and D
    C. A, B, and D   D. Both C and E

3. Which line(s) show(s) a positive vertical intercept?   3.____

    A. A and D *only*   B. B and C *only*
    C. A, D, and E   D. A, D, and B

4. Which line(s) show(s) a negative vertical intercept?   4.____

    A. C *only*   B. Both C and E
    C. B, C, and E   D. Both B and C

Questions 5-7.

DIRECTIONS: Questions 5 through 7 are to be answered on the basis of the following diagram.

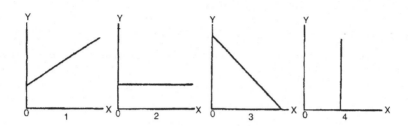

5.   The amount of Y is directly related to the amount of X in   5._____

   A.   both 1 and 3   B.   both 1 and 2
   C.   2 *only*   D.   1 *only*

6.   The amount of Y is inversely related to the amount of X in   6._____

   A.   2 *only*   B.   both 1 and 3
   C.   3 *only*   D.   1 *only*

7.   The amount of Y is unrelated to the amount of X in   7._____

   A.   both 2 and 4   B.   3 *only*
   C.   2 *only*   D.   1 *only*

8.   8._____

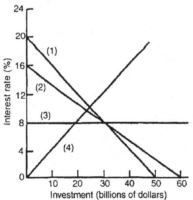

Assume that if the interest rate which businesses must pay to borrow funds were 20
percent, it would be unprofitable for businesses to invest in new machinery and equipment so that investment would be zero. But if the interest rate were 16 percent, businesses will find it profitable to invest $10 billion. If the interest rate were 12 percent,
$20 billion would be invested. Assume that total investment continues to increase by
$10 billion for each successive 4 percentage point decline in the interest rate. Refer to
the above graph. Which of the following is the correct graphical presentation of the
indicated relationship? Line

   A.   4   B.   3   C.   2   D.   1

Questions 9-11.

DIRECTIONS: Questions 9 through 11 are to be answered on the basis of the following data.

After-tax Income	Consumption
$1,000	$ 900
2,000	1,800
3,000	2,700
4,000	3,600
5,000	4,500

9. The above data suggest that 9.____

    A. consumption varies inversely with after-tax income
    B. consumption varies directly with after-tax income
    C. consumption and after-tax income are unrelated
    D. a tax increase will increase consumption

10. The above data indicate that 10.____

    A. consumers spend 80 percent of their after-tax incomes
    B. consumers spend 90 percent of their after-tax incomes
    C. a tax reduction will reduce consumption
    D. the relationship between consumption and after-tax income is random

11. The above data suggest that 11.____

    A. a policy of tax reduction will increase consumption
    B. a policy of tax increases will increase consumption
    C. tax changes will have no impact upon consumption
    D. after-tax income should be lowered in order to increase consumption

Questions 12-15.

DIRECTIONS: Questions 12 through 15 are to be answered on the basis of the following diagram.

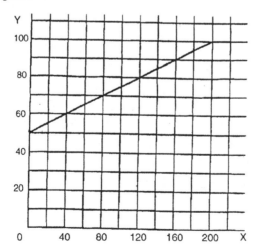

12. The variables X and Y are

  A. inversely related   B. directly related
  C. unrelated   D. negatively related

12.____

13. The vertical intercept

  A. is 40
  B. is 50
  C. is 60
  D. cannot be determined from the information given

13.____

14. The slope of the line

  A. is -1/4
  B. is +1/4
  C. is .40
  D. cannot be determined from the information given

14.____

15. The equation which shows the relationship between Y and X is

  A. Y = 50 + 1/4 X   B. X = 1/4 Y
  C. Y = 4X   D. Y = 1/4 X - 50

15.____

16. The movement from line A to
line A' represents a change in
  A. the slope *only*
  B. the intercept *only*
  C. both the slope and the intercept
  D. neither the slope nor the intercept

16.____

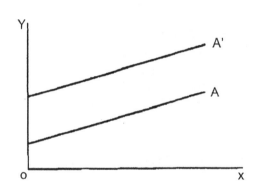

Questions 17-19.

DIRECTIONS: Questions 17 through 19 are to be answered on the basis of the following graph.

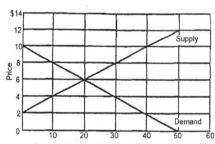

Quantity demanded (Qd) and Quantity supplied (Qs)

17. Which of the following statements is CORRECT   17.____

    A. Quantity demanded and quantity supplied are independent of price.
    B. Price and quantity demanded are directly related.
    C. Price and quantity supplied are directly related.
    D. Price and quantity supplied are inversely related.

18. Which of the following schedules correctly reflects *demand*?   18.____

A		B		C		D	
P	Qd	P	Qd	P	Qd	P	Qd
$12	0	$14	0	$14	60	$12	0
10	0	12	0	12	50	10	10
8	10	10	20	10	40-	8	20
6	20	8	40	8	30	6	30
4	30	6	60	6	20	4	40
2	40	4	80	4	10	2	50

19. Which of the following schedules correctly reflects *supply*?   19.____

A		B		C		D	
P	Qs	P	Qs	P	Qs	P	Qs
$12	50	$14	50	$12	50	$12	0
10	30	12	40	10	40	10	0
8	10	10	30	8	30	8	10
6	0	8	20	6	20	6	20
4	0	6	10	4	10	4	30
2	0	4	0	2	0	2	40

Questions 20-22.

DIRECTIONS: Questions 20 through 22 are to be answered on the basis of the following diagram.

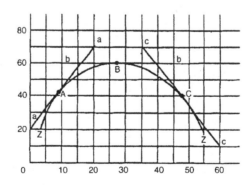

20. The slope of curve ZZ at point A is   20.____

    A. +2   B. +2 1/2   C. -2 1/2
    D. +4   E. none of the above

21. The slope of curve ZZ at point B is   21.____

    A. infinity   B. zero
    C. one   D. none of the above

22. The slope of curve ZZ at point C is   22.____

    A. -4   B. -2   C. -2 2/5
    D. +3   E. none of the above

23. Slopes of lines are especially important in economics because   23.____

    A. they measure marginal changes
    B. they always tell us something about profits
    C. positive slopes are always preferred to negative slopes
    D. they always relate to resource and output scarcity

24. The slope of a straight line can be determined by   24.____

    A. comparing the absolute horizontal change to the absolute vertical change between two points on the line
    B. comparing the absolute vertical change to the absolute horizontal change between two points on the line
    C. taking the reciprocal of the vertical intercept
    D. comparing the percentage vertical change to the percentage horizontal change between two points on the line

25. The measured slope of a line   25.____

    A. is independent of how the two variables are denominated
    B. will be affected by how the two variables are denominated
    C. necessarily diminishes as one moves rightward on the line
    D. necessarily increases as one moves rightward on the line

----

KEY (CORRECT ANSWERS)

1.	C		11.	A
2.	D		12.	B
3.	C		13.	B
4.	D		14.	B
5.	D		15.	A
6.	C		16.	B
7.	A		17.	C
8.	D		18.	A
9.	B		19.	C
10.	B		20.	A

21.	A
22.	B
23.	A
24.	B
25.	B

TEST 2

DIRECTIONS: Each question or incomplete statement is followed by several suggested answers or completions. Select the one that BEST answers the question or completes the statement. *PRINT THE LETTER OF THE CORRECT ANSWER IN THE SPACE AT THE RIGHT.*

Questions 1-3.

DIRECTIONS: Questions 1 through 3 are to be answered on the basis of the given supply and demand data for wheat.

Bushels Demanded Per Month	Price Per Bushel	Bushels Supplied Per Month
45	$5	77
50	4	73
56	3	68
61	2	61
67	1	57

1. Equilibrium price will be

    A. $4   B. $3   C. $2   D. $1

1.____

2. If the price in this market was $4,

    A. farmers would reduce the number of acres allocated to the growing of wheat
    B. buyers would want to purchase more wheat than is currently being supplied
    C. farmers would not be able to sell all of their wheat
    D. there would be a shortage of wheat

2.____

3. If price was initially $4, we would expect

    A. quantity supplied to continue to exceed quantity demanded
    B. the quantity of wheat supplied to decline as a result of the subsequent price change
    C. the quantity of wheat demanded to fall as a result of the subsequent price change
    D. the price of wheat to rise

3.____

Questions 4-6.

DIRECTIONS: Questions 4 through 6 are to be answered on the basis of the following diagram.

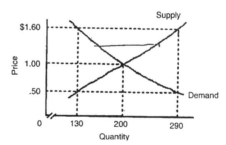

4. The equilibrium price and quantity in this market will be   4._____

    A. $1.00 and 130   B. $1.00 and 200
    C. $1.60 and 130   D. $.50 and 130

5. A surplus of 160 units would be encountered if price was   5._____

    A. $1.10, that is, $1.60 minus $.50
    B. $1.60
    C. $1.00
    D. $.50

6. A shortage of 160 units would be encountered if price was   6._____

    A. $1.10, that is, $1.60 minus $.50
    B. $1.60
    C. $1.00
    D. $.50

Questions 7-10.

DIRECTIONS: Questions 7 through 10 are to be answered on the basis of the following diagram.

7. A price of $60 in this market will result in a _____ of _____ units.   7._____

    A. shortage; 50   B. surplus; 50
    C. surplus; 100   D. shortage; 100

8. A price of $20 in this market will result in a _____ of _____ units.   8._____

    A. shortage; 50   B. surplus; 50
    C. surplus; 100   D. shortage; 100

9. The highest price that buyers will be willing and able to pay for 100 units of this product is   9._____

    A. $30   B. $60   C. $40   D. $20

10. If this is a competitive market, price and quantity will gravitate toward _____, respectively.   10._____

    A. $60 and 100   B. $60 and 200
    C. $40 and 150   D. $20 and 150

Questions 11-16.

DIRECTIONS: Questions 11 through 16 are to be answered on the basis of the following diagrams.

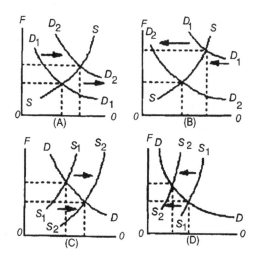

11.   Which of the above diagrams illustrate(s) the effect of an increase in automobile worker   11.____
      wages on the market for automobiles?

      A.   A   B.   B   C.   C   D.   D

12.   Which of the above diagrams illustrate(s) the effect of a decline in the price of personal   12.____
      computers upon the market for software?

      A.   A *only*   B.   A and D   C.   B *only*   D.   D *only*

13.   Which of the above diagrams illustrate(s) the effect of an increase in the price of Bud-   13.____
      weiser upon the market for Coors?

      A.   A   B.   B   C.   C   D.   D

14.   Which of the above diagrams illustrate(s) the effect of a decrease in incomes upon the   14.____
      market for secondhand clothing?

      A.   A   B.   B   C.   C   D.   D

15.   Which of the above diagrams illustrate(s) the effect of a governmental subsidy on the   15.____
      market for AIDS research?

      A.   A   B.   B   C.   C   D.   D

16.   Which of the above diagrams illustrate(s) the effect of a decline in the price of irrigation   16.____
      equipment upon the market for corn?

      A.   A   B.   B   C.   C   D.   D

Questions 17-21.

DIRECTIONS: Questions 17 through 21 are to be answered on the basis of the following cost data for a competitive seller.

Total Product	Total Fixed Cost	Total Variable Cost	Total Cost
0	$50	$ 0	$ 0
1	50	70	120
2	50	120	170
3	50	150	200
4	50	220	270
5	50	300	350
6	50	390	440

17. The above data are for

A. the long run
B. the short run
C. both the short run and the long run
D. the intermediate market period only

17.____

18. At 5 units of output average fixed cost, average variable cost, and average total cost are _____, respectively.

A. $10, $60, and $70   B. $50, $40, and $90
C. $10, $70, and $80   D. $5, $25, and $30

18.____

19. The marginal cost of the fifth unit of output

A. is $80
B. is $90
C. is $50
D. cannot be determined from the information given

19.____

20. If product price is $75, the firm will produce _____ units of output.

A. 3   B. 4   C. 5   D. 6

20.____

21. Given the $75 product price, at its optimal output the firm will realize a

A. $25 economic profit   B. $30 economic profit
C. $25 loss   D. $30 loss

21.____

Questions 22-24.

DIRECTIONS: Questions 22 through 24 are to be answered on the basis of the following
short-run data.

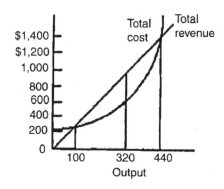

22.   The total fixed cost for this firm is

   A.   about $67   B. $300   C. $200   D. $100

23.   The shape of the total cost curve reflects

   A.   diminishing opportunity costs
   B.   the law of rising fixed costs
   C.   increasing and diminishing returns
   D.   economies and diseconomies of scale

24.   The profit-maximizing output for this firm is _____ units.

   A.   above 440   B.   440   C.   320   D.   100

25.   A competitive firm will maximize profits at that output at which

   A.   the excess of total revenue over total cost is greatest
   B.   total revenue and total cost are equal
   C.   price exceeds average total cost by the largest amount
   D.   the difference between marginal revenue and price is at a maximum

22.____

23.____

24.____

25.____

KEY (CORRECT ANSWERS)

1.	C	11.	D
2.	C	12.	A
3.	B	13.	A
4.	B	14.	A
5.	B	15.	C
6.	D	16.	C
7.	C	17.	B
8.	D	18.	A
9.	B	19.	A
10.	C	20.	B

21.	B
22.	C
23.	C
24.	B
25.	A

TEST 3

DIRECTIONS: Each question or incomplete statement is followed by several suggested answers or completions. Select the one that BEST answers the question or completes the statement. *PRINT THE LETTER OF THE CORRECT ANSWER IN THE SPACE AT THE RIGHT.*

1. Which of the following statements is CORRECT?   1.____

    A. The value of the independent variable is determined by the value of the dependent variable.

    B. The value of the dependent variable is determined by the value of the independent variable.

    C. The dependent variable designates the *cause* and the independent variable the *effect.*

    D. Dependent variables graph as upsloping lines; independent variables graph as downsloping lines.

Questions 2-4.

DIRECTIONS: Questions 2 through 4 are to be answered on the basis of the following cost data for a purely competitive seller.

Output	Total Cost
0	$ 50
1	90
2	120
3	140
4	170
5	210
6	260
7	330

2. If product price is $60, the firm will   2.____

    A. close down
    B. produce 4 units and realize a $120 profit
    C. produce 6 units and realize a $100 profit
    D. produce 3 units and realize a $40 loss

3. If product price is $45, the firm will   3.____

    A. close down
    B. produce 4 units and realize a $120 economic profit
    C. produce 5 units and realize a $15 economic profit
    D. produce 6 units and realize a $100 economic profit

4. If product price is $25, the firm will   4.____

    A. close down and realize a $90 loss
    B. close down and realize a $50 loss
    C. produce 3 units and realize a $65 loss
    D. produce 4 units and realize a $10 economic profit

Questions 5-6.

DIRECTIONS: Questions 5 and 6 are to be answered on the basis of the following diagrams.

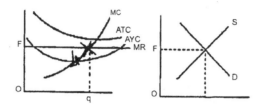

5. Referring to the above diagrams, which pertain to a purely competitive firm producing   5.____
    output Oq and the industry in which it operates, in the long run we should expect

    A.   firms to enter the industry, market supply to rise, and product price to fall
    B.   firms to leave the industry, market supply to rise, and product price to fall
    C.   firms to leave the industry, market supply to fall, and product price to rise
    D.   no change in the number of firms in this industry

6. Referring to the above diagrams, which pertain to a purely competitive firm producing   6.____
    output Oq and the industry in which it operates, the predicted long-run adjustments in
    this industry might be offset by

    A.   a decline in product demand
    B.   an increase in resource prices
    C.   a technological improvement in production methods
    D.   none of the above

Questions 7-8.

DIRECTIONS: Questions 7 and 8 are to be answered on the basis of the following diagram.

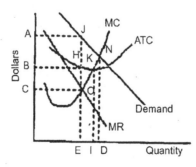

7. In order to maximize profits or minimize losses, this firm should produce _____ units   7.____
    and charge price _____.

    A.   OE; OC   B.   OE; OA   C.   OM; NM   D.   OL; LK

8. In equilibrium, total revenue will be　　　　　　　　　　　　　　　　　　　　8._____

    A.　NM times OM　　　　　　　　B.　OAJE
    C.　OEGC　　　　　　　　　　　　D.　OEHB

Questions 9-13.

DIRECTIONS:　Questions 9 through 13 are to be answered on the basis of the following list.

    A.　Monopolistic competition
    B.　Oligopoly
    C.　Pure monopoly
    D.　Pure competition

9. An industry comprised of 40 firms, none of which has more than 3 percent of the total　　9._____
market for a differentiated product.

10. A one-firm industry.　　　　　　　　　　　　　　　　　　　　　　　　　　10._____

11. An industry comprised of four firms, each of which has approximately 25 percent of the　　11._____
total market for a product.

12. An industry comprised of a very large number of sellers which are producing a standard-　　12._____
ized product.

13. An industry comprised of a small number of firms, each of which considers the potential　　13._____
reactions of its rivals in making price-output decisions.

Questions 14-15.

DIRECTIONS:　Questions 14 and 15 are to be answered on the basis of the information given
in the following table.

Employment	Total Product	Product Price
0	0	$3
1	12	3
2	22	3
3	30	3
4	36	3
5	40	3
6	42	3

14. If the firm is hiring workers under purely competitive conditions at a wage rate of $22, it　　14._____
will choose to employ _____ worker(s).

    A.　1　　　　　　　B.　2　　　　　　　C.　3　　　　　　　D.　4

15. If the firm is hiring workers under purely competitive conditions at a wage rate of $10, it　　15._____
will choose to employ _____ workers.

    A.　2　　　　　　　B.　3　　　　　　　C.　4　　　　　　　D.　5

16. The MRP curve for labor

    A. is downsloping and shows the relationship between wage rates and the quantity of labor demanded
    B. is perfectly elastic if the firm is selling its output competitively
    C. is upsloping and lies above the labor supply curve
    D. will shift location when the wage rate changes

16.____

Questions 17-19.

DIRECTIONS: Questions 17 through 19 are to be answered on the basis of the following information.

    A farmer who has fixed amounts of land and capital finds that total product is 24 for the first worker hired; 32 when two workers are hired; 37 when three are hired; and 40 when four are hired. The farmer's product sells for $3 per unit and the wage rate is $13 per worker.

17. The marginal product of the second worker

    A. is 24   B. is 8   C. is 5
    D. cannot be determined from the information given

17.____

18. The marginal revenue product of the second worker is

    A. $24   B. $8   C. $15   D. $9

18.____

19. How many workers should the farmer hire?

    A. 1   B. 2   C. 3   D. 4

19.____

20. A competitive employer is using labor in such an amount that labor's MRP is $10 and its wage rate is $8. We can conclude that the firm

    A. should hire more labor because this will increase profits
    B. should hire more labor, although this may either increase or decrease profits
    C. is currently hiring the profit-maximizing amount of labor
    D. none of the above

20.____

21.

21.____

Referring to the above diagrams, the firm

    A. is a monopsonist in the hire of labor
    B. must be selling its product in an imperfectly competitive market
    C. is a *wage taker*
    D. must pay a higher marginal resource cost for each successive worker

22.

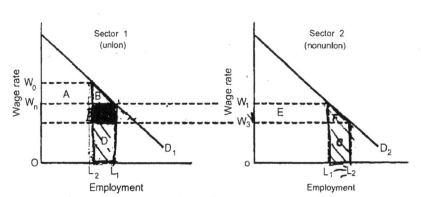

Referring to the above diagrams which show two sectors of the labor market for a particular kind of labor, relevant product markets are assumed to be competitive. The two labor demand curves are identical, and initially the quantities of labor employed in the two sectors are L_1 and L'_1 and the wage rate in each sector is Wn. This analysis suggests that the union wage advantage causes a net efficiency

A. loss equal to E-A
C. gain equal to C

B. loss equal to C
D. gain equal to B

22.____

23. Critics of unions argue that unions diminish efficiency and productivity by

A. engaging in featherbedding
B. precipitating strikes
C. causing a misallocation of labor
D. all of the above

23.____

Questions 24-25.

DIRECTIONS: Questions 24 and 25 are to be answered on the basis of the following diagrams.

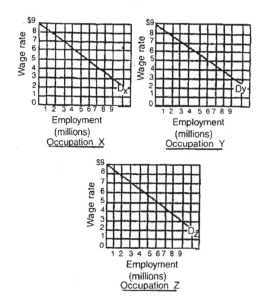

24. It is assumed that (1) the labor force is comprised of 9 million male and 9 million female   24._____
workers; (2) the economy is comprised of 3 occupations, X, Y, and Z, each having identical demand curves for labor; (3) male and female workers are homogeneous with
respect to their labor-market capabilities; (4) women are discriminated against in that
they are excluded from occupations X and Y and are confined to Z; and (5) aside from
discrimination, the economy is otherwise competitive. Under these circumstances, 9 million women will be employed in occupation Z

    A. 5 million men in X, and 4 million men in Y
    B. 3 million men in X, and 6 million men in Y
    C. 6 million men in X, and 3 million men in Y
    D. and 4 1/2 million men each in occupations X and Y

25. It is assumed that (1) the labor force is comprised of 9 million male and 9 million female   25._____
workers; (2) the economy is comprised of 3 occupations, X, Y, and Z, each having identical demand curves for labor; (3) male and female workers are homogeneous with
respect to their labor-market capabilities; (4) women are discriminated against in that
they are excluded from occupations X and Y and are confined to Z; and (5) aside from
discrimination, the economy is otherwise competitive. The elimination of gender discrimination

    A. may either increase or reduce real domestic output, depending upon what hap-
pens to the level of nominal wages
    B. will increase real domestic output
    C. will have no effect on real domestic output
    D. will reduce real domestic output

26. As applied to gender discrimination, the crowding model of occupational -segregation   26._____

    A. helps explain why women earn less than men
    B. predicts that men's wages would fall and women's wages would rise if occupational
segregation was eliminated
    C. predicts that the domestic output would increase if occupational segregation was
ended
    D. all of the above

Questions 27-29.

DIRECTIONS: Questions 27 through 29 are to be answered on the basis of the following figures.

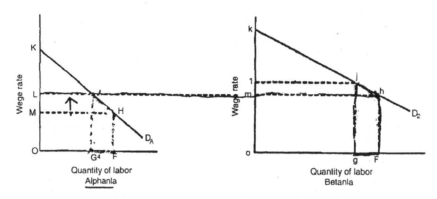

27.   It is assumed that (a) the demands for labor in Alphania and Betania are as shown by D_A 27.____
and DB, respectively; (b) Alphania's native labor force is OF and that of Betania is Og;
and (c) full employment exists in both countries. If migration is costless and unimpeded,

 A.   migration will cause the average level of wages to fall in Alphania
 B.   no migration will occur
 C.   fg workers will move from Betania to Alphania
 D.   GF workers will move from Alphania to Betania

28.   It is assumed that (a) the demands for labor in Alphania and Betania are as shown by D_A 28.____
and D_B, respectively; (b) Alphania's native labor force is OF and that of Betania is Og;
and (c) full employment exists in both countries. If migration is costless and unimpeded,
the average level of wages will

 A.   decrease in Betania, but remain unchanged in Alphania
 B.   increase in Alphania, but remain unchanged in Betania
 C.   increase in Alphania and decrease in Betania
 D.   increase in Betania and decrease in Alphania

29.   It is assumed that (a) the demands for labor in Alphania and Betania are as shown by D_A 29.____
and D_B, respectively; (b) Alphania's native labor force is OF and that of Betania is Og;
and (c) full employment exists in both countries. After migration has ceased,

 A.   world output will have increased by mljh-MLJH
 B.   Betania's output will have increased and Alphania's output will have decreased, but
  world output will not have changed
 C.   world output will have increased by gjhf-GJHF
 D.   world output will have decreased by gjhf-GJHF

30. Voluntary migration of skilled craftworkers from low-paying to high-paying nations is most likely to be opposed by   30.____

    A.   business groups in the high-paying nations
    B.   craft workers who stay in the low-paying nations
    C.   industrial unions in the high-paying nations
    D.   craft unions in the high-paying nations

KEY (CORRECT ANSWERS)

1.	B		16.	A
2.	C		17.	B
3.	C		18.	A
4.	B		19.	C
5.	D		20.	A
6.	C		21.	C
7.	A		22.	B
8.	A		23.	D
9.	A		24.	D
10.	C		25.	B
11.	B		26.	D
12.	D		27.	D
13.	B		28.	C
14.	C		29.	C
15.	D		30.	D

EXAMINATION SECTION
TEST 1

DIRECTIONS: Each question or incomplete statement is followed by several suggested answers or completions. Select the one that BEST answers the question or completes the statement. *PRINT THE LETTER OF THE CORRECT ANSWER IN THE SPACE AT THE RIGHT.*

1. Of the following workers, MOST likely to be classified as structurally unemployed would be a

    A. high school teacher who is unemployed during the summer months
    B. recent college graduate who is looking for her first job
    C. teenager who is seeking part-time employment at a fast-food restaurant
    D. worker who is unemployed because his skills are obsolete
    E. woman who reenters the job market after her child begins elementary school

1.____

2. According to the classical model, an increase in the money supply causes an increase in which of the following?
    I.   The price level
    II. Nominal gross national product
    III. Nominal wages
The CORRECT answer is:

    A. I *only*
    D. II, III
    B. II *only*
    E. I, II, III
    C. III *only*

2.____

3. If, in response to an increase in investment of $10 billion, equilibrium income rises by a total of $50 billion, then the marginal propensity to save is

    A. 0.1   B. 0.2   C. 0.5   D. 0.8   E. 0.9

3.____

4. In the circular flow diagram, which of the following is TRUE?

    A. Businesses pay wages, rent, interest, and profits to households in return for use of factors of production.
    B. Businesses purchase goods and services from households in return for money payments.
    C. Households pay wages, rent, interest, and profits to businesses in return for use of factors of production.
    D. The relationship between households and businesses exists only in a traditional society.
    E. The relationship between households and businesses exists only in a command economy.

4.____

5. Assume that the reserve requirement is 25 percent. If banks have excess reserves of $10,000, the MAXIMUM amount of additional money that can be created by the banking system through the lending process is $_____.

    A. 2,500   B. 10,000   C. 40,000   D. 50,000   E. 250,000

5.____

6. According to the Keynesian model, an increase in the money supply affects output more if

6.____

A. investment is sensitive to interest rates
B. money demand is sensitive to interest rates
C. the unemployment rate is low
D. consumption is sensitive to the Phillips curve
E. government spending is sensitive to public opinion

7. Which of the following combinations of monetary and fiscal policies is coordinated to increase output?

7.____

	Monetary Policy	Fiscal Policy
A.	Decrease the reserve requirement	Increase taxes
B.	Increase the discount rate	Increase government expenditures
C.	Sell securities	Increase taxes
D.	Sell securities	Decrease government expenditures
E.	Purchase securities	Decrease taxes

8. Which of the following is a possible cause of stagflation (simultaneous high unemployment and high inflation)?

8.____

A. Increase in labor productivity
B. Increase in price for raw materials
C. The rapid growth and development of the computer industry
D. A decline in labor union membership
E. A low growth rate of the money supply

9. If exchange rates are allowed to fluctuate freely and the United States demand for German marks increases, which of the following will MOST likely occur?

9.____

A. Americans will have to pay more for goods made in Germany.
B. Germans will find that American goods are getting more expensive.
C. The United States balance-of-payments deficit will increase.
D. The dollar price of marks will fall.
E. The dollar price of German goods will fall.

10. Which of the following would MOST likely be the immediate result if the United States increased tariffs on most foreign goods?

10.____

A. The United States standard of living would be higher.
B. More foreign goods would be purchased by Americans.
C. Prices of domestic goods would increase.
D. Large numbers of United States workers would be laid off.
E. The value of the United States dollar would decrease against foreign currencies.

11. Of the following, it is TRUE that a country operating inside its production possibilities frontier

11.____

A. has a market economy
B. has a command economy
C. is in the early stages of industrial development
D. is using resources inefficiently
E. has plentiful resources

12. Which of the following is an example of *investment* as the term is used by economists?   12.____

    A. A schoolteacher purchases 10,000 shares of stock in an automobile company.
    B. Newlyweds purchase a previously owned home.
    C. One large automobile firm purchases another large automobile firm.
    D. A farmer purchases $10,000 worth of government securities.
    E. An apparel company purchases 15 new sewing machines.

13. If the gross national product increased from $930 billion in 1969 to $975 billion in 1970   13.____
solely because of a rise in the price level, which of the following must be TRUE?

    A. Real gross national product increased between 1969 and 1970.
    B. Real gross national product decreased between 1969 and 1970.
    C. Nominal income increased between 1969 and 1970.
    D. Real income increased between 1969 and 1970.
    E. The rise in the price level between 1969 and 1970 was greater than 10 percent.

14.   14.____

REAL OUTPUT

The diagram above shows two aggregate supply curves, AS_1 and AS_2.
Which of the following statements MOST accurately characterizes the AS_1 curve relative to the AS_2 curve?
AS_1.

    A. is Keynesian because it reflects greater wage and price flexibility
    B. is classical because it reflects greater wage and price flexibility
    C. is Keynesian because it reflects less wage and price flexibility
    D. is classical because it reflects less wage and price flexibility
    E. could be either classical or Keynesian because it reflects greater wage flexibility but less price flexibility

15. If the marginal propensity to consume is 0.9, what is the MAXIMUM amount that the   15.____
equilibrium gross national product could change if government expenditures increase by
$1 billion?
It could _____ by up to $_____ billion.

    A. decrease; 9   B. increase; 0.9   C. increase; 1
    D. increase; 9   E. increase; 10

16.

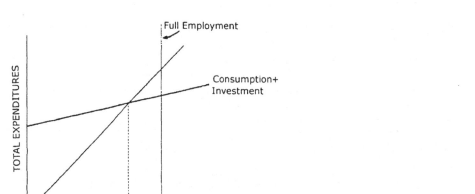

The figure above represents an economy with no government and no foreign sector. Which of the following statements about this economy is TRUE?
At

A. Y. planned investment is less than saving
B. Y. planned investment is equal to saving
C. Y. planned investment is greater than saving
D. full employment, total spending is equal to total income
E. full employment, planned investment is equal to saving

17. According to the classical economists, which of the following is MOST sensitive to interest rates?

A. Consumption
B. Investment
C. Government spending
D. Transfer payments
E. Intermediate goods

18. Expansionary fiscal policy will be MOST effective when

A. the aggregate supply curve is horizontal
B. the economy is at or above full-employment output
C. transfer payments are decreased, while taxes remain unchanged
D. wages and prices are very flexible
E. the Federal Reserve simultaneously increases the reserve requirement

19. Which of the following would increase the value of the multiplier?
A(n)

A. increase in government expenditure
B. increase in exports
C. decrease in government unemployment benefits
D. decrease in the marginal propensity to consume
E. decrease in the marginal propensity to save

20. According to the monetarists, inflation is MOST often the result of

A. high federal tax rates
B. increased production of capital goods

16.____

17.____

18.____

19.____

20.____

C. decreased production of capital goods
D. an excessive growth of the money supply
E. upward shifts in the consumption function

21. To counteract a recession, the Federal Reserve should 21.____

A. buy securities on the open market and raise the reserve requirement
B. buy securities on the open market and lower the reserve requirement
C. buy securities on the open market and raise the discount rate
D. sell securities on the open market and raise the discount rate
E. raise the reserve requirement and lower the discount rate

22. Which of the following would result in the LARGEST increase in aggregate demand? 22.____
A $30 billion _____ and a $30 billion _____ of government securities.

A. increase in military expenditure; open-market purchase
B. increase in military expenditure; open-market sale
C. tax cut; open-market sale
D. tax increase; open-market purchase
E. increase in social security payments; open-market sale

23. Which of the following will be TRUE if inflation can be accurately forecast and both prices 23.____
and wages are fully flexible?

A. Long periods of high unemployment will be possible.
B. The supply of labor will be insensitive to the real wage rate.
C. The Phillips curve will be vertical.
D. The equilibrium unemployment rate will be zero.
E. Real interest rates will be greater than nominal interest rates.

24. Which of the following policies is MOST likely to encourage long-run economic growth in 24.____
a country?
A(n)

A. embargo on high-technology imports
B. decline in the number of immigrants to the country
C. increase in government transfer payments
D. increase in the per capita savings rate
E. increase in defense spending

25. In one year, real gross national product fell by 3 percent, inflation rose to 10 percent, and 25.____
unemployment rose to 11 percent.
Which of the following may have caused these changes?
A(n)

A. decrease in the money supply and a decrease in government spending
B. decrease in inflationary expectations
C. increase in investment in inventories
D. increase in the money supply and an increase in government spending
E. increase in inflationary expectations

KEY (CORRECT ANSWERS)

1.	D		11.	D
2.	E		12.	E
3.	B		13.	C
4.	A		14.	C
5.	C		15.	E
6.	A		16.	B
7.	E		17.	B
8.	B		18.	A
9.	A		19.	E
10.	C		20.	D

21.	B
22.	A
23.	C
24.	D
25.	E

TEST 2

DIRECTIONS: Each question or incomplete statement is followed by several suggested
answers or completions. Select the one that BEST answers the question or
completes the statement. *PRINT THE LETTER OF THE CORRECT ANSWER
IN THE SPACE AT THE RIGHT.*

1.

1._____

QUANTITY OF SHOES PRODUCED PER YEAR

Which of the following is TRUE of an economy with the production possibilities frontier
shown above?

A.   Point Q is attainable but undesirable.
B.   Point R is unattainable but desirable.
C.   A technological improvement in the production of watches would move the econ-
omy from point T to point P.
D.   The opportunity cost of moving from point S to point T is the number of watches
given up.
E.   There is unemployment at point T because workers in the watch industry are with-
out jobs.

2.   Increases in real income per capita are made possible by

2._____

A.   improved productivity   B.   a high labor/capital ratio
C.   large trade surpluses   D.   stable interest rates
E.   high protective tariffs

3.   The sum of which of the following expenditures is equal to the value of the gross national
product?

3._____

A.   Consumer purchases, investment for capital goods, exports, and imports
B.   Consumer purchases, investment for capital goods, net exports, and inventories
C.   Consumer purchases, investment for capital goods, government purchases, and
net exports
D.   Consumer purchases, government purchases, exports, and natural income
E.   Investment for capital goods, government purchases, net exports, and
inventories

4. Of the following, MOST likely to lead to a decrease in aggregate demand, that is, shift the aggregate demand curve leftward, would be a(n)

    A. decrease in taxes
    B. decrease in interest rates
    C. increase in household savings
    D. increase in household consumption
    E. increase in business firms' purchases of capital equipment from retained earnings

4.____

5. According to the Keynesian model, equilibrium output of an economy may be less than the full-employment level of output because at full employment

    A. sufficient income may not be generated to keep workers above the subsistence level
    B. there might not be enough demand by firms and consumers to buy that output
    C. workers may not be willing to work the hours necessary to produce the output
    D. interest rates might not be high enough to provide the incentive to finance the production
    E. banks may not be willing to lend enough money to support the output

5.____

6. The principal reason for requiring commercial banks to maintain reserve balances with the Federal Reserve is that these balances

    A. provide the maximum amount of reserves a bank would ever need
    B. give the Federal Reserve more control over the money-creating operations of banks
    C. ensure that banks do not make excessive profits
    D. assist the Treasury in refinancing government debt
    E. enable the government to borrow cheaply from the Federal Reserve's discount window

6.____

7. If the Federal Reserve lowers the reserve requirement, which of the following is MOST likely to happen to interest rates and gross national product?

	Interest Rates	Gross National Product
A.	Increase	Decrease
B.	Increase	Increase
C.	Decrease	Decrease
D.	Decrease	Increase
E.	No change	No change

7.____

8. Which of the following measures might be used to reduce a federal budget deficit?
    I. Raising taxes
    II. Reducing federal spending
    III. Lowering interest rates
The CORRECT answer is:

    A. I only   B. II only   C. III only
    D. I, III   E. I, II, III

8.____

9. If the nominal interest rate is 6 percent and the expected inflation rate is 4 percent, the real interest rate is _____ percent.

    A. 10   B. 6   C. 4   D. 2   E. -2

9.____

10. Supply side economists argue that   10.____

    A. a cut in high tax rates results in an increased deficit and thus increases aggregate supply
    B. lower tax rates provide positive work incentives and thus shift the aggregate supply curve to the right
    C. the aggregate supply of goods can only be increased if the price level falls
    D. increased government spending should be used to stimulate the economy
    E. the government should regulate the supply of imports

11. If the dollar cost of the British pound decreases, United States imports from and exports   11.____
to the United Kingdom will change in which of the following ways?

	Imports	Exports
A.	Increase	Decrease
B.	Increase	Increase
C.	Increase	No change
D.	Decrease	Decrease
E.	Decrease	Increase

12. An economy that is fully employing all its productive resources but allocating less to investment than to consumption will be at which of the following positions on the production possibilities curve shown at the right?   12.____

    A. A
    B. B
    C. C
    D. D
    E. E

13. The United States government defines an individual as unemployed if the person   13.____

    A. does not hold a paying job
    B. has been recently fired
    C. works part-time but needs full-time work
    D. is without a job but is looking for work
    E. wants a job but is not searching because he or she thinks none is available

14. The gross national product is BEST described as a measure of   14.____

    A. economic welfare
    B. the full-employment output of an economy
    C. all monetary transactions in an economy
    D. current consumption in an economy
    E. current final output produced by an economy

15. An increase in which of the following would cause the long-run aggregate supply curve to shift to the right? 15.____

    A. Corporate income tax rates
    B. Aggregate demand
    C. Potential output
    D. The average wage rate
    E. The price level

16. Total spending in the economy is MOST likely to increase by the largest amount if which of the following occur to government spending and taxes? 16.____

	GovernmentSpending	Taxes
A.	Decrease	Increase
B.	Decrease	No change
C.	Increase	Increase
D.	Increase	Decrease
E.	No change	Increase

17. If businesses are experiencing an unplanned increase in inventories, which of the following is MOST likely to be true? 17.____

    A. Aggregate demand is greater than output, and the level of spending will increase.
    B. Aggregate demand is less than output, and the level of spending will decrease.
    C. The economy is growing and will continue to grow until a new equilibrium level of spending is reached.
    D. Planned investment is greater than planned saving, and the level of spending will decrease.
    E. Planned investment is less than planned saving, and the level of spending will increase.

18. The purchase of securities on the open market by the Federal Reserve will 18.____

    A. increase the supply of money
    B. increase the interest rate
    C. increase the discount rate
    D. decrease the number of Federal Reserve notes in circulation
    E. decrease the reserve requirement

19. If a banking system's reserves are $100 billion, demand deposits are $500 billion, and the system is fully loaned-up, then the reserve requirement must be _____ percent. 19.____

    A. 10   B. 12.5   C. 16.6   D. 20   E. 25

20. According to the Keynesian model, an expansionary fiscal policy would tend to cause which of the following changes in output and interest rates? 20.____

	Output	Interest Rates
A.	Increase	Increase
B.	Increase	Decrease
C.	Decrease	Increase
D.	Decrease	Decrease
E.	No change	Decrease

21. Which of the following policies would MOST likely be recommended in an economy with an annual inflation rate of 3 percent and an unemployment rate of 11 percent? A(n)

    21.____

    A. increase in transfer payments and an increase in the reserve requirement
    B. increase in defense spending and an increase in the discount rate
    C. increase in income tax rates and a decrease in the reserve requirement
    D. decrease in government spending and the open-market sale of government securities
    E. decrease in the tax rate on corporate profits and a decrease in the discount rate

22. The cost of reducing unemployment is accepting a higher rate of inflation.
The statement above would MOST likely be made by a person who believes in the

    22.____

    A. quantity theory of money
    B. Phillips curve
    C. theory of rational expectations
    D. paradox of value
    E. liquidity trap

23. Which of the following would occur if the international value of the United States dollar decreased?

    23.____

    A. United States exports would rise.
    B. More gold would flow into the United States.
    C. United States demand for foreign currencies would increase.
    D. The United States trade deficit would increase.
    E. Americans would pay less for foreign goods.

24. Which of the following will occur as a result of an improvement in technology?
The _____ curve will shift _____.

    24.____

    A. aggregate demand; to the right
    B. aggregate demand; to the left
    C. aggregate supply; to the right
    D. aggregate supply; to the left
    E. production possibilities; inward

25. Assume that land in an agricultural economy can be used either for producing grain or for grazing cattle to produce beef.
The opportunity cost of converting an acre from cattle grazing to grain production is the

    25.____

    A. market value of the extra grain that is produced
    B. total amount of beef produced
    C. number of extra bushels of grain that are produced
    D. amount by which beef production decreases
    E. profits generated by the extra production of grain

KEY (CORRECT ANSWERS)

1.	D		11.	A
2.	A		12.	C
3.	C		13.	D
4.	C		14.	E
5.	B		15.	C
6.	B		16.	D
7.	D		17.	B
8.	E		18.	A
9.	D		19.	D
10.	B		20.	A

21.	E
22.	B
23.	A
24.	C
25.	D

———

EXAMINATION SECTION

TEST 1

DIRECTIONS: Each question or incomplete statement is followed by several suggested answers or completions. Select the one that BEST answers the question or completes the statement. *PRINT THE LETTER OF THE CORRECT ANSWER IN THE SPACE AT THE RIGHT.*

1. Which of the following implies the law of diminishing returns?   1.____
   A. As all inputs are doubled, output less than doubles.
   B. As one input is increased, additions to output get smaller.
   C. As all inputs are doubled, output more than doubles.
   D. As one input is increased, output less than doubles.

2. Which of the following will NOT cause the economy's production possibility   2.____
   frontier to shift out?
   A. The discovery of previously unknown oil fields.
   B. An improvement in technology
   C. An increase in the stock of capital
   D. A decrease in the unemployment rate

3. In a two-good economy, if the opportunity cost of producing a good   3.____
   DECREASES as more of that good is produced, the economy's production
   possibility frontier will be
   A. "bowed inward" toward the origin
   B. "bowed outward" from the origin
   C. a straight line
   D. impossible to say whether a straight line or a bowed line

Questions 4a, 4b, 4c, 4d.

DIRECTIONS: Questions 4a, 4b, 4c, and 4d are to be answered on the basis of the following information.

    Fantasia is occupied by two tribes: Nates and Bens. Nates live in Nateland and Bens live in Benland, which are two geographically separate regions. Fantasia only grows wheat and soybeans. Wheat can only grow in Nateland and soybeans can only grow in Benland. Different tribes can work on each other's land. The following annual combinations constitute Fantasia's production possibilities' frontier (PPF).

Possibility	Wheat (in tons)	Soybeans (in tons)
A	0	14
B	2	12
C	4	9
D	6	5
E	8	0

4a. Draw Fantasia's PPF by plotting the points A, B, C, D, E and joining the dots (with wheat on the horizontal axis).

4b. The World Bank supplies Fantasia with a crop duster plane and a new insect spray that kills the insects that only prey on wheat (and does nothing to the insects that prey on soybeans). Once wheat crops are sprayed, the output of wheat will double. Draw the new PPF of Fantasia once the crop duster plane is in use.

4c. Now, thanks to new chemical additives, Fantasia gets a more effective spray that kills insects affecting *both* crops (so that the soybean yield could double, too, if sprayed).

    1)   Even though Fantasia now has new chemicals, the country has only one plane and thus can either spray Nateland or Benland, but not both. Draw the new PPF of Fantasia if only Nateland or Benland can be sprayed.

    2)   A huge swarm of insects is now approaching Fantasia. Unless sprayed with the new spray, these insects will eat the entire crop in Nateland and Benland. Recalling that Fantasia still has only one plane (and can only spray Nateland or Benland but not both), draw the new PPF of Fantasia once the insect threat is realized.

4d. Go back to the PPF in Part a. The people of Fantasia, Nates and Bens now embrace a new religion that strictly prohibits the consumption of soybeans. Explain how the PPF in Part a will change.

KEY (CORRECT ANSWERS)

1. (1 point)
    The answer is B. Other choices are fiddling around the concept of returns to scale.

2. (1 point)
    The answer is D. The PPF (production possibilities frontier) is a theoretical construct that demonstrates the limits of production possibilities in an ideal world, i.e., full and efficient use of all resources. Unemployment indicates less than full use of resources and hence corresponds to a point inside the PPF. Reducing unemployment moves the economy towards the PPF but does not shift it.

3. (2 points)
    The answer is A.

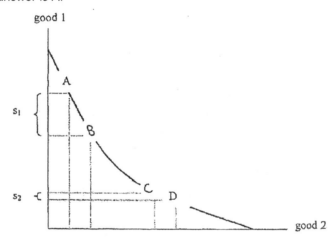

Examine the figure above. Starting from point A, if we want to produce more of good 2 (move from point A to B), we have to give up S_1 amount of good 1. However, at a point where more of good 2 is produced (point C), to have the same increase in good 2 that we had by moving from A to B (thus now moving from C to D), we sacrifice a smaller amount of good 1, only of the amount S_1.

4a.   (1 point)

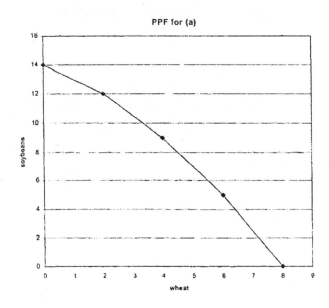

4b.   (1 point)

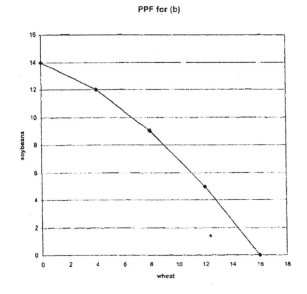

4c1.   (2 points)

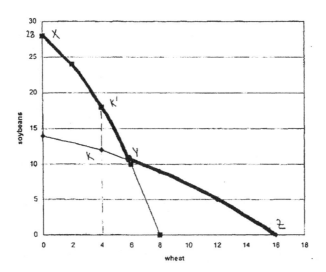

PPF for 4.c.1.

The new PPF is the outer envelope of the two PPF's, shown by the heavy line connecting the points X, Y, and Z. That is because the plane can spray Nateland or Benland, so we have two possibilities. In the first case, the wheat yield doubles but the soybean yield remains the same, and in the second case, vice versa. Since we are looking for the frontier, we are interested in those points where we get the best possible yield of wheat and soybeans. That is why we do not include the parts of the two intersecting PPF's that lie within the heavy-lined PPF (XYZ): We can always do better than those points. For example, take the point K. The point K' gives the same amount of wheat as point K, but more of soybeans. So, our "best" cannot be K since K' does better. If you try it yourself, you will see that we cannot do this with any point on XYZ. Along XYZ, if we want to increase the production of any crop, we have to reduce the production of the other.

4c2.   (1 point)

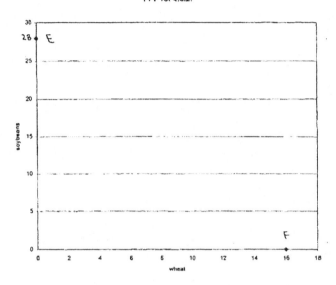

PPF for 4.c.2.

Now, if Nateland is sprayed, we get 16 tons of wheat (Idoubled yield), but the insects eat all of the soybeans. If Benland is sprayed, we get 28 tons of soybeans (doubled yield) but the insects eat all the wheat. So, the PPF collapses to 2 points, namely E and F.

4d.   (1 point)
Nothing changes. What is happening on the demand side does not alter the PPF in any way. Even if no one is consuming soybeans, Fantasia is still capable of producing just the same combinations of wheat and soybeans.

TEST 2

DIRECTIONS: Each question or incomplete statement is followed by several suggested answers or completions. Select the one that BEST answers the question or completes the statement. *PRINT THE LETTER OF THE CORRECT ANSWER IN THE SPACE AT THE RIGHT.*

1. Which of the following will necessarily occur when there is a simultaneous increase in demand and a decrease in supply (that is, the demand curve shifts right and the supply curve shifts left)?
   A. An increase in equilibrium price
   B. A decrease in equilibrium price
   C. An increase in equilibrium quantity
   D. A decrease in equilibrium quantity

1.____

2. The number of pizzas this restaurant sells per week increases from 500 to 700. This could be caused by
   A. an improvement in technology that reduces the cost of making pizza
   B. a decrease in the price of one of the ingredients used to make pizza
   C. an increase in the price of pizza
   D. a decrease in the demand for pizza

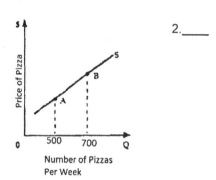

Number of Pizzas
Per Week

2.____

3. In the rollerblade market, you accurately predict that price will _____
   A. increase, the quantity demanded will fall, and the quantity supplied will rise
   B. increase, the quantity demanded will rise, and the quantity supplied will fall
   C. decrease, the quantity demanded will fall, and the quantity supplied will fall
   D. decrease, the quantity demanded will rise, and the quantity supplied will fall

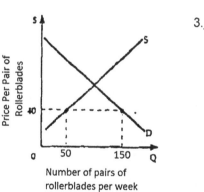

Number of pairs of
rollerblades per week

3.____

201

Questions 4a, 4b, 4c, 4d.

DIRECTIONS: Questions 4a, 4b, 4c, and 4d are to be answered on the basis of the following
information.

Suppose there are only two companies supplying "on-line services" (that is, access to the
internet) for a small island economy in the Pacific. They are willing to provide the following
amounts of on-line time at various prices:

Amarillo On-Line		Compus Werve	
Price ($/Hour)	Time Provided (Millions of Hours Per Week)	Price ($/Hour)	Time Provided (Millions of Hours Per Week)
1	5	1	5
2	12	2	8
3	16	3	14
4	22	4	18
5	27	5	23

4a.   Draw the aggregate supply curve for on-line services for this economy.

4b.   According to a reputable marketing research firm, the aggregate demand for the on-line
services in the economy is indicated by the following table:

Aggregate Demand	
Price ($/Hour)	Time Provided (Millions of Hours Per Week)
1	40
2	35
3	30
4	25
5	20

Draw and label the aggregate demand curve on the same diagram you drew in answer
to 4a. What is the equilibrium price and quantity?

4c.   Suppose the government imposes a price ceiling of $4 per hour on on-line services (i.e.,
nobody can sell on-line services above $4). Indicate the impact of this policy on the
price and quantity of on-line services, using a supply-and-demand diagram

4d.   On-line services and computers are complements. One of the two on-line service
companies is destroyed by fire, raising the price of on-line services. This rise in the price
of on-line services, claims an economist, will shift the supply curve for computers,
because at lower computer prices, computer suppliers will supply less. Justify, qualify,
or repudiate that claim. (Use a supply-and-demand diagram to illustrate your main
points.

KEY (CORRECT ANSWERS)

1.   (1 point) A.

2.   (1 point) C.

3.   (1 point) A.

4a.   (2 points)
Aggregate supply is found by horizontally adding up the supply curves of Amarillo On-Line and Compus Werve.

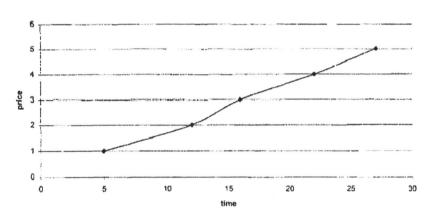

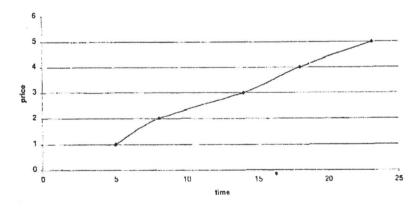

Aggregate Supply

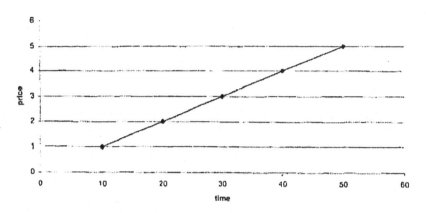

4b.   (1 point)
The equilibrium price and quantity are determined by the intersection of the aggregate demand and supply curves. The equilibrium price is $3 and the equilibrium quantity is 30.

Market Equilibrium

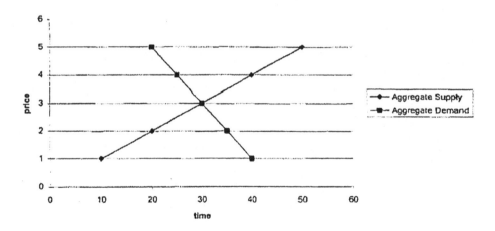

4c.   (2 points)
        Nothing changes. Since the equilibrium price is already below the price ceiling, the
        existing equilibrium is still available. The market will clear at the same equilibrium.

Effect of Price Ceiling

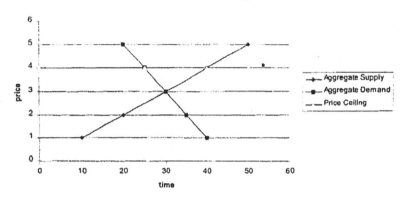

4d.   (2 points)
        The rise in the price of on-line services will shift the demand curve to the left because
        on-line services are complementary to computers. Hence, now people will demand
        fewer computers at any price. This will not affect the supply curve for computers but at
        the new equilibrium (point B) equilibrium price and quantity will be lower than those at
        the old equilibrium (point A)

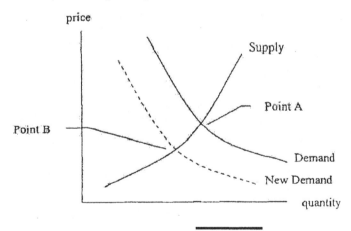

TEST 3

DIRECTIONS: Each question or incomplete statement is followed by several suggested answers or completions. Select the one that BEST answers the question or completes the statement. *PRINT THE LETTER OF THE CORRECT ANSWER IN THE SPACE AT THE RIGHT.*

1. Which of the following transactions would be counted in GDP?   1.____
   A. The wood you purchase to build yourself bookshelves in your room
   B. An economics textbook you purchase with the intent of selling it after your course is over
   C. Rent paid by Japanese tenants to an American who owns apartments in Tokyo
   D. The profit-sharing check that an employee receives this year
   E. The bicycles that a store adds to its inventory this year but is unable to sell
   F. Interest paid on consumer loans by households
   G. The commissions earned by a real estate agent in selling houses

2. Which of the following would NOT be counted as investment in the national   2.____
   income accounts?
   A. Building of a factory by General Motors
   B. Increase in General Motors inventories of raw materials
   C. Installation of a new assembly line at General Motors
   D. Purchase of a share of stock in General Motors by an employee of General Motors

3. Which of the following is NOT included in 2014's GDP?   3.____
   A. The value of a car produced in the United States and exported to England
   B. The profit earned in 2014 from selling a stock that you purchased in 2006
   C. The value of a computer chip that is used in the production of a personal computer
   D. The commission earned by an employment counselor when she locates a job for a client

Questions 4a, 4b, 4c, 4d, 4e.

DIRECTIONS: Questions 4a, 4b, 4c, 4d and 4e are to be answered on the basis of the following information.

Consider a simple economy consisting of consumers, farmers, a grocery store, and a restaurant. Assume the following transactions take place within a year.

1. Farmers sell $3,000 worth of potatoes to the grocery store, and $2,500 worth of potatoes to the restaurant.

2. Fishermen sell $5,000 worth of fish to the grocery store, and $3,500 worth of fish to the restaurant.

3. The grocery store, after cleaning and wrapping, sells potatoes (now worth $3,500) and fish (now worth $6,000) to consumers.

4. The restaurant serves "fish and chips" (worth $10,000) to their customers.

4a. What is the value of intermediate goods used by the
    (1)   Farmers
    (2)   Fishermen
    (3)   Grocery Store
    (4)   Restaurant

4b. What is the total "value added" in the economy?

4c. What are the total sales of final goods in the economy? (Give a dollar value)

4d. What, if any, is the relationship between "value added" and "total sales of final goods" in the economy? (Answer in one sentence.)

4e. A foreign firm how buys the restaurant. Under the new owners, the restaurant still uses the same amount of intermediate goods and sells the same amount of "fish and chips." But the new foreign owners realize that the previous owners had forgotten to charge $1,000 each year for the wearing out (or the depreciation) of the restaurant's cooking equipment. Explain how each of these changes ((i) new foreign ownership and (ii) restaurant depreciation charges) affect the value of GDP (gross domestic product). Use one sentence only for each explanation.

———

KEY (CORRECT ANSWERS)

1. (1.5 points)
    A, B, D, E, F and G are counted GDP, but C is not counted in GDP.)Case & Fair are ambiguous about F so we accepted both answers.)

2. (0.5 point) D.

3. (0.5 point) B.

4a. (2 points)
    (1) The value of intermediate goods used by the farmers is zero.
    (2) The value of intermediate goods used by the fishermen is zero.
    (3) The value of intermediate goods used by the grocery store is $3,000 + $5,000 = $8,000.
    (4) The value of intermediate goods used by the restaurant is $2,500 + $3,500 = $6,000.

4b. (2 points)
    The value added by the farmers is ($3,000 + $2,500) – 0 = $5,500.
    The value added by the fishermen is ($5,000 + $3,500) – 0 = $8,500.
    The value added by the grocery is ($3,500 + $6,000) – ($3,000 + $5,000) = $1,500.
    The value added by the restaurant is $10,000 – ($2,500 + $3,500) = $4,000.
    Therefore, the total value added in the economy is $5,500 + $8,500 + $1,500 + $4,000 = $19,500.

4c. (1 point)
    Sales of final goods by the farmers = 0
    Sales of final goods by the fishermen = 0
    Sales of final goods by the grocery = $9,500
    Sales of final goods by the restaurant = $10,000
    Therefore, the total sales of final goods in the economy is 0 + 0 + $9,500 + $10,000 = $19,500

4d. (0.5 point)
    "Value added" and the "total sales of final goods" in the economy are exactly equal.

4ei. (0.5 point)
    New foreign ownership does not affect the value of GDP.

4eii. (1 point)
    Restaurant depreciation charges do not affect the value of GDP.

TEST 4

DIRECTIONS: Each question is to be answered on the basis of the following information.

The General Accounting Office sends you the following U.S. economic data for 2014. (All figures are in billions of dollars.)

A	Payment of Factor Income to Rest of the World	128.4
B	Receipt of Factor Income from Rest of the World	121.6
C	Subsidies	40.1
D	Proprietors' Income	438
E	Personal Taxes	705.7
F	Rental Income	7.3
G	Capital Consumption Allowance (Depreciation)	610.5
H	Personal Consumption Expenditure on Services	2083.4
I	Total Expenditure on Durable Goods	1252
J	Total Expenditure on Non-Durable Goods	507.1
K	Indirect Taxes	522.4
L	Government Spending	1076.2
M	Exports	748.3
N	Transfer Payments	733.4
O	Imports	705.9
P	Dividends	40.8
Q	Social Insurance Payments	511.1
R	Corporate Profits	321.5
S	Personal Interest Income	221.3
T	Net Interest Income	487.6
U	Personal Consumption Expenditure	3842.5
V	Compensation of Employees	3404.5

1. Calculate Gross Domestic Product (GDP), Gross National Product (GNP), and Net National Product (NNP).

2. Calculate Gross Investment and Net Investment.

3. Calculate Personal Income and Disposable Income.

———

KEY (CORRECT ANSWERS)

1A. Calculate GDP (1 point)
Using the income approach (Table 7.3 from Case & Fair), we have:
GDP = National Income + Depreciation + Indirect Taxes minus Subsidies + Net Factor
   Payments to the Rest of the World
= [Compensation of Employees + Proprietors' Income + Corporate Profits + Net Interest
   + Rental Income] + Depreciation + Indirect Taxes minus Subsidies + Net Factor
   Payments to the Rest of the World
= [3404.5 + 438 + 321.5 + 487.6 + 7.3] + 610.5 + (522.4 − 40.1) + (128.4 − 121.6)
= 5758.5

1B. Calculate GNP (1 point)
From Table 7.4 from Case & Fair, we see
GNP = GDP + Receipts of Factor Income from the Rest of the World − Payments of
   Factor Income to the Rest of the World
= 57585 + 121.6 − 128.4 = 5751.7

1C. Calculate NNP (1 point)
NNP = GNP − Depreciation = 5751.7 − 610.5 = 5141.2

2A. Calculate Gross Investment (3 Points)
Using the expenditure approach (Table 7.2 from Case & Fair), we have
GDP = C + I+ G + (Ex − Im) = [Durable Goods + Non-Durable Goods + Services] +
   Gross Investment + Government Spending + Net Exports
= [1252 + 507.1 + 2083.4 + Gross Investment + 1076.2 + (748.3 − 705.9)
= 4961.1 + Gross Investment

Use the GNP figure we obtained from (1) to get
5751.7 − 4961.1 + Gross Investment, which gives Gross Investment = 797.4

2B. Calculate Net Investment (1 point)
Net Investment = Gross Investment − Depreciation
= 797.4 − 610.5 = 186.9

3A. Calculate Personal Income (2 points)
From Page 153 in Case & Fair, we see:
Personal Income = NNP − Indirect Taxes minus Subsidies −Corporate Profits minus
   Dividends − Social Insurance Payments + Personal Interest Income + Transfer
   Payments
= 5141.2 − (522.4 − 40.1) − (321.5 − 40.8) − 511.1 + 221.3 + 733.4 = 4821.8

3B. Calculate Disposable Income (1 point)
By Table 7.5 from Case & Fair, we have
Disposable Income = Personal Income − Personal Taxes = 4821.8 − 705.7 = 4116.1

TEST 5

DIRECTIONS: Each question or incomplete statement is followed by several suggested answers or completions. Select the one that BEST answers the question or completes the statement. *PRINT THE LETTER OF THE CORRECT ANSWER IN THE SPACE AT THE RIGHT.*

1. If income rises from $600 to $700 and consumption rises from S300 to S380, the marginal propensity to consume is

    A. 0.54   B. 0.80   C. 1.00   D. 0.65

1.____

2. If Total Expenditures exceeds Total Production at the current level of real GDP, inventories will

    A. build up above desired levels, so firms will cut production
    B. fall below desired levels, so firms will cut production
    C. build up above desired levels, so firms will increase production
    D. fall below desired levels, so firms will increase production

2.____

3. The government wishes to reduce total income by $80 billion. If the Keynesian multiplier for government spending is 2, what is the decrease in government purchases of goods and services that would do the job?

    A. $20 billion
    B. $40 billion
    C. $80 billion
    D. We don't have enough information

3.____

4. Referring to the figure shown at the right, this household's saving will be zero when income is

    A. $400
    B. $800
    C. $1,000
    D. $1,800

4.____

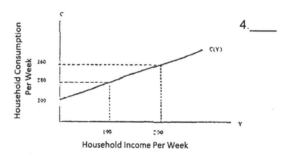

Household Income Per Week

Question 5a, 5b, 5c.

DIRECTIONS: Questions 5a, 5b, and 5c are to be answered on the basis of the following information.

    Assume an economy with no exports and no imports, in which consumers always spend $20 billion PLUS 50% of their after-tax income, or C = 20 + 0.5(Y-TX); investors always want to invest $120 billion, or I = $\bar{I}$ = 120; and the government has a balanced budget of $80 billion, or G = 80 – TX.

5a. What is the equilibrium level of national income (Y_1)? (Show your work.)

5b. Due to optimistic business expectations, investment spending increases by $30 billion, or now investment is $I = \bar{I} = 150$.
Assume everything else remains the same.
Compute the new equilibrium level of national income (Y_2). (Show your work.)

5c. Now suppose the government believes that this increase in investment spending (to $150 billion) may bring inflationary pressures. To combat this inflational threat, the government raises taxes by $20 billion. Assume that the government still has a balanced budget so that now $G = 100 = TX$.

  i. Using a circular flow diagram to derive the resulting <u>changes</u> in income, show how income will fall or rise as a result of this change in government fiscal policy. (Show your work for at least three successive changes in income.)
What will be the new equilibrium level of income (Y_3)?

  ii. What is the Keynesian multiplier for this change in taxes when the budget is balanced?

KEY (CORRECT ANSWERS)

1.   (1 point) B.

2.   (1 point) D.

3.   (1 point) B

4.   (1 point) C

    $S = Y - C$, where S = household savings, Y = Income, C = Consumption.
    This household's savings is zero, so
    $0 = Y - C$, or $Y = C$.
    From the information given on the graph, we find that the consumption function is:
    $C = 200 + 0.8Y$
    $\rightarrow Y = 200 + 0.8Y$ since $C = Y$
    $\rightarrow Y = 1000$

5a.   (1 point)
    $Y_1 = C + I + G$
    Plugging in, $Y_1 = 20 + 0.5(Y_1 - 80) + 120 + 80$
    $\rightarrow Y_1 = 0.5Y_1 + 180$
    $\rightarrow Y_1 = 360$

5b.   (2 points)
    $\Delta I = 30$

$$\rightarrow \Delta Y = \Delta I \left(\frac{1}{1 - MPC} \right)$$

    = 30 (1/0.5), since MFC = 0.5
    = 60
    So the new equilibrium level of national income is $Y_2 = 360 + 60$
    = 420

    An alternative solution would be to solve $Y_2 = C + I_2 + G$
    = $20 + 0.5(Y_2 - 80) + 150 + 80$
    which also gives $Y_2 = 420$.

5ci.   (2 points)

The first three rounds of changes in come when taxes change:

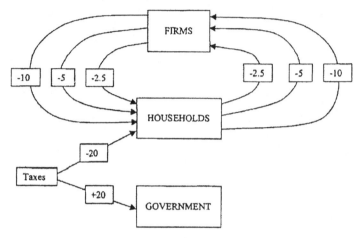

The first three rounds of changes in income when government spending changes:

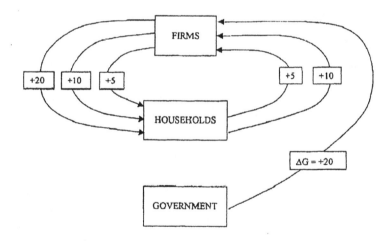

As a result of change in taxes,

$$\Delta Y = \Delta TX(\frac{-MPC}{1-MPC})$$

$$\rightarrow \Delta Y = 20(\frac{-0.5}{0.5})$$

$$= -20$$

As a result of change in government spending,

$$\Delta Y = \Delta G\left(\frac{1}{1-MPC}\right)$$

$$\rightarrow \Delta Y = 20\left(\frac{1}{0.5}\right)$$

$$= 40$$

Total change in Y = 40 − 20 = +20
Therefore, Y_3 = 420 + 20 = 440

5cii.   (1 point)
The combined multiplier for any simultaneous change in G and TX is:

$$\Delta Y = \Delta G\left(\frac{1}{1-MPC}\right) + \Delta TX\left(\frac{-MPC}{1-MPC}\right)$$

If the budget is balanced, then G = TX, and $\Delta G = \Delta TX$.

Substituting ΔTX for ΔG in (1) gives

$$\Delta Y = \Delta TX\left(\frac{1}{1-MPC}\right) + \Delta TX\left(\frac{-MPC}{1-MPC}\right)$$

$$= \frac{\Delta TX(1-MPC)}{(1-MPC)}$$

$\Delta TX \times (1)$

So, the Keynesian multiplier is 1.

EXAMINATION SECTION
TEST 1

DIRECTIONS: Each question or incomplete statement is followed by several suggested answers or completions. Select the one that BEST answers the question or completes the statement. *PRINT THE LETTER OF THE CORRECT ANSWER IN THE SPACE AT THE RIGHT.*

1. A company holds a ten-year maturity bond with a stated interest rate of 12%. If investors require a 10% yield on bonds of similar quality, the value of the bond in the coming month will   1.____

   A. decrease
   B. increase
   C. remain unchanged
   D. float along with the prime rate

2. Each of the following is considered to be a MAJOR financial management function EXCEPT   2.____

   A. raising funds
   B. financial planning and analysis
   C. managing the accounting system
   D. asset management

3. When used as a capital budgeting tool, the profitability index of a proposed investment project is determined by   3.____

   A. adding the present value of the investment and the cash outflow created by the cost of the investment
   B. dividing the cash outflow created by the cost of the investment by the investment's present value
   C. dividing the present value of the investment by the net present value
   D. dividing the present value of the investment by the cash outflow created by the cost of the investment

4. In what type of business do all owners have unlimited liability for the firm's debts?   4.____

   A. Proprietorship   B. Partnership
   C. Corporation   D. Limited partnership

5. For manufacturing firms, current assets have historically accounted for about _____% or more of total assets.   5.____

   A. 25   B. 40   C. 65   D. 80

6. Each of the following is a factor involved in the return-on-owners' equity model EXCEPT   6.____

   A. profit margin
   B. weighted average cost of capital
   C. equity multiplier
   D. asset turnover

7. What type of preferred stock gives a corporation the right to retire the preferred stock at its option?   7.____

   A. Noncumulative   B. Cumulative
   C. Convertible   D. Callable

8. The principle of hedging generally requires matching   8.____

   A. dollar amounts of current assets with fixed assets
   B. fixed assets with sales volume
   C. the average maturities of assets with liabilities and equity
   D. short-term financing with fixed assets

9. Which of the following is generally considered to be good practice in managing a company's investment portfolio?   9.____

   A. Considering securities with positive correlations to each other
   B. Investing primarily in creditor claims
   C. Adjusting upward to the extent to which an investment account can be realized in the case of market decline
   D. Staggering the maturity rates of securities

10. An ordinary annuity is one in which   10.____

   A. the interest rate is fixed for a specified period of time
   B. cash flows occur at the beginning of each time period
   C. cash flows occur over a period of several years
   D. cash flow amounts occur at the end of each period starting with the first cash flow at the end of the first year

11. A business's demand for the cash needed to carry out daily operations is referred to as its   11.____

   A. transactions motive   B. net working capital
   C. precautionary motive   D. current ratio

12. Which of the following forms of claim in foreign exchange is generally LEAST expensive?   12.____

   A. Bill of exchange   B. Time draft
   C. Cable order   D. Sight draft

13. Which of the following financial statements is best for capturing a *snapshot* of a company's overall status at a particular point in time?   13.____

   A. Cash flow statement   B. Income statement
   C. Trend analysis   D. Balance sheet

14. A financial manager should try to minimize the investment in current assets because of   14.____

   A. the need for acceptable credit terms
   B. the cost of financing them
   C. liquidity purposes
   D. the risk involved in holding them

15. The financing provided by accounts payable is estimated by means of   15.____
    - A. multiplying accounts payable by the average inventory turnover
    - B. subtracting accounts receivable from accounts payable
    - C. dividing the cost of goods sold by the average inventory turnover
    - D. dividing accounts payable by the cost of goods sold

16. Under current tax law, businesses are allowed to depreciate _____% of their fixed   16.____
    assets in the five-year property class during the first year.

    A. 6   B. 12   C. 20   D. 32

17. What is the term for the funds remaining after subtracting current liabilities from current   17.____
    assets?
    - A. Net working capital   B. Gross revenue
    - C. Retained earnings   D. Financial leverage

18. The management of receivables involves each of the following EXCEPT   18.____
    - A. conducting credit analysis
    - B. determining transactions motives
    - C. setting credit terms
    - D. carrying out collection efforts

Questions 19-20.

DIRECTIONS: Questions 19 and 20 refer to the information below.

Keller Manufacturing is a corporation with 50,000 shares of common stock outstanding. Its stock is currently traded at $40 per share. Its net sales total $1.4 million and its net income is $100,000.

19. What is the firm's earnings per share (EPS)?   19.____

    A. $1.00   B. $2.00   C. $2.50   D. $3.25

20. Keller's price-earnings (P/E) ratio is   20.____

    A. 2   B. 5   C. 10   D. 12

21. A loan on which the borrower agrees to make regular payments on principal as well as   21.____
    on interest is described as
    - A. compounding   B. combined
    - C. balanced   D. amortized

22. Most bonds pay interest   22.____
    - A. quarterly   B. semiannually
    - C. annually   D. biannually

23. The principal *current* assets of a business typically include each of the following   23.____
    EXCEPT
    - A. inventories   B. prepaid expenses
    - C. accounts receivable   D. cash and marketable securities

24. Which of the following is the most widely used source of short-term funds for businesses?   24.____

    A. Commercial paper
    B. Commercial finance companies
    C. Trade credits
    D. Commercial banks

25. Which of the following is typically used as a last resort for the financing of current assets?   25.____

    A. Accounts payable
    B. Marketable securities
    C. Accrued liabilities
    D. Short-term bank loans or long-term funds

KEY (CORRECT ANSWERS)

1.	B		11.	A
2.	C		12.	B
3.	D		13.	D
4.	B		14.	B
5.	B		15.	C
6.	B		16.	C
7.	D		17.	A
8.	C		18.	B
9.	D		19.	B
10.	D		20.	C

21.	D
22.	B
23.	B
24.	D
25.	D

TEST 2

DIRECTIONS: Each question or incomplete statement is followed by several suggested answers or completions. Select the one that BEST answers the question or completes the statement. *PRINT THE LETTER OF THE CORRECT ANSWER IN THE SPACE AT THE RIGHT.*

1. A limitation associated with the payback period method of capital budgeting is that it

    A. ignores all cash flows beyond the payback period
    B. does not include a specific estimate of an investment's initial outlay
    C. does not determine the time it will take to recover the initial investment
    D. does not presume the future benefits of an investment

1.____

2. Which of the following types of ratios is commonly used to determine a business's net working capital?
    I.   Financial leverage ratio
    II. Acid-test ratio
    III. Asset utilization ratio
    IV. Current ratio
    The CORRECT answer is:

    A. I, II   B. II, IV   C. I, II, III   D. I, III, IV

2.____

3. When a financial manager compares potential investment projects during the capital budgeting process, he or she is really comparing

    A. variance   B. net present values
    C. costs of investment   D. cash flows

3.____

4. Typically, the FIRST step in the financial planning process is to

    A. determine debt-equity fund mix
    B. forecast sales
    C. determine a liquidity ratio
    D. determine profitability

4.____

5. In general, which of the following investments involves the greatest risk of default?

    A. U.S. government bonds   B. Common stocks
    C. Municipal bonds   D. Corporate bonds

5.____

6. In which of the following situations would one most likely encounter a present-value annuity-due problem?

    A. Home mortgages   B. Facility rentals
    C. Leasing arrangements   D. Callable bonds

6.____

7. When a company's financial leverage is determined by using an equity multiplier ratio, it is calculated by

    A. multiplying total liabilities by owners' equity
    B. dividing total liabilities by total assets
    C. dividing owners' equity by total liabilities
    D. dividing the total assets by owners' equity

7.____

8. In the capital budgeting process, the *selection* stage typically involves   8.____

    A. applying the appropriate capital budgeting techniques to help make a final accept or reject decision
    B. reviewing past decisions
    C. discussing the pros and cons of each project
    D. finding potential capital investment opportunities and identifying whether a project involves a replacement decision and/or revenue expansion

9. The link between financial planning and the management of working capital, including   9.____
both current assets and current liabilities, can be described in terms of a business's

    A. short-term operating cycle
    B. retained earnings
    C. asset turnover ratio
    D. net working capital

10. _____ motives are NOT motives for which business firms hold cash and marketable   10.____
securities.

    A. Precautionary   B. Goodwill
    C. Speculative   D. Transactions

11. In a typical income statement, the starting point reflects   11.____

    A. current liabilities   B. current assets
    C. variable costs   D. revenues or sales

12. Which of the following stock market indicators demonstrates the health and trend of the   12.____
market?

    A. Trading volume   B. Odd-lot trading
    C. Charts   D. Market breadth

13. What is the term for the process by which savings are accumulated in financial institu-   13.____
tions and, in turn, lent or invested by them?

    A. Intermediation   B. Transition
    C. Interplay   D. Transubstantiation

Questions 14-15.

DIRECTIONS: Questions 14 and 15 refer to the information below.

    The Longbow Company is evaluating a project for possible inclusion in its capital budget. The project will require an $80,000 investment. After-tax cash inflows are estimated at $24,000 a year for the next four years.

14. What is the approximate payback period for the investment?   14.____
    _____ years.

    A. 1.2   B. 2.7   C. 3.3   D. 4.4

15. Calculate the net present value of the project based on a 10% cost of capital (PVIFA = 3.170).   15.____

    A. -$3,920   B. -$1,960   C. $7,840   D. $76,080

16. A finance computation involving cash flows that occur at the beginning of each time period is known as a(n) _____ problem.   16.____

    A. discounting   B. annuity due
    C. compounding   D. regular annuity

17. In general, the most critical element in the risk-return analysis of potential investment projects is the correct estimation of   17.____

    A. the amounts and probability of cash flows
    B. interest rates
    C. resources available for investment
    D. total costs

18. When information is taken from both the income statement and the balance sheet to show how the firm obtained funds during the accounting period and how those funds were used, this information is typically used to compose a(n)   18.____

    A. statement of cash flows
    B. time series analysis
    C. cash transactions statement
    D. asset utilization ratio

19. Which of the following is NOT a section that is included in a Dun & Bradstreet business credit report?   19.____

    A. History   B. Character assessment
    C. Operation and location   D. Trade payments

20. Amounts which are owed but not yet paid for are referred to as   20.____

    A. real liabilities   B. accrued liabilities
    C. current liabilities   D. amortized loans

21. A business firm's cost of common equity capital is considered to be the same as the   21.____

    A. weighted average cost of capital on all its investments
    B. internal rate of return on its long-term investments
    C. rate of return on long-term debt financing
    D. rate of return expected by investors in the firm's common stock

22. Each of the following is considered to be an internal business risk EXCEPT   22.____

    A. the death of a key employee
    B. theft
    C. bond market failure
    D. natural disasters

23. For most firms, retained earnings must first be used for   23.____

    A. paying out dividends   B. paying taxes
    C. repaying business loans   D. purchasing equipment

24. A company's break-even point for the sale of a particular product is revealed through the   24.____
process of

    A. time series analysis   B. sales forecasting
    C. comparative analysis   D. cost-volume analysis

25. When using the internal rate of return method for capital budgeting, the present value   25.____
interest factor (PVIFA) for an investment is found by

    A. dividing the initial outlay by the annual cash inflow of the investment
    B. dividing the cash inflow annuity amount (annual receipt) by the initial outlay
    C. dividing the initial outlay by the cash inflow annuity amount
    D. subtracting the initial outlay from the cash inflow annuity amount

---

KEY (CORRECT ANSWERS)

1.	A		11.	D
2.	B		12.	A
3.	B		13.	A
4.	B		14.	C
5.	B		15.	A
6.	C		16.	B
7.	D		17.	A
8.	A		18.	A
9.	A		19.	B
10.	B		20.	B

21.	D
22.	C
23.	A
24.	D
25.	C

TEST 3

DIRECTIONS: Each question or incomplete statement is followed by several suggested answers or completions. Select the one that BEST answers the question or completes the statement. *PRINT THE LETTER OF THE CORRECT ANSWER IN THE SPACE AT THE RIGHT.*

1. Solving for the future value of an amount deposited now will involve each of the following factors EXCEPT   1.____

    A. 1 divided by 1 plus the interest rate
    B. the number of periods to compound over
    C. 1 plus the interest rate
    D. present value amount

2. Which of the following is NOT a disadvantage associated with being a common stock-holder?   2.____

    A. When profits are low, other claims may completely absorb available funds
    B. Relatively little control over the firm's activities
    C. Less stability with respect to dividends
    D. Low priority during business liquidation

3. The purpose of a liquidity ratio is to   3.____

    A. show the ability of a business to meet its short-term obligations
    B. show how well the company uses its assets to support or generate sales
    C. indicate the extent to which assets are financed by borrowed funds and other liabilities
    D. compare profits with sales

4. An optimal capital structure   4.____

    A. makes maximum use of long-term debt
    B. minimizes the cost of debt and equity funds
    C. relies primarily on short-term funds
    D. stabilizes the value of the firm

5. A bank offers an 8% interest rate on its accounts which will compound semiannually. If $1,000 is invested for a period of ten years, what will be the future value of the investment?   5.____

    A. $1,763   B. $2,159   C. $2,191   D. $2,222

6. Which of the following is a selection technique used to evaluate long-term investment proposals?   6.____

    A. Capital budgeting   B. Working capital management
    C. Sensitivity analysis   D. Discounting analysis

7. Each of the following is a factor involved in calculating the future value of an investment EXCEPT the   7.____

    A. interest rate
    B. number of periods in years

C. difference between compounding and discounting rates
D. present value

8. In risk-return analysis, the dispersion of cash flows is denoted by the term   8._____

   A. variance   B. net present value
   C. standard deviation   D. expected value

Questions 9-10.

DIRECTIONS: Questions 9 and 10 refer to the information below.

In the previous year, the Earl Company earned $100,000 in net income on net sales of
$1.4 million. The company's balance sheet shows that accounts payable plus accrued liabili-
ties were about 15% of sales. Net sales are expected to rise by 10% next year, and the profit
margin is expected to hold.

9. Assuming that management at the Earl Company plans to pay out about half the com-   9._____
   pany's profits to the owners of the company, how much internally generated financing
   would be available to support Earl's assets?

   A. $45,000   B. $55,000   C. $70,000   D. $110,000

10. How much of Earl's assets would have to be financed with external funds?   10._____

   A. $45,000   B. $55,000   C. $70,000   D. $110,000

11. Which of the following is NOT typically a capital-budgeting decision?   11._____

   A. Ranking projects in terms of their expected returns
   B. Whether to expand existing product lines
   C. Whether to conduct credit analysis of a potential purchaser
   D. Whether to replace existing equipment with new equipment

12. What is the term for an option to buy a security at a specified price during a specified   12._____
    period of time?

   A. Bank acceptance   B. Futures contract
   C. Leverage contract   D. Call contract

13. Which of the following are indirect equity claims?   13._____

   A. Mutual funds   B. Money market funds
   C. Commercial paper   D. Bonds

14. Which of the following will be indicated by estimating the time it takes to complete a busi-   14._____
    ness's short-term operating cycle relative to the level of operations?
       I. The extent to which financing will take place through accounts payable
      II. The influence of asset turnover on inventories
     III. The size of the investment in accounts receivable and inventories
    The CORRECT answer is:

   A. I only   B. II only   C. I, III   D. II, III

15. What is the term for a company's need for funds to take advantage of unexpected price bargains or discounts?   15.____

    A. Incidental capital   B. Suppositional assets
    C. Speculative motive   D. Hedge

16. A company's asset turnover component is expressed as   16.____

    A. net income divided by net sales
    B. net sales divided by total assets
    C. total assets divided by net income
    D. net income divided by total assets

17. A financial manager must set a rate of return that the company needs to earn on its asset investments in order to cover the cost of debt and still leave an adequate rate of return for the owners. The combined rate necessary to cover the cost of debt and equity funds is referred to as the company's   17.____

    A. cost of capital   B. internal rate of return
    C. net present value   D. discount rate

18. Which of the following is NOT an advantage associated with short-term borrowing as opposed to other forms of financing?   18.____
It

    A. helps establish a close relationship with banks
    B. has more flexibility
    C. typically involves no prepayment penalties
    D. can usually be used to take care of future needs

Questions 19-20.

DIRECTIONS: Questions 19 and 20 refer to the information below.

Blake Industries' production process requires an average of 70 days to go from raw materials to finished products, and another 30 days before the finished goods are sold. Blake also extends credit to customers and has an accounts receivable cycle of 58 days based on its net sales. Materials for Blake are purchased on credit from suppliers, and the accounts payable cycle averages 50 days based on Blake's cost of goods sold.

19. What is Blake Industries' short-term operating cycle, in days?   19.____

    A. 100   B. 108   C. 158   D. 208

20. About how many times does Blake's short-term operating cycle turn over each year?   20.____

    A. 1.75   B. 2.31   C. 3.38   D. 3.65

21. Cost-push inflation typically occurs in response to   21.____

    A. lower wages accompanied by increased productivity
    B. higher production costs accompanied by increased productivity
    C. temporary resource shortages
    D. higher production costs without increased productivity

22. What is the term for an initial sale of newly issued debt or equity securities?   22.____

    A. Flotation   B. Hedging
    C. Turnover   D. Intermediation

23. When the rate of return on borrowed funds is higher than their cost to a firm, _____ has   23.____
occurred.

    A. negative financial leverage
    B. buying on margin
    C. positive financial leverage
    D. inflation

24. Which of the following is NOT a factor involved in determining the expected return of a   24.____
common stock?

    A. Growth   B. Present value
    C. Dividends   D. Stock price

25. Each of the following categories of risk is considered to affect the financing of business   25.____
firms EXCEPT _____ risk.

    A. transactions   B. macroeconomics business
    C. purchasing power   D. interest rate

KEY (CORRECT ANSWERS)

1.	A		11.	C
2.	B		12.	D
3.	A		13.	A
4.	B		14.	C
5.	C		15.	C
6.	A		16.	B
7.	C		17.	A
8.	A		18.	D
9.	B		19.	B
10.	A		20.	C

21. D
22. A
23. C
24. B
25. A

TEST 4

DIRECTIONS: Each question or incomplete statement is followed by several suggested answers or completions. Select the one that BEST answers the question or completes the statement. *PRINT THE LETTER OF THE CORRECT ANSWER IN THE SPACE AT THE RIGHT.*

1. In credit analysis, a borrower's financial ability to pay bills as they come due is described in terms of

   A. capital   B. collateral   C. capacity   D. character

1._____

2. Which of the following would NOT be considered a current liability for a business?

   A. Wages   B. Notes payable
   C. Mortgages   D. Interest

2._____

3. In general, stock prices change over time in response to changes in each of the following EXCEPT

   A. cash dividend levels
   B. weighted average cost of capital
   C. investor-expected returns
   D. growth rates

3._____

4. Which of the following typically constitutes the smallest proportion of a manufacturing firm's assets?

   A. Equipment and facilities
   B. Inventories
   C. Accounts receivable
   D. Cash and marketable securities

4._____

5. Which of the following typically accompanies a documentary draft in foreign exchange?

   A. Traveler's letter of credit
   B. Trust receipt
   C. Order bill of lading
   D. Manifest

5._____

6. A firm's inventory turnover is estimated by means of

   A. dividing inventories by accounts receivable
   B. dividing the cost of goods sold by inventories
   C. adding inventories and accounts receivable
   D. subtracting inventories from accounts receivable

6._____

7. A company is considering an investment project that is estimated to cost $8,000, and the incremental cost of capital is estimated at 12%. The investment cost will be incurred at the beginning of next year, and cash flows occur at the end of next year. The most likely cash flow for the coming year is estimated to be $10,000. If the term of the investment is a single year, what is the investment's net present value?

   A. -$857   B. $36   C. $929   D. $1,821

7._____

8. Which of the following business costs are primarily variable in nature?   8._____

    A. General and administrative expenses
    B. Cost of goods sold
    C. Interest expenses
    D. Depreciation expenses

9. For a corporation, the primary DISADVANTAGE associated with employing a liberal divi-   9._____
    dend policy is that it

    A. will lower the price of public issues of securities
    B. reduces internally generated funds available for investment
    C. increases the corporation's tax burden
    D. may appear unfavorable to stockholders

10. The most frequent justification given by lenders for requiring a compensating balance on   10._____
    unsecured loans is

    A. federal reserve requirements
    B. poor business credit
    C. inflation
    D. the inability to lend without deposits

11. What is the term for the promissory notes that can be issued or sold by large U.S. corpo-   11._____
    rations of high credit quality?

    A. Acceptances   B. Lines of credit
    C. Commercial paper   D. Stock or bond power

12. According to the recommendations of the Bank Management Commission of the Ameri-   12._____
    can Bankers Association, a loan based on the security of accounts receivable should
    generally be no more than _____% of the company's gross receivables.

    A. 60   B. 70   C. 80   D. 90

13. Which of the following is NOT an advantage associated with the use of bonds for financ-   13._____
    ing, rather than stocks?

    A. *Cheaper-dollar* paybacks due to inflation
    B. Equity interests remain intact
    C. No sinking fund requirements
    D. Tax-deductible interest

14. The Joan Company sells on credit terms of net/60 days.   14._____
    Its net sales total $1.5 million, and its accounts receivable balance is $300,000.
    What is the average collection period for this company, in days?

    A. 50   B. 72   C. 138   D. 180

15. Foreign exchange markets are   15._____

    A. major financial centers linked by exceptional communications
    B. located at specific locations in major industrial cities
    C. facilities set up by central banks for foreign exchanges
    D. money markets located outside of the United States

16. When a long-term debt is due within _____ from the date of the current balance sheet, it is generally transferred to the current liabilities section.

    A. 90 days   B. 6 months   C. 1 year   D. 3 years

16.____

17. A bond issued by a company with significant financial problems should be considered by a financial manager as a _____ risk.

    A. purchasing power   B. default
    C. liquidity   D. market

17.____

18. In capital budgeting, the payback period method is used primarily to

    A. determine the present value interest factor for a particular investment
    B. compare two investments to determine which one recovers its initial outlay more quickly
    C. determine the maximum initial cash outlay for a particular investment
    D. determine whether a risk premium should be added to a company's cost of capital

18.____

19. When a parcel of real estate has more than one mortgage lien against it, the bonds outstanding against mortgages filed after the first mortgage are

    A. debenture bonds   B. second mortgage bonds
    C. junior liens   D. indentures

19.____

20. Which of the following is true of industries that experience only minor operating changes and reverses over the business cycle?

    A. They generally have less long-term debt than companies with dramatic cyclical swings.
    B. Their investments generally have a profitability index of greater than 2.
    C. They make greater use of factoring services than less stable firms.
    D. They generally make greater use of borrowed capital than firms with wide cyclical swings.

20.____

21. Which of the following should be used as a company's discount rate for making future capital budgeting decisions?
The

    A. internal rate of return on its investment projects
    B. average yield to maturity of its investment projects
    C. weighted average cost of capital
    D. average face yield of its investment projects

21.____

22. The present value of an investment project is determined by

    A. dividing the initial outlay by the annual cash inflow of the investment
    B. subtracting the initial outlay from the present value of all cash inflows for the life of the investment
    C. dividing the initial outlay by the cash inflow annuity amount (annual receipt)
    D. subtracting the initial outlay from the cash inflow annuity amount

22.____

Questions 23-25.

DIRECTIONS: Questions 23 through 25 refer to the information below.

The company Technosoft is considering the development, manufacture, and sale of product for $200 each. The variable costs (raw materials and direct labor) are estimated at $100 per copy, and the fixed costs allocated to this product would be $80,000.

23. If sales reach 1,000 units per year, what would be the operating profits generated by this product

    A. $10,000   B. $20,000   C. $35,000   D. $45,000

23.____

24. How many units of the product will need to be sold in order for the company to break even?

    A. 150   B. 200   C. 400   D. 800

24.____

25. Expressed in dollars, Technosoft's break-even point for this product would be

    A. $40,000   B. $80,000   C. $160,000   D. $180,000

25.____

KEY (CORRECT ANSWERS)

1.	C	11.	C
2.	C	12.	C
3.	B	13.	C
4.	D	14.	B
5.	C	15.	A
6.	B	16.	C
7.	C	17.	B
8.	B	18.	B
9.	B	19.	C
10.	D	20.	D

21.	C
22.	B
23.	B
24.	D
25.	C

EXAMINATION SECTION
TEST 1

DIRECTIONS: Each question or incomplete statement is followed by several suggested answers or completions. Select the one that BEST answers the question or completes the statement. *PRINT THE LETTER OF THE CORRECT ANSWER IN THE SPACE AT THE RIGHT.*

1. The decision of whether to invest in a fixed asset begins with the 　　　　　　　　1.＿＿＿

   A. determination of inventory turnover
   B. estimation of current assets
   C. determination of the maximum possible cost for investment
   D. development of a schedule of relevant cash flows

2. The relation of net income to total assets reveals a(n) ＿＿＿＿ ratio. 　　　2.＿＿＿

   A. profitability   B. asset utilization
   C. liquidity   D. financial leverage

3. During the capital budgeting process, a risk-adjusted discount rate is most likely to be added to the company's cost of capital when estimating for 　　　3.＿＿＿

   A. the replacement of aging equipment used in production of existing products
   B. the best choice among equipment available from competing suppliers
   C. expansion projects involving new areas and product lines
   D. projects that are not in direct competition with one another

4. Which of the following are disadvantages associated with the use of factoring services for short-term funding? 　　　4.＿＿＿
   I.   Unknown costs of doing business through credit sales
   II. Higher overhead
   III. Relatively higher financing costs
   IV. The implication of financial weakness
   The CORRECT answer is:

   A. I, II   B. I, III   C. III, IV   D. I, II, IV

5. *Convertible* preferred stock is so named because 　　　5.＿＿＿

   A. dividends can be transferred to invest in long-term debt funds at the stockholder's option
   B. it can be converted to common stock of the corporation at the stockholder's option
   C. it can be retired by the corporation at its option
   D. it carries a previously stated dividend

6. The extent to which a company's assets are financed by liabilities is typically indicated by calculating the company's 　　　6.＿＿＿

   A. discount rate
   B. equity multiplier ratio
   C. negative financial leverage
   D. debt ratio

7. What is the term for credit extended to a business's customers for purchases of the com-   7.____
pany's products or services?

    A. Trade credit   B. Goodwill motive
    C. Purchase indemnity   D. Trade subsidy

8. A liquidity ratio that is calculated by dividing the residual of current assets minus invento-   8.____
ries by the firn's current liabilities is referred to as a(n) _____ ratio.

    A. cost-volume   B. acid-test
    C. asset turnover   D. equity

9. Each of the following is an advantage associated with the use of trade credit for short-   9.____
term financing EXCEPT it

    A. is easy to obtain
    B. involves zero or minimal financing costs
    C. is easily convertible
    D. has no collateral requirements

10. When a loan is offered that is not a mortgage, what is   10.____

    A. A deed of trust   B. All current assets
    C. A debenture bond   D. All fixed assets

11. The purpose of an income statement is to   11.____

    A. show the owners' equity accumulated as profits within the corporation
    B. show the assets and liabilities of a firm
    C. record cash received and disbursed
    D. itemize the net profit or loss of a firm during a specified time period

12. Which of the following types of drafts used in foreign exchanges requires immediate pay-   12.____
ment?
    _____ draft.

    A. Sight   B. Time
    C. Documentary   D. Clean

13. Generally, the purpose of financing some of a business's assets with long-term debt is to   13.____

    A. make use of current liabilities as well
    B. provide the owners with a rate of return on owners' equity that is higher than the
       rate of return on assets
    C. provide the owners with a rate of return on owners' equity that is the same as the
       return to the owners
    D. provide the owners with a rate of return on assets that is higher than the rate of
       return on owners' equity

14. The main limitation to the net present value method of capital budgeting is that it   14.____

    A. ignores all after-tax cash inflows
    B. does not consider the time value of money
    C. determines the annual receipt from the investment
    D. does not give the actual rates of return on the investment

15. Constant periodic annuity payments are most often determined in association with   15.____

    A. irrevocable trusts   B. municipal bonds
    C. securities   D. amortized loans

16. Investors in a company expect to receive cash dividends next year of $4 per share. The   16.____
common stock is currently selling for $60 a share. The stock value is expected to rise to
$64 a share over the next year.
What is the expected dividend yield?

    A. 3.3%   B. 6.7%   C. 11.1%   D. 15.0%

17. In determining the amount of new external funds needed to finance a company's asset   17.____
additions, which of the following would be performed FIRST?

    A. Subtracting the expected amount of internally generated profits from the planned
asset investments
    B. Subtracting the amount of spontaneous increases expected in accounts payable
and accrued liabilities from the planned asset investments
    C. Forecasting the dollar amount of expected sales increase
    D. Determining the dollar amount of new asset investments needed to support
increased sales

18. If a corporation wants to, obtain equity capital without diluting the control of current stock-   18.____
holders, it will typically

    A. reduce the work force   B. issue common stock
    C. finance with bonds   D. issue preferred stock

19. Which of the following is NOT in line with the principle of hedging?   19.____

    A. Fluctuating current assets associated with seasonal operations should be financed
with short-term liabilities.
    B. Permanent current assets should be financed with short-term debt.
    C. Fixed assets should be financed with long-term debt and owners' equity funds.
    D. Assets should mature as liabilities mature.

20. The agency in most cities that is set up by consumer finance companies to provide infor-   20.____
mation on loans is the credit

    A. union   B. league   C. exchange   D. bureau

21. Blake Industries' inventory turns over about 3.6 times a year, and its annual cost of   21.____
goods sold is $450,000. Accounts receivable turns over on average 7 times a year. What
would be the approximate average inventory on Blake's balance sheet?

    A. $64,285   B. $125,000   C. $231,430   D. $875,000

22. A company's balance sheet indicates the relationship of equality expressed as follows: 22.____
Assets = Liabilities +

    A. Accounts payable   B. Owners' equity
    C. Net revenues   D. Working capital

23. Typically, a commercial finance company advances funds to businesses in each of the following ways EXCEPT

    A. discounting accounts receivable
    B. financing deferred-payment sales of commercial and industrial equipment
    C. discounting acceptances
    D. making loans secured by chattel mortgages on machinery or liens on inventory

23.____

24. Improving a company's asset turnover ratio involves _____ its percentage of _____.

    A. *decreasing;* sales to income
    B. *decreasing;* assets to sales
    C. *increasing;* sales to income
    D. *increasing;* assets to sales

24.____

25. Which of the following aspects of a business's internal and external financing is generally considered to be most important?

    A. The capital market
    B. The firm's dividend policy
    C. Par value of common stock
    D. Taxes

25.____

KEY (CORRECT ANSWERS)

1.	D		11.	D
2.	A		12.	A
3.	C		13.	B
4.	C		14.	D
5.	B		15.	D
6.	D		16.	B
7.	A		17.	C
8.	B		18.	D
9.	C		19.	B
10.	A		20.	C

21.	B
22.	B
23.	C
24.	B
25.	B

TEST 2

DIRECTIONS: Each question or incomplete statement is followed by several suggested answers or completions. Select the one that BEST answers the question or completes the statement. *PRINT THE LETTER OF THE CORRECT ANSWER IN THE SPACE AT THE RIGHT.*

1. Accrued liabilities typically include the following EXCEPT   1.____

   A. interest on notes   B. accounts payable
   C. wages and salaries   D. taxes

2. The contractual terms associated with a bond issue are spelled out in detail in a(n)   2.____

   A. trust indenture   B. surety contract
   C. acceptance   D. trust receipt

Questions 3-5.

DIRECTIONS: Questions 3 through 5 refer to the information below.

A company's net sales for a single year total $1.4 million. Its variable costs, which the company keeps steady at 60% of net sales, totaled $840,000 and its fixed costs were $400,000.

3. What was the company's earnings before taxes?   3.____

   A. $160,000   B. $440,000
   C. $560,000   D. $1.4 million

4. If the company's sales increase by 10% in the coming year, what would be the percent   4.____
   change in the company's operating income?

   A. -35%   B. 0%   C. +17.5%   D. +35%

5. If the company's sales increase by 10%, what will be the company's degree of operating   5.____
   leverage?

   A. -3.5   B. 0   C. 1.75   D. 3.5

6. A statement by a bank guaranteeing acceptance and payment of a draft up to a stated   6.____
   amount is called a(n)

   A. commercial letter of credit
   B. promissory note
   C. acceptance
   D. clean draft

7. An annuity yields $1,000 a year for three years at a discount rate of 8%. The present   7.____
   value of the annuity is

   A. $2,382   B. $2,571   C. $2,577   D. $2,778

8. Short-term promissory notes of commercial bank customers, which can be discounted 8.____
with Federal Reserve banks, are known as

    A. commercial paper   B. eligible paper
    C. clean drafts   D. treasury notes

9. What type of financial ratio will be revealed by the turnover of accounts such as receiv- 9.____
ables and inventories?

    A. Asset utilization   B. Liquidity
    C. Profitability   D. Financial leverage

10. Which of the following offers the best explanation for why quotations of foreign exchange 10.____
rates are identical (or nearly so) in cities worldwide?

    A. Price fixing
    B. Central bank control
    C. Arbitrage activities
    D. Travelers' letters of credit

11. A lender agrees to a $1,000 receipt -- ten years in the future -- for a loan offered at an 8% 11.____
discount rate. What is the present value of the loan?

    A. $386   B. $463   C. $681   D. $800

12. Which of the following is NOT a source of long-term financing? 12.____

    A. Equity securities   B. Bonds
    C. Mortgages   D. Commercial paper

13. A company's financial officer is using a profitability index to determine whether a project 13.____
is a good candidate for investment. In order to be considered a good candidate, the
project should have a profitability index of AT LEAST

    A. 0.25   B. 0.5   C. 1   D. 2

Questions 14-15.

DIRECTIONS: Questions 14 and 15 refer to the information below.

A company plans to invest $10 each year for four years and will earn 10% per year.

14. If the first $100 is invested now, what will be the future value of the annuity? 14.____

    A. $146.40   B. $464.10   C. $510.50   D. $610.50

15. If the company waits a year to make its first investment, what will be the future value of 15.____
the annuity?

    A. $146.40   B. $464.10   C. $510.50   D. $610.50

16. Which of the following are NOT direct equity claims? 16.____

    A. Options   B. Warrants
    C. Preferred stocks   D. Common stocks

17. A lender offers a $20,000, 10%, three-year loan that is to be fully amortized with three annual payments. The first payment will be due one year from the loan date.
The present value interest factor (PVIFA) for 10% is 2.487. What is the approximate amount of each payment?

    A. $5,471.40   B. $7,333.33   C. $8,041.82   D. $8,846.00

17.____

18. Concentration risk refers to

    A. a lack of diversification in a company's investment portfolio
    B. factors such as financial condition and product demand that affect the value of an investment
    C. the variability in the value of an investment as interest rates, money market, or capital market conditions change
    D. the possibility that an investment may not be sold on short notice for its market value

18.____

19. Which of the following would be a typical use of a cash transaction statement?

    A. Measuring firm profitability as measured by the rate of return on assets
    B. Comparing the firm's ratios against industry ratios
    C. Showing the extent to which assets have been used to support revenue or sales
    D. Forecasting short-term borrowing needs

19.____

20. Which of the following stock market indicators relates the dispersion of general price fluctuation and is useful as an advance indicator of major price declines or advances?

    A. Relative strength analysis
    B. Trading volume
    C. Market breadth
    D. The *Barton's Confidence* index

20.____

21. A banker's acceptance

    A. depends entirely on the goodwill of the importer
    B. is always accompanied by a bank letter of credit
    C. is always less costly than a bill of exchange
    D. is not drawn on an importer

21.____

22. Which of the following U.S. Treasury obligations have the shortest maturities?

    A. Bills   B. Notes
    C. Certificates of deposit   D. Bonds

22.____

Questions 23-25.

DIRECTIONS: Questions 23 through 25 refer to the information below.

    The James Manufacturing Company's financial statement results for the previous year include the following: Net sales were $2 million with net income of $140,000. At year end, the total assets of the company amounted to $1.6 million.

23. What is the company's profit margin?

    A. 6.75%   B. 7%   C. 8%   D. 8.75%

23.____

24. What is the company's asset turnover ratio?   24.____

    A. 0.33   B. 0.75   C. 1.25   D. 1.50

25. The company's return on its assets would be expressed as which of the following per-   25.____
centages?

    A. 7.5%   B. 8.75%   C. 10.5%   D. 18.0%

_____

KEY (CORRECT ANSWERS)

1.	B		11.	B
2.	A		12.	D
3.	A		13.	C
4.	D		14.	C
5.	D		15.	B
6.	A		16.	C
7.	C		17.	C
8.	B		18.	A
9.	A		19.	D
10.	C		20.	C

21.	D
22.	A
23.	B
24.	C
25.	B

_____

TEST 3

DIRECTIONS: Each question or incomplete statement is followed by several suggested answers or completions. Select the one that BEST answers the question or completes the statement. *PRINT THE LETTER OF THE CORRECT ANSWER IN THE SPACE AT THE RIGHT.*

1. The primary basis for a manufacturing firm's earning power or profitability is its

    A. working capital management
    B. liquidity ratio
    C. investment in current assets
    D. investment in fixed assets

1.____

2. In terms of liquidity, quality, and marketability, which of the following tends to best serve businesses as a marketable security?

    A. Money market accounts
    B. U.S. Treasury bills
    C. Negotiable certificates of deposit (CDs)
    D. Commercial paper

2.____

3. Which of the following is an organization that engages in accounts receivable financing by purchasing accounts and assuming all risks?

    A. Factor
    B. Commercial finance company
    C. Commercial bank
    D. Surety company

3.____

Questions 4-5.

DIRECTIONS: Questions 4 and 5 refer to the information below.

The Laker Corporation's balance sheet reveals that the company's assets total $1 million. Its liabilities total $450,000. The owners' equity totals $550,000,

4. What is the Laker Corporation's debt ratio?

    A. 0.33   B. 0.45   C. 0.55   D. 0.82

4.____

5. What is the Laker Corporation's equity multiplier ratio?

    A. 0.45   B. 0.82   C. 1.82   D. 2.22

5.____

6. Most often, the largest single current liability of a business is

    A. the tax accrual   B. wages and salaries
    C. accounts payable   D. notes payable

6.____

7. Investors in a company expect a 12.5% rate of return on their common stock. The expected growth rate is 7.5% annually, and the stock is expected to pay $4 in cash dividends next year. What is the present value of the stock?

    A. $20   B. $40   C. $60   D. $80

7.____

8. Bonds which are dependent upon the general credit and strength of the corporation for their security are referred to as _____ bonds. 8.____

    A. tied   B. creditor
    C. debenture   D. property-dependent

Questions 9-10.

DIRECTIONS: Questions 9 and 10 refer to the information below.

Spacely, Inc. has total current assets of $500,000 and total current liabilities of $250,000. Its inventories also total $250,000.

9. What is Spacely's current ratio? 9.____

    A. 1:3   B. 1:2   C. 1:1   D. 2:l

10. What is Spacely's acid-test ratio? 10.____

    A. 1:3   B. 1:2   C. 1:1   D. 2:1

11. Under current tax law, businesses are allowed to depreciate _____% of their fixed assets in the seven-year property class during the first year. 11.____

    A. 4   B. 9   C. 14   D. 25

12. What is the purpose of calculating a company's degree of operating leverage? 12.____

    A. Determining the decrease or increase in sales
    B. Determining fixed costs as a percentage of sales
    C. Quantifying the responsiveness of operating expenses to the level of output
    D. Quantifying the responsiveness of operating income to the level of output

13. A firm's ability to generate earnings adequate to pay cash dividends and allow for some earnings retention is influenced to a large extent by the firm's 13.____

    A. net revenue   B. inventories
    C. profit margin   D. asset turnover

14. An asset in the form of money due to a firm by a certain date is known as a(n) 14.____

    A. note receivable   B. fixed asset
    C. account receivable   D. intangible asset

15. In general, the activity considered to be of greatest importance to most financial officers is 15.____

    A. receivables management
    B. planning and budgeting
    C. debt valuation
    D. working capital management

16. What is the term for a type of receivable instrument that arises out of the sale of merchandise to a business customer and which may be sold to a bank? 16.____

    A. Acceptance   B. Outlay
    C. Market order   D. Commercial paper

17. When a financial analyst looks at the direction and magnitude of the market in terms of   17.____
what to buy or sell, a(n) _____ analysis is being conducted.

   A. technical   B. time series
   C. off-budget   D. trend

18. Internally generated funds for financing new asset investments come generally from   18.____

   A. long-term debt   B. short-term debt
   C. equity funds   D. profits

Questions 19-20.

DIRECTIONS: Questions 19 and 20 refer to the information below.

   The Kingsley Group is considering the purchase of a hammermill for a total cost of
$40,000 that will have a five-year life before it is discarded. Cash revenues from the sale of
inventories are expected to be $24,000 a year, and cash operating expenses associated with
the use of the hammermill are estimated at $11,200 per year. The company, which is in the
25% tax bracket, is entitled to depreciate the hammermill for income tax purposes assume
that the company takes advantage of this deduction.

19. What will be the Kingsley Group's annual after-tax cash earnings if the hammermill is   19.____
purchased?

   A. $2,800   B. $3,600   C. $4,800   D. $8,000

20. What would be the company's annual cash inflow after taxes?   20.____

   A. $5,600   B. $8,000   C. $11,600   D. $12,200

21. In order to determine an investment's present value, it is sometimes necessary to trans-   21.____
late future cash benefits to the present. This process is known as

   A. remission   B. discounting
   C. rebating   D. hedging

22. Which stage in the capital budgeting process typically involves the estimation of relevant   22.____
cash inflows and outflows?

   A. Development   B. Implementation
   C. Identification   D. Selection

23. In a financial leverage ratio, total liabilities are often expressed as a percentage of   23.____
   I.   stockholders' equity
   II.   total assets
   III. Net income
   The CORRECT answer is:

   A. I only   B. I, II   C. II only   D. II, III

24. What is the term for an instrument through which a bank retains title to goods until they   24.____
are paid for?

   A. Time draft   B. Arbitrage
   C. Trust receipt   D. Documentary draft

25. It is generally true that as price levels increase, the increased costs for a business will be   25.____
    offset to the extent that

    A.   current assets are financed by current or long-term borrowing
    B.   the rate of asset turnover is increased
    C.   its products remain competitive
    D.   accounts receivable hold stable

KEY (CORRECT ANSWERS)

1.	D		11.	C
2.	B		12.	D
3.	A		13.	C
4.	B		14.	A
5.	C		15.	B
6.	A		16.	A
7.	D		17.	A
8.	C		18.	D
9.	D		19.	B
10.	C		20.	C

21.	B
22.	A
23.	B
24.	C
25.	A

TEST 4

DIRECTIONS: Each question or incomplete statement is followed by several suggested answers or completions. Select the one that BEST answers the question or completes the statement. *PRINT THE LETTER OF THE CORRECT ANSWER IN THE SPACE AT THE RIGHT.*

1. Practically all modern preferred stock is   1._____

    A. callable   B. noncumulative
    C. convertible   D. cumulative

2. In general, the profitability of a firm is affected to the greatest extent by the success of its   2._____
    financial manager in

    A. making current asset investment decisions
    B. creating a capital budget
    C. making fixed-asset investment decisions
    D. avoiding long-term liabilities

3. Which of the following is/are ways in which the Small Business Administration assists in   3._____
    the financing of small businesses?
            I.   Guaranteeing bank loans to businesses
            II. Participating jointly with banks in extending loans to businesses
            III. Making direct loans to businesses
    The CORRECT answer is:

    A. I *only*   B. I, II   C. II, III   D. I, II, III

4. Over time, a company's level of investment in fixed assets will be consistent with   4._____

    A. working capital   B. mortgage debt
    C. inventories   D. sales

5. Macroeconomic business risk is reflected in   5._____

    A. the importance of key employees
    B. short-term financing policies
    C. the degree of variability in a firm's sales and profits
    D. interest rates

6. The main DISADVANTAGE of using debt capital over equity capital is   6._____

    A. fewer special provisions such as conversion rights
    B. lower priority in the case of liquidation
    C. little or no control over firm activities
    D. generally lower yields

7. The process of using debt funds in an effort to increase the rate of return to owners or   7._____
    stockholders is

    A. trading on equity
    B. determining the weighted cost of capital
    C. buying on margin
    D. determining optimal capital structure

8. A company's marketable securities are held primarily to meet _____ motives.   8.____

    A. capacity   B. speculative
    C. precautionary   D. transactions

9. When the cash flow stream of an investment is constant or level in each time period, the   9.____
investment is called a(n)

    A. annuity   B. real asset
    C. floater   D. trust

10. Which of the following is NOT a disadvantage associated with short-term borrowing as   10.____
opposed to other forms of financing?

    A. Added element of financial risk
    B. Possibility of rising borrowing costs
    C. It tends to create inflexible operations
    D. Frequent renewals

11. The comparison of a firm's financial ratios over several years is known as a(n)   11.____

    A. statement of cash flows
    B. industry comparative analysis
    C. asset turnover statement
    D. trend analysis

12. In terms of a company's investment portfolio, changes in stock prices would be dis-   12.____
cussed as _____ risk.

    A. market   B. liquidity   C. business   D. default

13. When determining whether or not to extend credit to a business, creditors generally   13.____
place the greatest emphasis on

    A. total fixed assets   B. net working capital
    C. retained earnings   D. the prime rate

14. Secured long-term debt obligations are generally referred to as   14.____

    A. debenture bonds   B. mortgage bonds
    C. callable bonds   D. tied loans

15. Which of the following capital budgeting techniques does not explicitly consider the time   15.____
value of money?

    A. Internal rate of return   B. Net present value
    C. Payback period   D. Profitability index

16. When an investment earns interest that is reinvented along with the principal, _____   16.____
occurs.

    A. discounting   B. splitting
    C. compounding   D. special assessment

17. In risk-return analysis, standard deviation is used to measure the   17.____

    A. average dispersion of individual cash flows
    B. net present value of an investment

C. expected value of the cash flows
D. weighted cost of the investment

18. Which of the following type of business is characterized by relatively high current asset to fixed asset mixes?   18.____

    A. Retail store   B. Electric power
    C. Manufacturing   D. Railroad

19. A borrower offers to pay a lender $1,000 at the end of one year in return for a loan of $1,000 now. The lender agrees to receive exactly $1,000 a year from now, but insists on an 8% return on the loan.   19.____
What amount would be lended?

    A. $800   B. $909   C. $926   D. $1,000

20. Which of the following types of corporations tend to rely almost exclusively on internally generated funds for financing?   20.____

    A. Corporations that invest heavily in fixed assets
    B. Rapidly growing firms such as high-technology firms
    C. Companies with high capital needs
    D. Corporations that require little investment in fixed assets

21. In the case of corporations, the owners' equity is usually broken down into several accounts. Which of the following is NOT one of these accounts?   21.____

    A. Capital earnings   B. Retained earnings
    C. Transfer payments   D. Common stock account

22. What type of long-term debt instrument allows for continuing sale of bonds secured by the same mortgage?   22.____

    A. Closed-end mortgage bond
    B. Debenture bond
    C. Open-end mortgage bond
    D. Trust indenture

23. Each of the following are thrift institutions EXCEPT   23.____

    A. mutual savings banks
    B. commercial finance companies
    C. savings and loan associations
    D. credit unions

24. Whenever a company cannot or will not undertake all investment projects with a net present value greater than or equal to zero, _____ occurs.   24.____

    A. capital rationing   B. discounting
    C. hedging   D. sensitivity analysis

25. If a business relied entirely on short-term financing for its current asset requirements, the   25._____
    total current assets of the firm would

    A. be equal to the total current liabilities
    B. be less than the total current liabilities
    C. remain unchanged
    D. fluctuate depending on inventories

_____

KEY (CORRECT ANSWERS)

1.	B		11.	D
2.	C		12.	A
3.	D		13.	B
4.	D		14.	B
5.	C		15.	C
6.	D		16.	C
7.	A		17.	A
8.	C		18.	A
9.	A		19.	C
10.	C		20.	D

21.	C
22.	C
23.	B
24.	A
25.	A

_____

EXAMINATION SECTION
TEST 1

DIRECTIONS: Each question or incomplete statement is followed by several suggested answers or completions. Select the one that BEST answers the question or completes the Statement. *PRINT THE LETTER OF THE CORRECT ANSWER IN THE SPACE AT THE RIGHT.*

1. Gross income of an individual for Federal income tax purposes does NOT include

    A. interest credited to a bank savings account
    B. gain from the sale of sewer authority bonds
    C. back pay received as a result of job reinstatement
    D. interest received from State Dormitory Authority bonds

1.____

2. A cash-basis, calendar-year taxpayer purchased an annuity policy at a total cost of $20,000. Starting on January 1 of 2015, he began to receive annual payments of $1,500. His life expectancy as of that date was 16 years.
The amount of annuity income to be included in his gross income for the taxable year 2015 is

    A. none   B. $250   C. $1,250   D. $1,500

2.____

3. The transactions related to a municipal police retirement system should be included in a(n)

    A. intra-governmental service fund
    B. trust fund
    C. general fund
    D. special revenue fund

3.____

4. The budget for a given cost during a given period was $100,000. The actual cost for the period was $90,000. Based upon these facts, one should say that the responsible manager has done a better than expected job in controlling the cost if the cost is

    A. variable and actual production equaled budgeted production
    B. a discretionary fixed cost and actual production equaled budgeted production
    C. variable and actual production was 90% of budgeted production
    D. variable and actual production was 80% of budgeted production

4.____

5. In the conduct of an audit, the *most practical* method by which an accountant can satisfy himself as to the physical existence of inventory is to

    A. be present and observe personally the audited firm's physical inventory being taken
    B. independently verify an adequate proportion of all inventory operations performed by the audited firm
    C. mail confirmation requests to vendors of merchandise sold to the audited firm within the inventory year
    D. review beforehand the adequacy of the audited firm's plan for inventory taking, and during the actual inventory-taking stages, verify that this plan is being followed

5.____

Questions 6-7.

DIRECTIONS: The following information applies to Questions 6 and 7.

For the month of March, the ABC Manufacturing Corporation's estimated factory overhead for an expected volume of 15,000 lbs. of a product was as follows:

	Amount	Overhead Rate Per Unit
Fixed Overhead	$3,000	$.20
Variable Overhead	$9,000	$.60

Actual volume was 10,000 lbs. and actual overhead expense was $7,700.

6. The Spending (Budget) Variance was   6.____

    A. $1,300 (Favorable)   B. $6,000 (Favorable)
    C. $7,700 (Favorable)   D. $9,000 (Favorable)

7. The Idle Capacity Variance was   7.____

    A. $300 (Favorable)   B. $1,000 (Unfavorable)
    C. $1,300 (Favorable)   D. $8,000 (Unfavorable)

Questions 8-11.

DIRECTIONS: Answer Questions 8 through 11 on the basis of the information given below.

A bookkeeper, who was not familiar with proper accounting procedures, prepared the following financial report for Largor Corporation as of December 31, 2015. In addition to the errors in presentation, additional data below was not considered in the preparation of the report. Restate this balance sheet in proper form, giving recognition to the additional data, so that you will be able to determine the required information to answer Questions 8 through 11.

LARGOR CORPORATION
December 31, 2015

Current Assets			
Cash		$110,000	
Marketable Securities		53,000	
Accounts Receivable	$261,400		
Accounts Payable	125,000	136,400	
Inventories		274,000	
Prepaid Expenses		24,000	
Treasury Stock		20,000	
Cash Surrender Value of			
Officers' Life Insuranc Policies		105,000	$722 , 400
Plant Assets			
Equipment		350,000	
Building	200,000		
Reserve for Plant			
Expansion	75,000	125,000	
Land		47,500	522,500
TOTAL ASSETS			$1,244,900

Liabilities

Salaries Payable		16,500	
Cash Dividend Payable		50,000	
Stock Dividend Payable		70,000	
Bonds Payable	200,000		
Less Sinking Fund	90,000	110,000	
TOTAL LIABILITIES			$246,500

Stockholders' Equity:

Paid In Capital

Common Stock		350,000

Retained Earnings and Reserves

Reserve for Income Taxes	90,000		
Reserve for Doubtful Accounts	6,500		
Reserve for Treasury Stock	20,000		
Reserve for Depreciation Equipment	70,000		
Reserve for Depreciation Building	80,000		
Premium on Common stock	15,000		
Retained Earnings	366,900	648,400	998,400

TOTAL LIABILITIES & EQUITY	$1,244,900

Additional Data

A. Bond Payable will mature eight (8) years from Balance Sheet date.

B. The Stock Dividend Payable was declared on December 31, 2015.

C. The Reserve for Income Taxes represents the balance due on the estimated liability for taxes on income for the year ended December 31.

D. Advances from Customers at the Balance Sheet date totaled $13,600. This total is still credited against Accounts Receivable.

E. Prepaid Expenses include Unamortized Mortgage Costs of $15,000.

F. Marketable Securities were recorded at cost. Their market value at December 31, 2015 was $50,800.

8. After restatement of the balance sheet in proper form and giving recognition to the additional data, the Total Current Assets should be   8.____

   A. $597,400   B. $702,400   C. $712,300   D. $827,300

9. After restatement of the balance sheet in proper form and giving recognition to the additional data, the Total Current Liabilities should be   9.____

   A. $261,500   B. $281,500   C. $295,100   D. . D. $370,100

10. After restatement of the balance sheet in proper form and giving recognition to the additional data, the net book value of plant and equipment should be   10.____

   A. $400,000   B. B, $447,500   C. $550,000   D. $597,500

11. After restatement of the balance sheet in proper form and giving recognition to the additional data, the Stockholders Equity should be   11.____

   A. $320,000   B. $335,000   C. $764,700   D. $874,700

12. When preparing the financial statement, dividends in arrears on preferred stock should be treated as a   12.____

    A. contingent liability   B. deduction from capital
    C. parenthetical remark   D. valuation reserve

13. The IPC Corporation has an intangible asset which it values at $1,000,000 and has a life expectancy of 60 years. The *appropriate* span of write-off, as determined by good accounting practice, should be _____ years.   13.____

    A. 17   B. 34   C. 40   D. 60

14. The following information was used in costing inventory on October 31:   14.____

October	1 -	Beginning inventory -	800 units	@	$1.20
	4 -	Received	200 units	@	$1.40
	16 -	Issued	400 units		
	24 -	Received	200 units	@	$1.60
	27 -	Issued	500 units		

Using the LIFO method of inventory evaluation (end-of-month method), the total dollar value of the inventory at October 31 was   14.____

    A. $360   B. $460   C. $600   D. $1,200

15. If a $400,000 par value bond issue paying 8%, with interest dates of June 30 and December 31, is sold in November 1 for par plus accrued interest, the cash proceeds received by the issuer on November 1 should be *approximately*   15.____

    A. $405,000   B. $408,000   C. $411,000   D. $416,000

16. The TOTAL interest cost to the issuer of a bond issue sold for more than its face value is the periodic interest payment   16.____

    A. *plus* the discount amortization
    B. *plus* the premium amortization
    C. *minus* the discount amortization
    D. *minus* the premium amortization

17. If shareholders donate shares of stock back to the company, such stock received by the company is *properly* classified as   17.____

    A. Treasury stock
    B. Unissued stock
    C. Other assets - investment
    D. Current assets - investment

18. Assume the following transactions have occurred: 18.____
    1. 10,000 shares of capital stock of Omer Corp., par value $50, have been sold and issued on initial sale @ $55 per share during the month of June
    2. 2,000 shares of previously issued stock were purchased from shareholders during the month of September @ $58 per share.

As of September 30, the stockholders' equity section TOTAL should be

    A. $434,000   B. $450,000   C. $480,000   D. $550,000

19. Mr. Diak, a calendar-year taxpayer in the construction business, agrees to construct a   19.____
building for the Supermat Corporation to cost a total of $500,000 and to require about
two years to complete. By December 31, 2015, he has expended $150,000 in costs, and
it was determined that the building was 35% completed.
If Mr. Diak is reporting income under the completed contract method, the amount of
gross income he will report for 2015 is

    A. none   B. $25,000   C. $175,000   D. $350,000

20. When the Board of Directors of a firm uses the present-value technique to aid in deciding   20.____
whether or not to buy a new plant asset, it needs to have information reflecting

    A. the cost of the new asset only
    B. the increased production from use of new asset only
    C. an estimated rate of return
    D. the book value of the asset

KEY (CORRECT ANSWERS)

1.	D	11.	D
2.	B	12.	C
3.	B	13.	C
4.	A	14.	A
5.	D	15.	C
6.	A	16.	D
7.	B	17.	A
8.	C	18.	A
9.	C	19.	A
10.	B	20.	C

TEST 2

DIRECTIONS: Each question or incomplete statement is followed by several suggested answers or completions. Select the one that BEST answers the question or completes the statement. *PRINT THE LETTER OF THE CORRECT ANSWER IN THE SPACE AT THE RIGHT.*

Questions 1-3.

DIRECTIONS: The following information applies to Questions 1 through 3.

During your audit of the Avon Company, you find the following errors in the records of the company:

1. Incorrect exclusion from the final inventory of items costing $3,000 for which the purchase was not recorded.
2. Inclusion in the final inventory of goods costing $5,000, although a purchase was not recorded. The goods in question were being held on consignment from Reldrey Company.
3. Incorrect exclusion of $2,000 from the inventory count at the end of the period. The goods were in transit (F.O.B. shipping point); the invoice had been received and the purchase recorded.
4. Inclusion of items on the receiving dock that were being held for return to the vendor because of damage. In counting the goods in the receiving department, these items were incorrectly included. With respect to these goods, a purchase of $4,000 had been recorded.

The records (uncorrected) showed the following amounts:
1. Purchases, $170,000
2. Pretax income, $15,000
3. Accounts payable, $20,000; and
4. Inventory at the end of the period, $40,000.

1. The *corrected* inventory is   1.____

   A. $36,000   B. $42,000   C. $43,000   D. $44,000

2. The *corrected* income for the year is   2.____

   A. $12,000   B. $15,000   C. $17,000   D. $18,000

3. The *correct* accounts payable liabilities are   3.____

   A. $16,000   B. $17,000   C. $19,000   D. $23,000

4. An auditing procedure that is *most likely* to reveal the existence of a contingent liability is   4.____

   A. a review of vouchers paid during the month following the year end
   B. confirmation of accounts payable
   C. an inquiry directed to legal counsel
   D. confirmation of mortgage notes

Questions 5-6.

DIRECTIONS: The following information is to be used in answering Questions 5 and 6.

Mr. Zelev operates a business as a sole proprietor and uses the cash basis for reporting income for income tax purposes. His bank account during 2015 for the business shows receipts totaling $285,000 and cash payments totaling $240,000. Included in the cash payments were payments for three-year business insurance policies whose premiums totaled $1,575. It was determined that the expired premiums for this year were $475. Further examination of the accounts and discussion with Mr. Zelev revealed the fact that included in the receipts were the following items, as well as the proceeds received from customers:

$15,000 which Mr. Zelev took from his savings account and deposited in the business account.

$20,000 which Mr. Zelev received from the bank as a loan which will be repaid next year.

Included in the cash payments were $10,000 which Mr. Zelev took on a weekly basis from the business receipts to use for his personal expenses.

5. The amount of net income to be reported for income tax purposes for calendar year 2006   5._____
    for Mr. Zelev is

    A. $21,100   B. $26,100   C. $31,100   D. $46,100

6. Assuming the same facts as those reported above, Mr. Zelev would be required to pay a   6._____
    self-employment tax for 2006 of

    A. $895.05   B. $1,208.70   C. $1,234.35   D. $1,666.90

7. For the year ended December 31, 2015, you are given the following information relative   7._____
    to the income and expense statements for the Sungam Manufacturers, Inc.:
    Sales $1,000,000
        Sales Returns 95,000

Cost of Sales
Opening Inventories $200,000
Purchases During the Year   567,000
Direct Labor Costs   240,000
Factory Overhead   24,400
Inventories End of Year   235,000

On June 15, 2015, a fire destroyed the plant and all of the inventories then on hand. You are given the following information and asked to ascertain the amount of the estimated inventory loss.

Sales up to June 15 $545,000
Purchased to June 15   254,500
Direct Labor   233,000
Overhead   14,550
Salvaged Inventory   95,000
The *estimated* inventory loss is

    A. $95,000   B. $162,450   C. $189,450   D. $257,450

8. Losses and excessive costs with regard to inventory can occur in any one of several   8.____
   operating functions of an organization.
   The operating function which bears the GREATEST responsibility for the failure to give
   proper consideration to transportation costs of material acquisitions is

   A. accounting   B. purchasing
   C. receiving   D. shipping

Questions 9-17.

DIRECTIONS: Questions 9 through 17 are to be answered on the basis of the information
              given below.

You are conducting an audit of the PAP Company, which has a contract to supply the
municipal hospitals with specialty refrigerators on a cost-plus basis. The following information
is available:

Materials purchased	$1,946,700

Inventories, January 1
Materials	268,000
Finished Goods (100 units)	43,000
Direct Labor	2,125,800
Factory Overhead (40% variable)	764,000
Marketing Expenses (all fixed)	516,000
Administrative Expenses (all fixed)	461,000
Sales (12,400 units)	6,634,000

Inventories, March 31
Materials	167,000
Finished Goods (200 units)	(omitted)
No Work In Process	

9. The *net income* for the period is   9.____

   A. $755,500   B. $1,237,500
   C. $1,732,500   D. $4,980,500

10. The *number* of units manufactured is   10.____

   A. 12,400   B. 12,500   C. 12,600   D. 12,700

11. The *unit cost* of refrigerators manufactured is *most nearly*   11.____

   A. $389.00   B. $395.00   C. $398.00   D. $400.00

12. The *total* variable costs are   12.____

   A. $305,600   B. $764,000
   C. $4,479,100   D. $4,937,500

13. The *total* fixed costs are   13.____

   A. $458,400   B. $1,435,400
   C. $1,471,800   D. $1,741,000

While you are conducting your audit, the PAP Company advises you that they have changed their inventory costing from FIFO to LIFO. You are interested in pursuing the matter further because this change will affect the cost of the refrigerators. An examination of material part 2-317 inventory card shows the following activity:

May 2 - Received 100 units @ $5.40 per unit
May 8 - Received 30 units @ $8.00 per unit
May 15 - Issued 50 units
May 22 - Received 120 units @ $9.00 per unit
May 29 - Issued 100 units

14. Using the FIFO method under a perpetual inventory control system, the *total* cost of the units issued in May is   14.____

    A. $690   B. $960   C. $1,590   D. $1,860

15. Using the FIFO method under a perpetual inventory control system, the *value* of the clos-   15.____
    ing inventory is

    A. $780   B. $900   C. $1,080   D. $1,590

16. Using the LIFO method under a perpetual inventory control system, the *total* cost of the   16.____
    units issued in May is

    A. $1,248   B. $1,428   C. $1,720   D. $1,860

17. Using the LIFO method under a perpetual inventory control system, the *value* of the clos-   17.____
    ing inventory is

    A. $612   B. $780   C. $1,512   D. $1,680

Questions 18-20.

DIRECTIONS: For Questions 18 through 20, consider that the EEF Corporation has a fully
               integrated cost accounting system.

18. Unit cost of manufacturing dresses was $7.00. Spoiled dresses numbered 400 with a   18.____
    sales value of $800. When it is not customary to have a Spoiled Work account, the *most*
    appropriate account to be credited is

    A. Work In Process   B. Cost of Sales
    C. Manufacturing Overhead   D. Finished Goods

19. Overtime premium for factory workers (direct labor) totaled $400 for the payroll period.   19.____
    This was due to inadequate plant capacity. The account to be *debited* is

    A. Work In Process   B. Cost of Sales
    C. Manufacturing Overhead   D. Finished Goods

20. A month-end physical inventory of stores shows a shortage of $175. The account to be   20.____
    debited to correct this shortage is

    A. Stores   B. Work In Process
    C. Cost of Sales   D. Manufacturing Overhead

KEY (CORRECT ANSWERS)

1.	A	11.	B
2.	A	12.	C
3.	C	13.	B
4.	C	14.	B
5.	A	15.	B
6.	D	16.	A
7.	B	17.	A
8.	B	18.	A
9.	A	19.	C
10.	B	20.	C

———

EXAMINATION SECTION
TEST 1

DIRECTIONS: Each question or incomplete statement is followed by several suggested answers or completions. Select the one that BEST answers the question or completes the statement. *PRINT THE LETTER OF THE CORRECT ANSWER IN THE SPACE AT THE RIGHT.*

1. An upward cumulative frequency curve does NOT

    A. consist of several connected line segments
    B. provide relative frequencies directly
    C. touch the horizontal axis exactly once
    D. indicate how many observations lie below a particular value

1.____

2. The city tabulates sales tax collections according to various industry groupings - retail trade, manufacturing, etc.
Which one of the following statements is INCORRECT? The

    A. relative frequency of retail firms to the total of all firms is .45
    B. frequency of retail food stores is 130,000
    C. cumulative frequency of manufacturing firms is .32
    D. total number of firms is 653,000

2.____

3. Assume that the distribution of ages of employees in the department of social services is positively skewed.
It may, therefore, be concluded that for the distribution of ages the

    A. mean is less than the median
    B. mean is greater than the median
    C. mean is less than the mode
    D. mode and the mean are equal

3.____

4. The range in average daily temperature in the city during a given year was 93°.
If the *highest* recorded average daily temperature was 95°, the *lowest* recorded average daily temperature was

    A. 0°   B. -2°   C. 2°   D. 32°

4.____

5. A head of a research unit has to send two of his six employees to a meeting of a professional society. How many possible different groups of two are there?

    A. 12   B. 15   C. 30   D. 36

5.____

6. The probability that an employee in a given agency would be late is .05 and the probability that an employee would be absent is .02.
The probability that an employee would be *either* late or absent is

    A. less than .07   B. more than .07
    C. .07   D. .03

6.____

7. The one of the following variables which CANNOT have a continuous probability distribution is the

7.____

A. time of run from the 14th Street station to the 168th Street station on the IND *A* line
B. average age of recruits in the police department
C. number of retirees from the fire department in fiscal 1994-95
D. average height of sanitation men to be hired in fiscal 1995-96

8. You have been asked to prepare a frequency distribution of the cost of furniture repair
jobs for hospitals. Open-ended class intervals in the distribution should be *avoided*
because the _____ cannot be computed.   8.____

    A. median   B. mean
    C. mode   D. interquartile range

9. A continuous random variable has a uniform probability distribution and the variable
ranges from -5 to 15. The probability that the value of this random variable will be *positive* is   9.____

    A. .1875   B. .75   C. .25   D. .50

10. The median family income in the city was estimated to be $29,503.
The average (arithmetic mean) family income was   10.____

    A. less than $29,503
    B. higher than $29,503
    C. either higher or lower than $29,503
    D. equal to $29,503

11. The process of removing errors from the coding of a computer program is known as   11.____

    A. flowcharting   B. compiling
    C. verifying   D. debugging

12. Which of the following is NOT primarily a simulation language?   12.____

    A. Fortran   B. GPSS   C. Simscript   D. Dynamo

13. The FASTEST retrieval of data in a computer is from   13.____

    A. tape   B. disc   C. cards   D. core

14. Remote access terminals are also known as   14.____

    A. batch processing terminals
    B. data processing centers
    C. time sharing terminals
    D. inhouse terminals

15. The *first* card of an input deck submitted to a batch processing computer center is a(n)   15.____
_____ card.

    A. executive   B. job   C. format   D. language

16. A Type I error is committed when we   16.____

    A. accept a null hypothesis which should be rejected
    B. reject a null hypothesis which should be accepted
    C. make only one mistake in a problem
    D. fail to make a decision

17. Of the following, the number of characters to be included in a field is BEST described as _____ the field.   17.____

    A. smaller than
    B. exactly the same size of
    C. the same size or smaller than
    D. the same size or larger than

18. The one of the following publications which contains an extensive guide to sources of data in addition to many tables is the   18.____

    A. SURVEY OF CURRENT BUSINESS
    B. MONTHLY LABOR REVIEW
    C. FEDERAL RESERVE BULLETIN
    D. STATISTICAL ABSTRACT OF THE U.S.

19. Possible biases caused by low response rate in mail questionnaires can often be *avoided* by   19.____

    A. contacting more people initially
    B. conducting a follow-up study of nonrespondents
    C. conducting a follow-up study on a sample of respondents
    D. discarding by an objective method a certain percentage of the replies to balance the percentage of non-response

20. Assume that the city comptroller's office made the following investments: 20.____
        $30,000 invested at 10%
        $10,000 invested at 6%
        $10,000 invested at 5%
The *mean return* on the total investment will be

    A. 7.0%   B. 7.5%   C. 8.0%   D. 8.2%

KEY (CORRECT ANSWERS)

1.	B	11.	D
2.	C	12.	A
3.	B	13.	D
4.	C	14.	C
5.	B	15.	B
6.	C	16.	B
7.	C	17.	C
8.	B	18.	D
9.	B	19.	B
10.	B	20.	D

TEST 2

DIRECTIONS: Each question or incomplete statement is followed by several suggested answers or completions. Select the one that BEST answers the question or completes the statement. *PRINT THE LETTER OF THE CORRECT ANSWER IN THE SPACE AT THE RIGHT.*

1. Which of the following statements concerning the Consumer Price Index (CPI) is NOT correct?   1.____

   A. The CPI is prepared by the Bureau of Labor Statistics.
   B. The CPI is published in the Survey of Current Business.
   C. The CPI makes possible the comparison of the level of living costs among major American cities.
   D. A rise in the CPI from 125.0 to 130.0 indicates that the index increased by 4 percent.

2. A certain city negotiated a union contract with an escalator clause to maintain buying power for hourly workers. The Consumer Price Index at the time of the contract was at 125.   2.____
   What increase in wages should be granted to an employee whose wage rate was $4.50 at the time of the contract, for each one point increase in the Index?
   _____ cents.

   A. 0.8   B. 2.8   C. 3.6   D. 8.0

3. In using the simplex method for solving a linear programming problem, it is possible for a tie to occur for the entering basic variable.   3.____
   Under such circumstances, the entering variable is determined

   A. arbitrarily from among the *ties*
   B. from the equation with the largest constant term
   C. from the equation with the smallest constant term
   D. by choosing a different variable to enter

4. Both PERT and CPM determine a   4.____

   A. critical path
   B. variance of activity times
   C. minimum and a maximum finishing time
   D. sequencing of events

5. Zero-sum game theory problems can be solved by means of   5.____

   A. linear programming   B. calculus
   C. inventory theory   D. queueing theory

6. The following system of equations: $2x + 4y = 15$ and $x + 2y = 5$, has _____ solution(s).   6.____

   A. no   B. 1
   C. 2   D. an infinity of

7. The following system of equations: $2x + 3y = 10$ and $x + 1.5y = 5$, has _____ solution(s).   7.____

   A. no   B. 1
   C. 2   D. an infinity of

8. The simplex method requires the use of   8.____

   A. basis variables
   B. slack variables of the *less than* or *equal to* variety
   C. the *northwest corner* rule
   D. the identity matrix

9. The binomial distribution may be approximated by the normal curve.   9.____
   The approximation is MOST precise for a given sample size when the population

   A. is most variable
   B. is completely uniform
   C. is skewed
   D. proportion is greater than .75

10. The coefficients of artificial variables in the objective function of a linear programming   10.____
    problem are equal to

   A. -1   B. 0
   C. +1   D. plus or minus infinity

11. The coefficients of the slack variables in the objective function of linear programming   11.____
    problems are equal to

   A. -1   B. 0   C. +1   D. infinity

12. The function of slack variables in linear programming is to   12.____

   A. remove the inequality signs
   B. obtain an initial feasible solution
   C. create new variables to increase the dimensions of the problem
   D. eliminate the need for artificial variables

13. A set of steps to be taken in solving a particular problem is known as a(n)   13.____

   A. corollary   B. theorem
   C. algorithm   D. proposal

14. Raw test scores (x) are very often expressed as standard test scores (y). where   14.____

   $$y = \frac{x - \bar{x}}{\sigma_x}$$

   The variance of the standard test scores is

   A. $\Sigma \dfrac{(x - \bar{x})^2}{\sigma x^2}$

   B. 0
   C. I
   D. always less than the variance of the raw scores

15. The determinant of the matrix is equal to   15.____

   A. -1   B. 0   C. 1   D. infinity

16. Assume that a Poisson distribution has been fitted to data on the number of on-the-job accidents per month in the department of social services.
A test of the goodness of fit will be given by a(n) _____ test.

    A. *F*
    C. *t*
    B. Kolmogoroff-Smirnov
    D. variance-ratio

16.____

17. The Federal Reserve Board's Index of Industrial Production may BEST be classified as a _____ index.

    A. quantity
    C. Paasche
    B. price
    D. simple aggregative

17.____

18. The expected value of the Student's *t statistic*

    A. depends on the number of degrees of freedom
    B. is zero
    C. is distributed normally
    D. should be expressed as a percentage

18.____

19. Assume that a four-quarter moving average was taken as a first step in computing a quarterly seasonal index. This step was taken PRIMARILY to remove from the data the _____ movement.

    A. cyclical
    B. trend
    C. seasonal
    D. random

19.____

20. If the probability that any one bullet in a policeman's 6-chamber revolver is defective is P, the probability that two of the six bullets in the revolver are defective is

    A. $15P^2(1-P)^4$
    C. $6P(1-P)^5$
    B. $30P^4(1-P)^2$
    D. P/3

20.____

KEY (CORRECT ANSWERS)

1.	C	11.	B
2.	C	12.	A
3.	A	13.	C
4.	A	14.	C
5.	A	15.	B
6.	A	16.	B
7.	D	17.	A
8.	A	18.	B
9.	A	19.	C
10.	D	20.	A

BASIC FUNDAMENTALS OF A FINANCIAL STATEMENT

TABLE OF CONTENTS

BASIC FUNDAMENTALS
OF A FINANCIAL STATEMENT

COMMENTARY

The ability to read and understand a financial statement is a basic requirement for the accountant, auditor, account clerk, bookkeeper, bank examiner. budget examiner, and, of course, for the executive who must manage and administer departmental affairs.

FINANCIAL REPORTS

Are financial reports really as difficult as all that? Well, if you know they are not so difficult because you have worked with them before, this section will be of auxiliary help for you. However, if you find financial statements a bit murky, but realize their great importance to you, we ought to get along fine together. For "mathematics," all we'll use is fourth-grade arithmetic.

Accountants, like all other professionals, have developed a specialized vocabulary. Sometimes this is helpful and sometimes plain confusing (like their practice of calling the income account, "Statement of Profit and Loss," when it is bound to be one or the other). But there are really only a score or so technical terms that you will have to get straight in mind. After that is done, the whole foggy business will begin to clear and in no time at all you'll be able to talk as wisely as the next fellow.

BALANCE SHEET

Look at the sample balance sheet printed on page 2, and we'll have an insight into how it is put together. This particular report is neither the simplest that could be issued, nor the most complicated. It is a good average sample of the kind of report issued by an up-to-date manufacturing company.

Note particularly that the *balance sheet* represents the situation as it stood on one particular day, December 31, not the record of a year's operation. This balance sheet is broken into two parts: on the left are shown *ASSETS* and on the right *LIABILITIES.* Under the asset column, you will find listed the value of things the company owns or are owed to the company. Under liabilities, are listed the things the company owes to others, plus reserves, surplus, and the stated value of the stockholders' interest in the company.

One frequently hears the comment, "Well, I don't see what a good balance sheet is anyway, because the assets and liabilities are always the same whether the company is successful or not."

It is true that they always balance and, by itself, a balance sheet doesn't tell much until it is analyzed. Fortunately, we can make a balance sheet tell its story without too much effort -- often an extremely revealing story, particularly, if we compare the records of several years. ASSETS The first notation on the asset side of the balance sheet is *CURRENT* ASSETS (item 1). In general, current assets include cash and things that can be turned into cash in a hurry, or that, in the normal course of business, will be turned into cash in the reasonably near future, usually within a year.

Item 2 on our sample sheet is *CASH.* Cash is just what you would expect -bills and silver in the till and money on deposit in the bank.

UNITED STATES GOVERNMENT SECURITIES is item 3. The general practice is to show securities listed as current assets at cost or market value, whichever is lower. The figure, for all reasonable purposes, represents the amount by which total cash could be easily increased if the company wanted to sell these securities.

The next entry is *ACCOUNTS RECEIVABLE* (item 4). Here we find the total amount of money owed to the company by its regular business creditors and collectable within the next year. Most of the money is owed to the company by its customers for goods that the company delivered on credit. If this were a department store instead of a manufacturer, what you owed the store on your charge account would be included here. Because some people fail to pay their bills, the company sets up a reserve for doubtful accounts, which it subtracts from all the money owed.

THE ABC MANUFACTURING COMPANY, INC.
CONSOLIDATED BALANCE SHEET -- DECEMBER 31

Item			Item		
1.	CURRENT ASSETS		16.	CURRENT LIABILITIES	
2.	Cash		17.	Accts. Payable	$ 300,000
3.	U.S. Government Securities		18.	Accrued Taxes	800,000
4.	Accounts Receivable (less reserves)	2,000,000	19.	Accrued Wages, Interest and Other Expenses	370,000
5.	Inventories (at lower of cost or market)	2,000,000	20.	Total Current Liabilities	$1,470,000
6.	Total Current Assets	$7,000,000	21.	FIRST MORTGAGE SINK-ING FUND BONDS, 3 1/2% DUE 2002	2,000,000
7.	INVESTMENT IN AFFIL-IATED COMPANY Not consolidated (at cost, not in ex-cess of net assets)	200,000	22.	RESERVE FOR CON-TINGENCIES	200,000
8.	OTHER INVESTMENTS At cost, less than market	100,000	23.	CAPITAL STOCK:	
9.	PLANT IMPROVEMENT FUND	550,000	24.	5% Preferred Stock (author-ized and issued 10,000 shares of $100 par value)	$1,000,000
10.	PROPERTY, PLANT AND EQUIPMENT: Cost	$8,000,000	25.	Common stock (author-ized and issued 400,000 shares of no par value)	1,000,000
11.	Less Reserve for Deprecia-tion	5,000,000			2,000,000
12.	NET PROPERTY	3,000,000	26.	SURPLUS:	
13.	PREPAYMENTS	50,000	27.	Earned	3,530,000
14.	DEFERRED CHARGES	100,000	28.	Capital (arising from sale of common capital stock at price in excess of stated value	1,900,000
15.	PATENTS AND GOODWILL	100,000			5,430,000
	TOTAL	$11,100,000		TOTAL	$11,100,000

(Handwritten annotations:)

- cash that would be available if assets were sold
- what is owed to the company (customers' bills, awaiting payment)
- value of raw product on hand
- companies that the parent org. owns
- ex. gov. bonds
- is put aside for improvement
- (−) wear depreciation of equipment
- value of land, business machinery, buildings
- all debts due w/in next year
- unpaid bills
- unpaid taxes past year
- owed in next 12 mos.
- pensions

Item 5, *INVENTORIES,* is the value the company places on the supplies it owns. The inventory of a manufacturer may contain raw materials that it uses in making the things it sells, partially finished goods in process of manufacture and, finally, completed merchandise that it is ready to sell. Several methods are used to arrive at the value placed on these various items. The most common is to value them at their cost or present market value, whichever is lower. You can be reasonably confident, however, that the figure given is an honest and significant one for the particular industry if the report is certified by a reputable firm of public accountants.

Next on the asset side is *TOTAL CURRENT ASSETS* (item 6). This is an extremely important figure when used in connection with other items in the report, which we will come to presently. Then we will discover how to make total current assets tell their story.

INVESTMENT IN AFFILIATED COMPANY (item 7) represents the cost to our parent company of the capital stock of its *subsidiary* or affiliated company. A subsidiary is simply one company that is controlled by another. Most corporations that own other companies outright, lump the figures in a *CONSOLIDATED BALANCE SHEET.* This means that, under cash, for example, one would find a total figure that represented *all* of the cash of the parent company and of its wholly owned subsidiary. This is a perfectly reasonable procedure because, in the last analysis, all of the money is controlled by the same persons.

Our typical company shows that it has *OTHER INVESTMENTS* (item 8), in addition to its affiliated company. Sometimes good marketable securities other than Government bonds are carried as current assets, but the more conservative practice is to list these other security holdings separately. If they have been bought as a permanent investment, they would always be shown by themselves. "At cost, less than market" means that our company paid $100,000 for these other investments, but they are now worth more.

Among our assets is a *PLANT IMPROVEMENT FUND* (item 9). Of course, this item does not appear in all company balance sheets, but is typical of *special funds* that companies set up for one purpose or another. For example, money set aside to pay off part of the bonded debt of a company might be segregated into a special fund. The money our directors have put aside to improve the plant would often be invested in Government bonds.

FIXED ASSETS

The next item (10), is *PROPERTY, PLANT AND EQUIPMENT,* but it might just as well be labeled *Fixed Assets* as these terms are used more or less interchangeably. Under item 10, the report gives the value of land, buildings, and machinery and such movable things as trucks, furniture, and hand tools. Historically, probably more sins were committed against this balance sheet item than any other.

In olden days, cattlemen used to drive their stock to market in the city. It was a common trick to stop outside of town, spread out some salt for the cattle to make them thirsty and then let them drink all the water they could hold. When they were weighed for sale, the cattlemen would collect cash for the water the stock had drunk. Business buccaneers, taking the cue from their farmer friends, would often "write up" the value of their fixed assets. In other words, they would increase the value shown on the balance sheet, making the capital stock appear to be worth a lot more than it was. *Watered stock* proved a bad investment for most stockholders. The practice has, fortunately, been stopped, though it took major financial reorganizations to squeeze the water out of some securities.

The most common practice today is to list fixed assets at cost. Often, there is no ready market for most of the things that fall under this heading, so it is not possible to give market value. A good report will tell what is included under fixed assets and how it has been valued. If the value has been increased by *write-up* or decreased by *write-down,* a footnote explanation is usually given. A *write-up* might occur, for instance, if the value of real estate increased substantially. A *write-down* might follow the invention of a new machine that put an important part of the company's equipment out of date.

DEPRECIATION

Naturally, all of the fixed property of a company will wear out in time (except, of course, non-agricultural land). In recognition of this fact, companies set up a *RESERVE FOR DEPRECIATION* (item 11). If a truck costs $4,000 and is expected to last four years, it will be depreciated at the rate of $1,000 a year.

Two other terms also frequently occur in connection with depreciation -*depletion* and *obsolescence*. Companies may lump depreciation, depletion, and obsolescence under a single title, or list them separately.

Depletion is a term used primarily by mining and oil companies (or any of the so-called extractive industries). Depletion means exhaust or use up. As the oil or other natural resource is used up, a reserve is set up, to compensate for the natural wealth the company no longer owns. This reserve is set up in recognition of the fact that, as the company sells its natural product, it must get back not only the cost of extracting but also the original cost of the natural resource.

Obsolescence represents the loss in value because a piece of property has gone out of date before it wore out. Airplanes are modern examples of assets that tend to get behind the times long before the parts wear out. (Women and husbands will be familiar with the speed at which ladies' hats "obsolesce.")

In our sample balance sheet we have placed the reserve for depreciation under fixed assets and then subtracted, giving us *NET PROPERTY* (item 12), which we add into the asset column. Sometimes, companies put the reserve for depreciation in the liability column. As you can see, the effect is just the same whether it is *subtracted* from assets or *added* to liabilities.

The manufacturer, whose balance sheet we use, rents a New York showroom and pays his rent yearly, in advance. Consequently, he has listed under assets *PREPAYMENTS* (item 13). This is listed as an asset because he has paid for the use of the showroom, but has not yet received the benefit from its use. The use is something coming to the firm in the following year and, hence, is an asset. The dollar value of this asset will decrease by one-twelfth each month during the coming year.

DEFERRED CHARGES (item 14) represents a type of expenditure similar to prepayment. For example, our manufacturer brought out a new product last year, spending $100,000 introducing it to the market. As the benefit from this expenditure will be returned over months or even years to come, the manufacturer did not think it reasonable to charge the full expenditure against costs during the year. He has *deferred* the charges and will write them off gradually.

INTANGIBLES

The last entry in our asset column is *PATENTS AND GOODWILL* (item 15). If our company were a young one, set up to manufacture some new patented prod uct, it would probably carry its patents at a substantial figure. in fact, *intangibles* of both old and new companies are often of great but generally unmeasurable worth.

Company practice varies considerably in assigning value to intangibles. Procter & Gamble, despite the tremendous goodwill that has been built up for IVORY SOAP, has reduced all of its intangibles to the nominal $1. Some of the big cigarette companies, on the contrary, place a high dollar value on the goodwill their brand names enjoy. Companies that spend a good deal for research and the development of new products are more inclined than others to reflect this fact in the value assigned to patents, license agreements, etc.

What is your patent worth?

LIABILITIES

The liability side of the balance sheet appears a little deceptive at first glance. Several of the entries simply don't sound like liabilities by any ordinary definition of the term.

The first term on the liability side of any balance sheet is usually *CURRENT LIABILITIES* (item 16). This is a companion to the *Current Assets* item across the page and includes all debts that fall due within the next year. The relation between current assets and current liabilities is one of the most revealing things to be gotten from the balance sheet, but we will go into that quite thoroughly later on.

ACCOUNTS PAYABLE (item 17) represents the money that the company owes to its ordinary business creditors -- unpaid bills for materials, supplies, insurance, and the like. Many companies itemize the money they owe in a much more detailed fashion than we have done, but, as you will see, the totals are the most interesting thing to us.

Item 18, *ACCRUED TAXES,* is the tax bill that the company estimates it still owes for the past year. We have lumped all taxes in our balance sheet, as many companies do. However, sometimes you will find each type of tax given separately. If the detailed procedure is followed, the description of the tax is usually quite sufficient to identify the separate items.

Accounts Payable was defined as the money the company owed to its regular business creditors. The company also owes, on any given day, wages to its own employees; interest to its bondholders and to banks from which it may have borrowed money; fees to its attorneys; pensions, etc. These are all totaled under *ACCRUED WAGES, INTEREST AND OTHER EXPENSES* (item 19).

TOTAL CURRENT LIABILITIES (item 20) is just the sum of everything that the company owed on December 31 and which must be paid sometime in the next twelve months.

It is quite clear that all of the things discussed above are liabilities. The rest of the entries on the liability side of the balance sheet, however, do not seem at first glance to be liabilities.

Our balance sheet shows that the company, on December 31, had $2,000,000 of 3 1/2 percent First Mortgage *BONDS* outstanding (item 21). Legally, the money received by a company when it sells bonds is considered a loan to the company. Therefore, it is obvious that the company owes to the bondholders an amount equal to the face value or the *call price* of the bonds it has outstanding. The call price is a figure usually larger than the face value of the bonds at which price the company can *call* the bonds in from the bondholders and pay them off before they ordinarily fall due. The date that often occurs as part of the name of a bond is the date at which the company has promised to pay off the loan from the bondholders.

RESERVES

The next heading, *RESERVE FOR CONTINGENCIES* (item 22), sounds more like an asset than a liability. "My reserves," you might say, "are dollars in the bank, and dollars in the bank are assets."

No one would deny that you have something there. In fact, the corporation treasurer also has his reserve for contingencies balanced by either cash or some kind of unspecified investment on the asset side of the ledger. His reason for setting up a reserve on the liability side of the balance sheet is a precaution against making his financial position seem better than it is. He decided that the company might have to pay out this money during the coming year if certain things happened. If he did not set up the "reserve," his surplus would appear larger by an amount equal to his reserve.

A very large reserve for contingencies or a sharp increase in this figure from the previous year should be examined closely by the investor. Often, in the past, companies tried to hide their true earnings by transferring funds into a contingency reserve. As a reserve looks somewhat like a true liability, stockholders were confused about the real value of their securities. When a reserve is not set up for protection against some very probable loss or expenditure, it should be considered by the investor as part of surplus.

CAPITAL STOCK

Below reserves there is a major heading, *CAPITAL STOCK* (item 23). Companies may have one type of security outstanding, or they may have a dozen. All of the issues that represent shares of ownership are capital, regardless of what they are called on the balance sheet -- preferred stock, preference stock, common stock, founders' shares, capital stock, or something else.

Our typical company has one issue of 5 per cent *PREFERRED STOCK* (item 24). It is called *preferred* because those who own it have a right to dividends and assets before the *common* stockholders -- that is, the holders are in a preferred position as owners. Usually, preferred stockholders do not have a voice in company affairs unless the company fails to pay them dividends at the promised rate. Their rights to dividends are almost always *cumulative*. This simply means that all past dividends must be paid before the other stockholders can receive anything. Preferred stockholders are not creditors of the company so it cannot properly be said that the company *owes* them the value of their holdings. However, in case the company decided to go out of business, preferred stockholders would have a prior claim on anything that was left in the company treasury after all of the creditors, including the bondholders, were paid off. In practice, this right does not always mean much, but it does explain why the book value of their holdings is carried as a liability.

COMMON STOCK (item 25) is simple enough as far as definition is concerned it represents the rights of the ordinary owner of the company. Each company has as many owners as it has stockholders. The proportion of the company that each stockholder owns is determined by the number of shares he has. However, neither the book value of a no-par common stock, nor the par value of an issue that has a given par, can be considered as representing either the original sale price, the market value, or what would be left for the stockholders if the company were liquidated.

A profitable company will seldom be dissolved. Once things have taken such a turn that dissolution appears desirable, the stated value of the stock is generally nothing but a fiction. Even if the company is profitable as a going institution, once it ceases to function even its tangible assets drop in value because there is not usually a ready market for its inventory of raw materials and semi-finished goods, or its plant and machinery.

SURPLUS

The last major heading on the liability side of the balance sheet is *SURPLUS* (item 26). The surplus, of course, is not a liability in the popular sense at all. It represents, on our balance sheet, the difference between the stated value of our common stock and the net assets behind the stock.

Two different kinds of surplus frequently appear on company balance sheets, and our company has both kinds. The first type listed is *EARNED* surplus (item 27). Earned surplus is roughly similar to your own savings. To the corporation, earned surplus is that part of net income which has not been paid to stockholders as dividends. It still *belongs* to you, but the directors have decided that it is best for the company and the stockholders to keep it in the business. The surplus may be invested in the plant just as you might invest part of your savings in your home. It may also be in cash or securities.

In addition to the earned surplus, our company also has a *CAPITAL* surplus (item 28) of $1,900.00, which the balance sheet explains arose from selling the stock at a higher cost per share than is given as its stated value. A little arithmetic shows that the stock is carried on the books at $2.50 a share while the capital surplus amounts to $4.75 a share. From this we know that the company actually received an average of $7.25 net a share for the stock when it was sold.

WHAT DOES THE BALANCE SHEET SHOW?

Before we undertake to analyze the balance sheet figures, a word on just what an investor can expect to learn is in order. A generation or more ago, before present accounting standards had gained wide acceptance, considerable imagination went into the preparation of balance sheets. This, naturally, made the public skeptical of financial reports. Today, there is no substantial ground for skepticism. The certified public accountant, the listing requirements of the national stock exchanges, and the regulations of the Securities and Exchange Commission have, for all practical purposes, removed the grounds for doubting the good faith of financial reports.

The investor, however, is still faced with the task of determining the significance of the figures. As we have already seen, a number of items are based, to a large degree, upon estimates, while others are, of necessity, somewhat arbitrary.

NET WORKING CAPITAL *can be twisted on balance sheet*

There is one very important thing that we can find from the balance sheet and accept with the full confidence that we know what we are dealing with. That is net working capital, sometimes simply called working capital.

On the asset side of our balance sheet we have added up all of the current assets and show the total as item 6. On the liability side, item 20 gives the total of current liabilities. *Net working capital* or *net current assets* is the difference left after subtracting current liabilities from current assets. If you consider yourself an investor rather than a speculator, you should always insist that any company in which you invest have a comfortable amount of working capital. The ability of a company to meet its obligations with ease, expand its volume as business expands and take advantage of opportunities as they present themselves, is, to an important degree, determined by its working capital.

Probably the question in your mind is: *"Just what does 'comfortable amount' of working capital mean?"* Well, there are several methods used by analysts to judge whether a particular company has a sound working capital position. The first rough test for an industrial company is to compare the working capital figure with the current liability total. Most analysts say that minimum safety requires that net working capital at least equal current liabilities. Or, put another way, that current assets should be at least twice as large as current liabilities.

There are so many different kinds of companies, however, that this test requires a great deal of modification if it is to be really helpful in analyzing companies in different industries. To help you interpret the *current position* of a company in which you are considering investing, the *current ratio* is more helpful than the dollar total of working capital. The current ratio is current assets divided by current liabilities.

In addition to working capital and current ratio, there are two other ways of testing the adequacy of the current position. *Net quick assets* provide a rigorous and important test of a company's ability to meet its current obligations. Net quick assets are found by taking total current assets (item 6) and subtracting the value of inventories (item 5). A well-fixed industrial company should show a reasonable excess of quick assets over current liabilities..

Finally, many analysts say that a good industrial company should have at least as much working capital (current assets less current liabilities) as the total book value of its bonds and preferred stock. In other words, current liabilities, bonded debt, and preferred stock *altogether* should not exceed the current assets.

INVENTORY AND INVENTORY TURNOVER

In the recent past, there has been much talk of inventories. Many commentators have said that these carry a serious danger to company earnings if management allows them to increase too much. Of course, this has always been true, but present high prices have made everyone more inventory-conscious than usual.

There are several dangers in a large inventory position. In the first place, a sharp drop in price may cause serious losses; also, a large inventory may indicate that the company has accumulated a big supply of unsalable merchandise. The question still remains, however: *"What do we mean by large inventory?"*

As you certainly realize, an inventory is large or small only in terms of the yearly turnover and the type of business. We can discover the annual turnover of our sample company by dividing inventories (item 5) into total annual sales (item "a" on the income account).

It is also interesting to compare the value of the inventory of a company being studied with total current assets. Again, however, there is considerable variation between different types of companies, so that the relationship becomes significant only when compared with similar companies.

NET BOOK VALUE OF SECURITIES

There is one other very important thing that can be gotten from the balance sheet, and that is the net book or equity value of the company's securities. We can calculate the net book value of each of the three types of securities our company has outstanding by a little very simple arithmetic. *Book value means the value at which something is carried on the books of the company.*

The full rights of the bondholders come before any of the rights of the stockholders, so, to find the net book value or net tangible assets backing up the bonds we add together the balance sheet value of the bonds, preferred stock, common stock, reserve, and surplus. This gives us a total of $9,630,000. (We would not include contingency reserve if we were reasonably sure the contingency was going to arise, but, as general reserves are often equivalent to surplus, it is, usually, best to treat the reserve just as though it were surplus.) However, part of this value represents the goodwill and patents carried at $100,000, which is not a tangible item, so, to be conservative, we subtract this amount, leaving $9,530,000 as the total net book value of the bonds. This is equivalent to $4,765 for each $1,000 bond, a generous figure. To calculate the net book value of the preferred stock, we must eliminate the face value of the bonds, and then, following the same procedure, add the value of the preferred stock, common stock, reserve, and surplus, and subtract goodwill. This gives us a total net book value for the preferred stock of $7,530,000 or $753 for each share of $100 par value preferred. This is also very good coverage for the preferred stock, but we must examine current earnings before becoming too enthusiastic about the *value* of any security.

The net book value of the common stock, while an interesting figure, is not so important as the coverage on the senior securities. In case of liquidation, there is seldom much left for the common stockholders because of the normal loss in value of company assets when they are put up for sale, as mentioned before. The book value figure, however, does give us a basis for comparison with other companies. Comparisons of net book value over a period of years also show us if the company is a soundly growing one or, on the other hand, is losing ground. Earnings, however, are our important measure of common stock values, as we will see shortly.

The net book value of the common stock is found by adding the stated value of the common stock, reserves, and surplus and then subtracting patents and goodwill. This gives us a total net book value of $6,530,000. As there are 400,000 shares of common outstanding, each share has a net book value of $16.32. You must be careful not to be misled by book value figures, particularly of common stock. Profitable companies (Coca-Cola, for example) often show a very low net book value and very substantial earnings. Railroads, on the other hand, may show a high book value for their common stock but have such low or irregular earnings that the market price of the stock is much less than its apparent book value. Banks, insurance companies, and investment -trusts are exceptions to what we have said about common stock net book value. As their assets are largely liquid (i.e., cash, accounts receivable, and marketable securities), the book value of their common stock sometimes indicates its value very accurately.

PROPORTION OF BONDS, PREFERRED AND COMMON STOCK

Before investing, you will want to know the proportion of each kind of security issued by the company you are considering. A high proportion of bonds reduces the attractiveness of both the preferred and common stock, while too large an amount of preferred detracts from the value of the common.

The *bond ratio* is found by dividing the face value of the bonds (item 21), or $2,000,000, by the total value of the bonds, preferred stock, common stock, reserve, and surplus, or $9,630,000. This shows that bonds amount to about 20 per cent of the total of bonds, capital, and surplus.

The *preferred stock ratio* is found in the same way, only we divide the stated value of the preferred stock by the total of the other five items. Since we have half as much preferred stock as we have bonds, the preferred ratio is roughly 10.

Naturally, the *common stock ratio* will be the difference between 100 per cent and the totals of the bonds and preferred, or 70 per cent in our sample company. You will want to remember that the most valuable method of determining the common stock ratio is in combination with reserve and surplus. The surplus, as we have noted, is additional backing for the common stock and usually represents either original funds paid in to the company in excess of the stated value of the common stock (capital surplus), or undistributed earnings (earned surplus).

Most investment analysts carefully examine industrial companies that have more than about a quarter of their capitalization represented by bonds, while common stock should total at least as much as all senior securities (bonds and preferred issues). When this is not the case, companies often find it difficult to raise new capital. Banks don't like to lend them money because of the already large debt, and it is sometimes difficult to sell common stock because of all the bond interest or preferred dividends that must be paid before anything is available for the common stockholder.

Railroads and public utility companies are exceptions to most of the rules of thumb that we use in discussing The ABC Manufacturing Company, Inc. Their situation is different because of the tremendous amounts of money they have invested in their fixed assets., their small inventories and the ease with which they can collect their receivables. Senior securities of railroads and utility companies frequently amount to more than half of their capitalization. Speculators often interest themselves in companies that have a high proportion of debt or preferred stock because of the *leverage factor*. A simple illustration will show why. Let us take, for example, a company with $10,000,000 of 4 per cent bonds outstanding. If the company is earning $440,000 before bond interest, there will be only $40,000 left for the common stock ($10,000,000 at 4% equals $400,000). However, an increase of only 10 per cent in earnings (to $484,000) will leave $84,000 for common stock dividends, or an increase of more than 100 per cent. If there is only a small common issue, the increase in earnings per share would appear very impressive.

You have probably already noticed that a decline of 10 per cent in earnings would not only wipe out everything available for the common stock, but result in the company being unable to cover its full interest on its bonds without dipping into surplus. This is the great danger of so-called high leverage stocks and also illustrates the fundamental weakness of companies that have a disproportionate amount of debt or preferred stock. Investors would do well to steer clear of them. Speculators, however, will continue to be fascinated by the market opportunities they offer.

THE INCOME ACCOUNT

The fundamental soundness of a company, as shown by its balance sheet, is important to investors, but of even greater interest is the record of its operation. Its financial structure shows much of its ability to weather storms and pick up speed when times are good. It is the income record, however, that shows us how a company is actually doing and gives us our best guide to the future.

The *Consolidated Income and Earned Surplus* account of our company is stated on the next page. Follow the items given there and we will find out just how our company earned its money, what it did with its earnings, and what it all means in terms of our three classes of securities. We have used a combined income and surplus account because that is the form most frequently followed by industrial companies. However, sometimes the two statements are given separately. Also, a variety of names are used to describe this same part of the financial report. Sometimes it is called profit and loss account, sometimes *record of earnings,* and, often, simply *income account.* They are all the same thing.

The details that you will find on different income statements also vary a great deal. Some companies show only eight or ten separate items, while others will give a page or more of closely spaced entries that break down each individual type of revenue or cost. We have tried to strike a balance between extremes; give the major items that are in most income statements, omitting details that are only interesting to the expert analyst.

The most important source of revenue always makes up the first item on the income statement. In our company, it is *Net Sales* (item "a"). If it were a railroad or a utility instead of a manufacturer, this item would be called *gross revenues.* In any case, it represents the money paid into the company by its customers. Net sales are given to show that the figure represents the amount of money actually received after allowing for discounts and returned goods.

Net sales or gross revenues, you will note, is given before any kind of miscellaneous revenue that might have been received from investments, the sale of company property, tax refunds, or the like. A well-prepared income statement is always set up this way so that the stockholder can estimate the success of the company in fulfilling its major job of selling goods or service. If this were not so, you could not tell whether the company was really losing or making money on its operations, particularly over the last few years when tax rebates and other unusual things have often had great influence on final net income figures.

COST OF SALES

A general heading, *Cost of Sales, Expenses and Other Operating Charges* (item "b") is characteristic of a manufacturing company, but a utility company or railroad would call all of these things *operating expenses.*

The most important subdivision is *Cost of Goods Sold* (item "c"). Included under cost of goods sold are all of the expenses that go directly into the manufacture of the products the company sells -- raw materials, wages, freight, power, and rent. We have lumped these expenses together, as many companies do. Sometimes, however, you will find each item listed separately. Analyzing a detailed income account is a pretty technical operation and had best be left to the expert.

The ABC Manufacturing Company, Inc.
CONSOLIDATED INCOME AND EARNED SURPLUS
For the Year Ended December 31

Item			
a.	Sales		$10,000,000
b.	COST OF SALES, EXPENSES AND OTHER OPERATING CHARGES:		
c.	Cost of Goods Sold	$7,000,000	
d.	Selling, Administrative & Gen. Expenses	500,000	
e.	Depreciation	200,000	
f.	Maintenance and Repairs	400,000	
g.	Taxes (Other than Federal Inc. Taxes)	300,000	8,400,000
h.	NET PROFIT FROM OPERATIONS		$ 1,600,000
i.	OTHER INCOME:		
j.	Royalties and Dividends	$ 250,000	
k.	Interest	25,000	275,000
l.	TOTAL		$ 1,875,000
m.	INTEREST CHARGES:		
n.	Interest on Funded Debt	$ 70,000	
o.	Other Interest	20,000	90,000
p.	NET INCOME BEFORE PROVISION FOR FED. INCOME TAXES		$ 1,785,000
q.	PROVISION FOR FEDERAL INCOME TAXES		678,300
r.	NET INCOME		$ 1,106,700
s.	DIVIDENDS:		
t.	Preferred Stock - $5.00 Per Share	$ 50,000	
u.	Common Stock - $1.00 Per Share	400,000	
v.	PROVISION FOR CONTINGENCIES	200,000	650,000
w.	BALANCE CARRIED TO EARNED SURPLUS		$ 456,700
x.	EARNED SURPLUS – JANUARY 1		3,073,000
y.	EARNED SURPLUS – DECEMBER 31		$ 3,530,000

We have shown separately, opposite "d," the *Selling, Administrative and General Expenses* of the past year. Unfortunately, there is little uniformity among companies in their treatment of these important non-manufacturing costs. Our figure includes the expenses of management; that is, executive salaries and clerical costs; commissions and salaries paid to salesmen; advertising expenses, and the like.

Depreciation ("e") shows us the amount that the company transferred from income during the year to the depreciation reserve that we ran across before as item "11" on the balance sheet (page 2). Depreciation must be charged against income unless the company is going to live on its own fat, something that no company can do for long and stay out of bankruptcy.

MAINTENANCE

Maintenance and Repairs (item "f") represents the money spent to keep the plant in good operating order. For example, the truck that we mentioned under depreciation must be kept running day by day. The cost of new tires, recharging the battery, painting and mechanical repairs are all maintenance costs. Despite this day-to-day work on the truck, the company must still provide for the time when it wears out -- hence, the reserve for depreciation.

You can readily understand from your own experience the close connection between maintenance and depreciation. If you do not take good care of your own car, you will have to buy a new one sooner than you would had you maintained it well. Corporations face the same problem with all of their equipment. If they do not do a good job of maintenance, much more will have to be set aside for depreciation to replace the abused tools and property.

Taxes are always with us. A profitable company always pays at least two types of taxes. One group of taxes are paid without regard to profits, and include real estate taxes, excise taxes, social security, and the like (item "g"). As these payments are a direct part of the cost of doing business, they must be included before we can determine the *Net Profit From Operations* (item "h").

Net Profit from Operations (sometimes called *gross profit)* tells us what the company made from manufacturing and selling its products. It is an interesting figure to investors because it indicates .how efficiently and successfully the company operates in its primary purpose as a creator of wealth. As a glance at the income account will tell you, there are still several other items to be deducted before the stockholder can hope to get anything. You can also easily imagine that for many companies these other items may spell the difference between profit and loss. For these reasons, we use net profit from operations as an indicator of progress in manufacturing and merchandising efficiency, not as a judge of the investment quality of securities.

Miscellaneous Income not connected with the major purpose of the company is generally listed after net profit from operations. There are quite a number of ways that corporations increase their income, including interest and dividends on securities they own, fees for special services performed, royalties on patents they allow others to use, and tax refunds. Our income statement shows *Other Income* as item "i," under which is shown income from *Royalties and Dividends* (item "j"), and, as a separate entry, *Interest* (item "k") which the company received from its bond investments. The *Total* of other income (item t1t?) shows us how much The ABC Manufacturing Company received from so-called *outside activities.* Corporations with diversified interests often receive tremendous amounts of *other income.*

INTEREST CHARGES

There is one other class of expenses that must be deducted from our income before we can determine the base on which taxes are paid, and that is *Interest Charges* (item "m"). As our company has $2,000,000 worth of 3 1/2 per cent bonds outstanding, it will pay *Interest on Funded Debt* of $70,000 (item "n"). During the year, the company also borrowed money from the bank, on which it, of course, paid interest, shown as *Other Interest* (item "o").

Net Income Before Provision for Federal Income Taxes (item "p") is an interesting figure for historical comparison. It shows us how profitable the company was in all of its various operations. A comparison of this entry over a period of years will enable you to see how well the company had been doing as a business institution before the Government stepped in for its share of net earnings. Federal taxes have varied so much in recent years that earnings before taxes are often a real help in judging business progress.

A few paragraphs back we mentioned that a profitable corporation pays two general types of taxes. We have already discussed those that are paid without reference to profits. *Provision for Federal Income Taxes* (item "q") is ordinarily figured on the total income of the company after normal business expenses, and so appears on our income account below these charges. Bond interest, for example, as it is payment on a loan, is deducted beforehand. Preferred and common stock dividends, which are *profits* that go to owners of the company, come after all charges and taxes.

NET INCOME

After we have deducted all of our expenses and income taxes from total income, we get *Net Income* (item "r"). Net income is the most interesting figure of all to the investor. Net income is the amount available to pay dividends on the preferred and common stock. From the balance sheet, we have learned a good deal about the company's stability and soundness of structure; from net profit from operations, we judge whether the company is improving in industrial efficiency. Net income tells us whether the securities of the company are likely to be a profitable investment.

The figure given for a single year is not nearly all of the story, however. As we have noted before, the historical record is usually more important than the figure for any given year. This is just as true of net income as any other item. So many things change from year to year that care must be taken not to draw hasty conclusions. During the war, Excess Profits Taxes had a tremendous effect on the earnings of many companies. In the next few years, *carryback tax credits* allowed some companies to show a net profit despite the fact that they had operated at a loss. Even net income can be a misleading figure unless one examines it carefully. A rough and easy way of judging how *sound* a figure it is would be to compare it with previous years.

The investor in stocks has a vital interest in *Dividends* (item "s"). The first dividend that our company must pay is that on its *Preferred Stock* (item "t"). Some companies will even pay preferred dividends out of earned surplus accumulated in the past if the net income is not large enough, but such a company is skating on thin ice unless the situation is most unusual.

The directors of our company decided to pay dividends totaling $400,000 on the *Common Stock,* or $1 a share (item "u"). As we have noted before, the amount of dividends paid is not determined by net income, but by a decision of the stockholders' representatives - the company's directors. Common dividends, just like preferred dividends, can be paid out of surplus if there is little or no net income. Sometimes companies do this if they have a long history of regular payments and don't want to spoil the record because of some special temporary situation that caused them to lose money. This occurs even less frequently and is more *dangerous* than paying preferred dividends out of surplus.

It is much more common, on the contrary, to *plough earnings back into the business* -- a phrase you frequently see on the financial pages and in company reports. The directors of our typical company have decided to pay only $1 on the common stock, though net income would have permitted them to pay much more. They decided that the company should *save* the difference.

The next entry on our income account, *Provision for Contingencies* (item "v"), shows us where our reserve for contingencies arose. The treasurer of our typical company has put the provision for contingencies after dividends. However, you will discover, if you look at very many financial reports, that it is sometimes placed above net income.

All of the net income that was not paid out as dividends, or set aside for contingencies, is shown as *Balance Carried to Earned Surplus* (item "w"). In other words, it is kept in the business. In previous years, the company had also earned more than it paid out so it had already accumulated by the beginning of the year an earned surplus of $3,073,000 (item "x"). When we total the earned surplus accumulated during the year to that which the company had at the first of the year, we get the total earned surplus at the end' of the year (item "y"). You will notice that the total here is the same as that which we ran across on the balance sheet as item 27.

Not all companies combine their income and surplus account. When they do not, you will find that *balance carried to surplus will* be the last item on the income account. The statement of consolidated surplus would appear as a third section of the corporation's financial report. A separate surplus account might be used if the company shifted funds for reserves to surplus during the year or made any other major changes in its method of treating the surplus account.

ANALYZING THE INCOME ACCOUNT

The income account, like the balance sheet, will tell us a lot more if we make a few detailed comparisons. The size of the totals on an income account doesn't mean much by itself. A company can have hundreds of millions of dollars in net sales and be a very bad investment. On the other hand, even a very modest profit in round figures may make a security attractive if there are only a small number of shares outstanding.

Before you select a company for investment, you will want to know something of its *margin of profit,* and how this figure has changed over the years. Finding the margin of profit is very simple. We just divide the net profit from operations (item "h") by net sales (item "a"). The figure we get (0.16) shows us that the company make a profit of 16 per cent from operations. By itself, though, this is not very helpful. We can make it significant in two ways.

In the first place, we can compare it with the margin of profit in previous years, and, from this comparison, learn if the company excels other companies that do a similar type of business. If the margin of profit of our company is very low in comparison with other companies in the same field, it is an unhealthy sign. Naturally, if it is high, we have grounds to be optimistic.

Analysts also frequently use *operating ratio* for the same purpose. The operating ratio is the complement of the margin of profit. The margin of profit of our typical company is 16. The operating ratio is 84. You can find the operating ratio either by subtracting the margin of profit from 100 or dividing the total of operating costs ($8,400,000) by net sales ($10,000,000).

The margin of profit figure and the operating ratio, like all of those ratios we examined in connection with the balance sheet, give us general information about the company, help us judge its prospects for the future. All of these comparisons have significance for the long term as they tell us about the fundamental economic condition of the company. But you still have the right to ask: *"Are the securities good investments for me now?"*

Investors, as opposed to speculators, are primarily interested in two things. The first is safety for their capital and the second, regularity of income. They are also interested in the rate of return on their investment but, as you will see, the rate of return will be affected by the importance placed on safety and regularity. High income implies risk. Safety must be bought by accepting a lower return.

The safety of any security is determined primarily by the earnings of the company that are available to pay interest or dividends on the particular issue. Again, though, round dollar figures aren't of much help to us. What we want to know is the relationship between the total money available and the requirements for each of the securities issued by the company.

INTEREST COVERAGE

As the bonds of our company represent part of its debt, the first thing we want to know is how easily the company can pay the interest. From the income account we see that the company had total income of $1,875,000 (item "1"). The interest charge on our bonds each year is $70,000 (3 1/2 per cent of $2,000,000 - item 21 on the balance sheet). Dividing total income by bond interest charges ($1,875,000 by $70,000) shows us that the company earned its bond interest 26 times over. Even after income taxes, bond interest was earned 17 times, a method of testing employed by conservative analysts. Before an industrial bond should be considered a safe investment, most analysts say that the company should earn interest charges several times over, so our company has a wide margin of safety.

To calculate the *preferred dividend coverage* (i.e., the number of times preferred dividends were earned), we must use net income as our base, as Federal Income Taxes and all interest charges must be paid before anything is available for stockholders. As we have 10,000 shares of $100 par value of preferred stock which pays a dividend of 5 per cent, the total dividend requirement for the preferred stock is $50,000 (items 24 on the balance sheet and "t" on the income account).

EARNINGS PER COMMON SHARE

The buyer of common stocks is often more concerned with the earnings per share of his stock than he is with the dividend. It is usually earnings per share or, rather, prospective earnings per share, that influence stock market prices. Our income account does not show the earnings available for the common stock, so we must calculate it ourselves. It is net income less preferred dividends (items "r" - "t"), or $1,056,700. From the balance sheet, we know that there are 400,000 shares outstanding, so the company earned about $2.64 per share.

All of these ratios have been calculated for a single year. It cannot be emphasized too strongly, however, that the *record* is more important to the investor than the report of any single year. By all the tests we have employed, both the bonds and the preferred stock of our typical company appear to be very good investments,, if their market prices were not too high. The investor would want to look back, however, to determine whether the operations were reasonably typical of the company.

Bonds and preferred stocks that are very safe usually sell at pretty high prices, so the yield to the investor is small. For example, if our company has been showing about the same coverage on its preferred dividends for many years and there is good reason to believe that the future will be equally kind, the company would probably replace the old 5 per cent preferred with a new issue paying a lower rate, perhaps 4 per cent.

STOCK PRICES

As the common stock does not receive a guaranteed dividend, its market value is determined by a great variety of influences in addition to the present yield of the stock measured by its dividends. The stock market, by bringing together buyers and sellers from all over the world, reflects their composite judgment of the present and future value of the stock. We cannot attempt here to write a treatise on the stock market. There is one important ratio, however, that every common stock buyer considers. That is the ratio of earnings to market price.

The so-called *price-earnings ratio is* simply the earnings per share on the common stock divided into the market price. Our typical company earned $2.64 a common share in the year, If the stock were selling at $30 a share, its price-earnings ratio would be about 11.4. This is the basic figure that you would want to use in comparing the common stock of this particular company with other similar stocks.

IMPORTANT TERMS AND CONCEPTS

LIABILITIES
WHAT THE COMPANY OWES -- + RESERVES + SURPLUS + STOCKHOLDERS INTEREST IN THE COMPANY

ASSETS
WHAT THE COMPANY OWNS -- + WHAT IS OWED TO THE COMPANY

FIXED ASSETS
MACHINERY, EQUIPMENT, BUILDINGS, ETC.

EXAMPLES OF FIXED ASSETS
DESKS, TABLES, FILING CABINETS, BUILDINGS, LAND, TIMBERLAND, CARS AND TRUCKS, LOCOMOTIVES AND FREIGHT CARS, SHIPYARDS, OIL LANDS, ORE DEPOSITS, FOUNDRIES

EXAMPLES OF:
PREPAID EXPENSES
PREPAID INSURANCE, PREPAID RENT, PREPAID ROYALTIES AND PREPAID INTEREST

DEFERRED CHARGES
AMORTIZATION OF BOND DISCOUNT, ORGANIZATION EXPENSE, MOVING EXPENSES, DEVELOPMENT EXPENSES

ACCOUNTS PAYABLE
BILLS THE COMPANY OWES TO OTHERS

BONDHOLDERS ARE CREDITORS
BOND CERTIFICATES ARE IOU'S ISSUED BY A COMPANY BACKED BY A PLEDGE

BONDHOLDERS ARE OWNERS
A STOCK CERTIFICATE IS EVIDENCE OF THE SHAREHOLDER'S OWNERSHIP

EARNED SURPLUS
INCOME PLOWED BACK INTO THE BUSINESS

NET SALES
GROSS SALES MINUS DISCOUNTS AND RETURNED GOODS

NET INCOME
= TOTAL INCOME MINUS ALL EXPENSES AND INCOME TAXES

PRINCIPLES AND PRACTICES OF
ADMINISTRATION, SUPERVISION & MANAGEMENT

TABLE OF CONTENTS

PRINCIPLES AND PRACTICES OF ADMINISTRATION, SUPERVISION & MANAGEMENT

Most people are inclined to think of administration as something that only a few persons are responsible for in a large organization. Perhaps this is true if you are thinking of Administration with a capital *A*, but administration with a lower case *a* is a responsibility of supervisors at all levels each working day.

All of us feel we are pretty good supervisors and that we do a good job of administering the workings of our agency. By and large, this is true, but every so often it is good to check up on ourselves. Checklists appear from time to time in various publications which psychologists say, tell whether or not a person will make a good wife, husband, doctor, lawyer, or supervisor.

The following questions are an excellent checklist to test yourself as a supervisor and administrator.

Remember, Administration gives direction and points the way but administration carries the ideas to fruition. Each is dependent on the other for its success. Remember, too, that no unit is too small for these departmental functions to be carried out. These statements apply equally as well to the Chief Librarian as to the Department Head with but one or two persons to supervise.

GENERAL ADMINISTRATION - General Responsibilities of Supervisors

1. Have I prepared written statements of functions, activities, and duties for my organizational unit?

2. Have I prepared procedural guides for operating activities?

3. Have I established clearly in writing, lines of authority and responsibility for my organizational unit?

4. Do I make recommendations for improvements in organization, policies, administrative and operating routines and procedures, including simplification of work and elimination of non-essential operations?

5. Have I designated and trained an understudy to function in my absence?

6. Do I supervise and train personnel within the unit to effectively perform their assignments?

7. Do I assign personnel and distribute work on such a basis as to carry out the organizational unit's assignment or mission in the most effective and efficient manner?

8. Have I established administrative controls by:

    a. Fixing responsibility and accountability on all supervisors under my direction for the proper performance of their functions and duties.

b. Preparing and submitting periodic work load and progress reports covering the operations of the unit to my immediate superior.

c. Analysis and evaluation of such reports received from subordinate units.

d. Submission of significant developments and problems arising within the organizational unit to my immediate superior.

e. Conducting conferences, inspections, etc., as to the status and efficiency of unit operations.

9. Do I maintain an adequate and competent working force?

10. Have I fostered good employee-department relations, seeing that established rules, regulations, and instructions are being carried out properly?

11. Do I collaborate and consult with other organizational units performing related functions to insure harmonious and efficient working relationships?

12. Do I maintain liaison through prescribed channels with city departments and other governmental agencies concerned with the activities of the unit?

13. Do I maintain contact with and keep abreast of the latest developments and techniques of administration (professional societies, groups, periodicals, etc.) as to their applicability to the activities of the unit?

14. Do I communicate with superiors and subordinates through prescribed organizational channels?

15. Do I notify superiors and subordinates in instances where bypassing is necessary as soon thereafter as practicable?

16. Do I keep my superior informed of significant developments and problems?

SEVEN BASIC FUNCTIONS OF THE SUPERVISOR

1. PLANNING
This means working out goals and means to obtain goals. What needs to be done, who will do it, how, when, and where it is to be done.

SEVEN STEPS IN PLANNING

1. Define job or problem clearly.
2. Consider priority of job.
3. Consider time-limit - starting and completing.
4. Consider minimum distraction to, or interference with, other activities.
5. Consider and provide for contingencies - possible emergencies.
6. Break job down into components.
7. Consider the 5 W's and H:

WHY	...	is it necessary to do the job? (Is the purpose clearly defined?)
WHAT	...	needs to be done to accomplish the defined purpose?
	...	is needed to do the job? (money, materials, etc.)
WHO	...	is needed to do the job?
	...	will have responsibilities?
WHERE	...	is the work to be done?
WHEN	...	is the job to begin and end? (schedules, etc.)
HOW	...	is the job to be done? (methods, controls, records, etc.)

2. ORGANIZING

This means dividing up the work, establishing clear lines of responsibility and authority and coordinating efforts to get the job done.

3. STAFFING

The whole personnel function of bringing in and training staff, getting the right man and fitting him to the right job - the job to which he is best suited.

In the normal situation, the supervisor's responsibility regarding staffing normally includes providing accurate job descriptions, that is, duties of the jobs, requirements, education and experience, skills, physical, etc.; assigning the work for maximum use of skills; and proper utilization of the probationary period to weed out unsatisfactory employees.

4. DIRECTING

Providing the necessary leadership to the group supervised. Important work gets done to the supervisor's satisfaction.

5. COORDINATING

The all-important duty of inter-relating the various parts of the work.

The supervisor is also responsible for controlling the coordinated activities. This means measuring performance according to a time schedule and setting quotas to see that the goals previously set are being reached. Reports from workers should be analyzed, evaluated, and made part of all future plans.

6. REPORTING

This means proper and effective communication to your superiors, subordinates, and your peers (in definition of the job of the supervisor). Reports should be read and information contained therein should be used not be filed away and forgotten. Reports should be written in such a way that the desired action recommended by the report is forthcoming.

7. BUDGETING

This means controlling current costs and forecasting future costs. This forecast is based on past experience, future plans and programs, as well as current costs.

You will note that these seven functions can fall under three topics:

Planning	)	
Organizing	)	Make a Plan
Staffing	)	
Directing	)	Get things done
Controlling	)	

Reporting   )
Budgeting   )   Watch it work

PLANNING TO MEET MANAGEMENT GOALS

I.   WHAT IS PLANNING?
    A.   Thinking a job through before new work is done to determine the best way to do it
    B.   A method of doing something
    C.   Ways and means for achieving set goals
    D.   A means of enabling a supervisor to deliver with a minimum of effort, all details involved in coordinating his work

II. WHO SHOULD MAKE PLANS?
Everybody!
All levels of supervision must plan work. (Top management, heads of divisions or bureaus, first line supervisors, and individual employees.) The higher the level, the more planning required.

III. WHAT ARE THE RESULTS OF POOR PLANNING?
    A.   Failure to meet deadline
    B.   Low employee morale
    C.   Lack of job coordination
    D.   Overtime is frequently necessary
    E.   Excessive cost, waste of material and manhours

IV. PRINCIPLES OF PLANNING
    A.   Getting a clear picture of your objectives. What exactly are you trying to accomplish?
    B.   Plan the whole job, then the parts, in proper sequence.
    C.   Delegate the planning of details to those responsible for executing them.
    D.   Make your plan flexible.
    E.   Coordinate your plan with the plans of others so that the work may be processed with a minimum of delay.
    F.   Sell your plan before you execute it.
    G.   Sell your plan to your superior, subordinate, in order to gain maximum participation and coordination.
    H.   Your plan should take precedence. Use knowledge and skills that others have brought to a similar job.
    I.   Your plan should take account of future contingencies; allow for future expansion.
    J.   Plans should include minor details. Leave nothing to chance that can be anticipated.
    K.   Your plan should be simple and provide standards and controls. Establish quality and quantity standards and set a standard method of doing the job. The controls will indicate whether the job is proceeding according to plan.
    L.   Consider possible bottlenecks, breakdowns, or other difficulties that are likely to arise.

V.   Q.   WHAT ARE THE *YARDSTICKS* BY WHICH PLANNING SHOULD BE MEASURED?
    A.   Any plan should:
       - Clearly state a definite course of action to be followed and goal to be achieved, with consideration for emergencies.
       - Be realistic and practical.

- State what's to be done, when it's to be done, where, how, and by whom.
- Establish the most efficient sequence of operating steps so that more is accomplished in less time, with the least effort, and with the best quality results.
- Assure meeting deliveries without delays.
- Establish the standard by which performance is to be judged.

Q.   WHAT KINDS OF PLANS DOES EFFECTIVE SUPERVISION REQUIRE?
A.   Plans should cover such factors as:
- Manpower - right number of properly trained employees on the job.
- Materials - adequate supply of the right materials and supplies.
- Machines - full utilization of machines and equipment, with proper maintenance.
- Methods - most efficient handling of operations.
- Deliveries - making deliveries on time.
- Tools - sufficient well-conditioned tools
- Layout - most effective use of space.
- Reports - maintaining proper records and reports.
- Supervision - planning work for employees and organizing supervisor's own time.

I.   MANAGEMENT

Question: *What do we mean by management?*

Answer: *Getting work done through others.*

Management could also be defined as planning, directing, and controlling the operations of a bureau or division so that all factors will function properly and all persons cooperate efficiently for a common objective.

II.   MANAGEMENT PRINCIPLES

1.   There should be a hierarchy - wherein authority and responsibility run upward and downward through several levels - with a broad base at the bottom and a single head at the top.

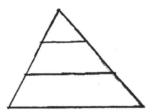

2.   Each and every unit or person in the organization should be answerable ultimately to the manager at the apex. In other words, *The buck stops here!*

3.   Every necessary function involved in the bureau's objectives is assigned to a unit in that bureau.

4.   Responsibilities assigned to a unit are specifically clear-cut and understood.

5.   Consistent methods of organizational structure should be applied at each level of the organization.

6. Each member of the bureau from top to bottom knows:
    to whom he reports
    who reports to him.

7. No member of one bureau reports to more than one supervisor.
    No dual functions

8. Responsibility for a function is matched by authority necessary to perform that function.
    Weight of authority

9. Individuals or units reporting to a supervisor do not exceed the number which can be feasibly and effectively coordinated and directed.
    Concept of *span of control*

10. Channels of command (management) are not violated by staff units, although there should be staff services to facilitate and coordinate management functions.

11. Authority and responsibility should be decentralized to units and individuals who are responsible for the actual performance of operations.
    Welfare - down to Welfare Centers
    Hospitals - down to local hospitals

12. Management should exercise control through attention to policy problems of exceptional importance, rather than through review of routine actions of subordinates.

13. Organizations should never be permitted to grow so elaborate as to hinder work accomplishments.
    Empire building

II. ORGANIZATION STRUCTURE
Types of Organizations.
The purest form is a leader and a few followers, such as:

```
                    ┌─────────────┐
                    │ Supervisor  │
                    └─────────────┘
═══════════════════════════════════════════════
┌──────────┐  ┌──────────┐  ┌──────────┐  ┌──────────┐
│  Worker  │  │  Worker  │  │  Worker  │  │  Worker  │
└──────────┘  └──────────┘  └──────────┘  └──────────┘
```

(Refer to organization chart) from supervisor to workers.

The line of authority is direct,
The workers know exactly where they stand in relation to their boss, to whom they report for instructions and direction.

Unfortunately, in our present complex society, few organizations are similar to this example of a pure line organization. In this era of specialization, other people are often needed in the simplest of organizations. These specialists are known as staff. The sole purpose for their existence (staff) is to assist, advise, suggest, help or counsel line organizations. Staff has no authority to direct line people - nor do they give them direct instructions.

```
                          ┌─────────────┐
                          │ SUPERVISOR  │
                          └─────────────┘
                                 │
   ┌──────────────┬──────────────┴──────────┬──────────────┐
┌───────────┐ ┌───────────┐         ┌───────────┐    ┌───────────┐
│ Personnel │ │ Accounting│         │ Inspection│    │  Legal    │
└───────────┘ └───────────┘         └───────────┘    └───────────┘
┌───────────┐ ┌───────────┐         ┌───────────┐    ┌───────────┐
│  Worker   │ │  Worker   │         │  Worker   │    │  Worker   │
└───────────┘ └───────────┘         └───────────┘    └───────────┘
```

Line Functions	Staff Functions
1. Directs	1. Advises
2. Orders	2. Persuades and sells
3. Responsibility for carrying out activities from beginning to end	3. Staff studies, reports, recommends but does not carry out
4. Follows chain of command	4. May advise across department lines
5. Is identified with what it does	5. May find its ideas identified with others
6. Decides when and how to use staff advice	6. Has to persuade line to want its advice
7. Line executes	7. Staff - Conducts studies and research. Provides advice and instructions in technical matters. Serves as technical specialist to render specific services

Types and Functions of Organization Charts.
An organization chart is a picture of the arrangement and inter-relationship of the subdivisions of an organization.

1. Types of Charts:
   a. Structural - basic relationships only
   b. Functional - includes functions or duties
   c. Personnel - positions, salaries, status, etc.
   d. Process Chart - work performed
   e. Gantt Chart - actual performance against planned
   f. Flow Chart - flow and distribution of work

2. Functions of Charts:
   a. Assist in management planning and control
   b. Indicate duplication of functions
   c. Indicate incorrect stressing of functions
   d. Indicate neglect of important functions
   e. Correct unclear authority
   f. Establish proper span of control

3. Limitations of Charts:
   a. Seldom maintained on current basis

b. Chart is oversimplified
c. Human factors cannot adequately be charted

4. Organization Charts should be:
   a. Simple
   b. Symmetrical
   c. Indicate authority
   d. Line and staff relationship differentiated
   e. Chart should be dated and bear signature of approving officer
   f. Chart should be displayed, not hidden

ORGANIZATION

There are four basic principles of organization:

1. Unity of command
2. Span of control
3. Uniformity of assignment
4. Assignment of responsibility and delegation of authority

Unity of Command

Unity of command means that each person in the organization should receive orders from one, and only one, supervisor. When a person has to take orders from two or more people, (a) the orders may be in conflict and the employee is upset because he does not know which he should obey, or, (b) different orders may reach him at the same time and he does not know which he should carry out first.

Equally as bad as having two bosses is the situation where the supervisor is by-passed. Let us suppose you are a supervisor whose boss by-passes you (deals directly with people reporting to you). To the worker, it is the same as having two bosses; but to you, the supervisor, it is equally serious. By-passing on the part of your boss will undermine your authority, and the people under you will begin looking to your boss for decisions and even for routine orders.

You can prevent by-passing by telling the people you supervise that if anyone tries to give them orders, they should direct that person to you.

Span of Control

Span of control on a given level involves:

a. The number of people belng supervised
b. The distance
c. The time involved in supervising the people. (One supervisor cannot supervise too many workers effectively.)

Span of control means that a supervisor has the right number (not too many and not too few) of subordinates that he can supervise well.

Uniformity of Assignment

In assigning work, you as the supervisor should assign to each person jobs that are similar in nature. An employee who is assigned too many different types of jobs will waste time in going from one kind of work to another. It takes time for him to get to top production in one kind of task and, before he does so, he has to start on another.

When you assign work to people, remember that:

a. Job duties should be definite. Make it clear from the beginning <u>what</u> they are to do, <u>how</u> they are to do it, and <u>why</u> they are to do it. Let them know how much they are expected to do and how well they are expected to do it.

b. Check your assignments to be certain that there are no workers with too many unrelated duties, and that no two people have been given overlapping responsibilities. Your aim should be to have every task assigned to a specific person with the work fairly distributed and with each person doing his part.

<u>Assignment of Responsibility and Delegation of Authority</u>

A supervisor cannot delegate his final responsibility for the work of his department. The experienced supervisor knows that he gets his work done through people. He can't do it all himself. So he must assign the work and the responsibility for the work to his employees. Then they must be given the authority to carry out their responsibilities.

By assigning responsibility and delegating authority to carry out the responsibility, the supervisor builds in his workers initiative, resourcefulness, enthusiasm, and interest in their work. He is treating them as responsible adults. They can find satisfaction in their work, and they will respect the supervisor and be loyal to the supervisor.

PRINCIPLES OF ORGANIZATION

1. <u>Definition</u>
   Organization is the method of dividing up the work to provide the best channels for coordinated effort to get the agency's mission accomplished.

2. <u>Purpose of Organization</u>
   a. To enable each employee within the organization to clearly know his responsibilities and relationships to his fellow employees and to organizational units.
   b. To avoid conflicts of authority and overlapping of jurisdiction.
   c. To ensure teamwork.

3. <u>Basic Considerations in Organizational Planning</u>
   a. The basic plans and objectives of the agency should be determined, and the organizational structure should be adapted to carry out effectively such plans and objectives.
   b. The organization should be built around the major functions of the agency and not individuals or groups of individuals.
   c. The organization should be sufficiently flexible to meet new and changing conditions which may be brought about from within or outside the department.
   d. The organizational structure should be as simple as possible and the number of organizational units kept at a minimum.
   e. The number of levels of authority should be kept at a minimum. Each additional management level lengthens the chain of authority and responsibility and increases the time for instructions to be distributed to operating levels and for decisions to be obtained from higher authority.

    f.   The form of organization should permit each executive to exercise maximum initiative within the limits of delegated authority.

4.   <u>Bases for Organization</u>
    a.   Purpose (Examples: education, police, sanitation)
    b.   Process (Examples: accounting, legal, purchasing)
    c.   Clientele (Examples: welfare, parks, veteran)
    d.   Geographic (Examples: borough offices, precincts, libraries)

5.   <u>Assignments of Functions</u>
    a.   Every function of the agency should be assigned to a specific organizational unit. Under normal circumstances, no single function should be assigned to more than one organizational unit.
    b.   There should be no overlapping, duplication, or conflict between organizational elements.
    c.   Line functions should be separated from staff functions, and proper emphasis should be placed on staff activities.
    d.   Functions which are closely related or similar should normally be assigned to a single organizational unit.
    e.   Functions should be properly distributed to promote balance, and to avoid overemphasis of less important functions and underemphasis of more essential functions.

6.   <u>Delegation of Authority and Responsibility</u>
    a.   Responsibilities assigned to a specific individual or organizational unit should carry corresponding authority, and all statements of authority or limitations thereof should be as specific as possible.
    b.   Authority and responsibility for action should be decentralized to organizational units and individuals responsible for actual performance to the greatest extent possible, without relaxing necessary control over policy or the standardization of procedures. Delegation of authority will be consistent with decentralization of responsibility but such delegation will not divest an executive in higher authority of his overall responsibility.
    c.   The heads of organizational units should concern themselves with important matters and should delegate to the maximum extent details and routines performed in the ordinary course of business.
    d.   All responsibilities, authorities, and relationships should be stated in simple language to avoid misinterpretation.
    e.   Each individual or organizational unit charged with a specific responsibility will be held responsible for results.

7.   <u>Employee Relationships</u>
    a.   The employees reporting to one executive should not exceed the number which can be effectively directed and coordinated. The number will depend largely upon the scope and extent of the responsibilities of the subordinates.
    b.   No person should report to more than one supervisor. Every supervisor should know who reports to him, and every employee should know to whom he reports. Channels of authority and responsibility should not be violated by staff units.
    c.   Relationships between organizational units within the agency and with outside organizations and associations should be clearly stated and thoroughly understood to avoid misunderstanding.

DELEGATING

1. <u>What is Delegating?</u>
   Delegating is assigning a job to an employee, giving him the authority to get that job done, and giving him the responsibility for seeing to it that the job is done.

   a. <u>What to Delegate</u>
      (1) Routine details
      (2) Jobs which may be necessary and take a lot of time, but do not have to be done by the supervisor personally (preparing reports, attending meetings, etc.)
      (3) Routine decision-making (making decisions which do not require the supervisor's personal attention)

   b. <u>What Not to Delegate</u>
      (1) Job details which are *executive functions* (setting goals, organizing employees into a good team, analyzing results so as to plan for the future)
      (2) Disciplinary power (handling grievances, preparing service ratings, reprimands, etc.)
      (3) Decision-making which involves large numbers of employees or other bureaus and departments
      (4) Final and complete responsibility for the job done by the unit being supervised

   c. <u>Why Delegate?</u>
      (1) To strengthen the organization by developing a greater number of skilled employees
      (2) To improve the employee's performance by giving him the chance to learn more about the job, handle some responsibility, and become more interested in getting the job done
      (3) To improve a supervisor's performance by relieving him of routine jobs and giving him more time for *executive functions* (planning, organizing, controlling, etc.) which cannot be delegated

2. <u>To Whom to Delegate</u>
   People with abilities not being used. Selection should be based on ability, not on favoritism.

REPORTS

<u>Definition</u>
   A report is an orderly presentation of factual information directed to a specific reader for a specific purpose.

<u>Purpose</u>
   The general purpose of a report is to bring to the reader useful and factual information about a condition or a problem. Some specific purposes of a report may be:

1. To enable the reader to appraise the efficiency or effectiveness of a person or an operation
2. To provide a basis for establishing standards
3. To reflect the results of expenditures of time, effort, and money
4. To provide a basis for developing or altering programs

<u>Types</u>
1. Information Report - Contains facts arranged in sequence
2. Summary (Examination) Report - Contains facts plus an analysis or discussion of the significance of the facts. Analysis may give advantages and disadvantages or give qualitative and quantitative comparisons
3. Recommendation Report - Contains facts, analysis, and conclusion logically drawn from the facts and analysis, plus a recommendation based upon the facts, analysis, and conclusions

<u>Factors to Consider Before Writing Report</u>

1. <u>Why</u> write the report - The purpose of the report should be clearly defined.
2. <u>Who</u> will read the report - What level of language should be used? Will the reader understand professional or technical language?
3. <u>What</u> should be said - What does the reader need or want to know about the subject?
4. <u>How</u> should it be said - Should the subject be presented tactfully? Convincingly? In a stimulating manner?

<u>Preparatory Steps</u>

1. Assemble the facts - Find out who, why, what, where, when, and how.
2. Organize the facts - Eliminate unnecessary information.
3. Prepare an outline - Check for orderliness, logical sequence.
4. Prepare a draft - Check for correctness, clearness, completeness, conciseness, and tone.
5. Prepare it in final form - Check for grammar, punctuation, appearance.

<u>Outline For a Recommendation Report</u>
   Is the report:

1. Correct in information, grammar, and tone?
2. Clear?
3. Complete?
4. Concise?
5. Timely?
6. Worth its cost?

Will the report accomplish its purpose?

MANAGEMENT CONTROLS

1. <u>Control</u>
What is control? What is controlled? Who controls?

The essence of control is action which adjusts operations to predetermined standards, and its basis is information in the hands of managers. Control is checking to determine whether plans are being observed and suitable progress toward stated objectives is being made, and action is taken, if necessary, to correct deviations.

We have a ready-made model for this concept of control in the automatic systems which are widely used for process control in the chemical and petroleum industries. A process control system works this way. Suppose, for example, it is desired to maintain a constant rate of flow of oil through a pipe at a predetermined or set-point value. A signal, whose strength represents the rate of flow, can be produced in a measuring device and transmitted to a control mechanism. The control mechanism, when it detects any deviation of the actual from the set-point signal, will reposition the value regulating flow rate.

2. Basis For Control

A process control mechanism thus acts to adjust operations to predetermined standards and does so on the basis of information it receives. In a parallel way, information reaching a manager gives him the opportunity for corrective action and is his basis for control. He cannot exercise control without such information, and he cannot do a complete job of managing without controlling.

3. Policy

What is policy?

Policy is simply a statement of an organization's intention to act in certain ways when specified types of circumstances arise. It represents a general decision, predetermined and expressed as a principle or rule, establishing a normal pattern of conduct for dealing with given types of business events - usually recurrent. A statement is therefore useful in economizing the time of managers and in assisting them to discharge their responsibilities equitably and consistently.

Policy is not a means of control, but policy does generate the need for control.

Adherence to policies is not guaranteed nor can it be taken on faith. It has to be verified. Without verification, there is no basis for control. Policy and procedures, although closely related and interdependent to a certain extent, are not synonymous. A policy may be adopted, for example, to maintain a materials inventory not to exceed one million dollars. A procedure for inventory control would interpret that policy and convert it into methods for keeping within that limit, with consideration, too, of possible but foreseeable expedient deviation.

4. Procedure

What is procedure?

A procedure specifically prescribes:

    a. What work is to be performed by the various participants
    b. Who are the respective participants
    c. When and where the various steps in the different processes are to be performed
    d. The sequence of operations that will insure uniform handling of recurring transactions
    e. The *paper* that is involved, its origin, transition, and disposition

Necessary appurtenances to a procedure are:

    a. Detailed organizational chart

    b.   Flow charts

    c.   Exhibits of forms, all presented in close proximity to the text of the procedure

5.   <u>Basis of Control - Information in the Hands of Managers</u>
If the basis of control is information in the hands of managers, then <u>reporting</u> is elevated to a level of very considerable importance.

Types of reporting may include:

    a.   Special reports and routine reports

    b.   Written, oral, and graphic reports

    c.   Staff meetings

    d.   Conferences

    e.   Television screens

    f.   Non-receipt of information, as where management is by exception

    g.   Any other means whereby information is transmitted to a manager as a basis for control action

FRAMEWORK OF MANAGEMENT

<u>Elements</u>

1.   <u>Policy</u> - It has to be verified, controlled.

2.   <u>Organization</u> - is part of the giving of an assignment. The organizational chart gives to each individual in his title, a first approximation of the nature of his assignment and orients him as being accountable to a certain individual. Organization is not in a true sense a means of control. Control is checking to ascertain whether the assignment is executed as intended and acting on the basis of that information.

3.   <u>Budgets</u> - perform three functions:

    a.   They present the objectives, plans, and programs of the organization in financial terms.

    b.   They report the progress of actual performance against these predetermined objectives, plans, and programs.

    c.   Like organizational charts, delegations of authority, procedures and job descriptions, they define the assignments which have flowed from the Chief Executive. Budgets are a means of control in the respect that they report progress of actual performance against the program. They provide information which enables managers to take action directed toward bringing actual results into conformity with the program.

4.   <u>Internal Check</u> - provides in practice for the principle that the same person should not have responsibility for all phases of a transaction. This makes it clearly an aspect of organization rather than of control. Internal Check is static, or built-in.

5.   <u>Plans, Programs, Objectives</u>
People must know what they are trying to do. <u>Objectives</u> fulfill this need. Without them, people may work industriously and yet, working aimlessly, accomplish little.

Plans and Programs complement Objectives, since they propose how and according to what time schedule the objectives are to be reached.

6. Delegations of Authority

Among the ways we have for supplementing the titles and lines of authority of an organizational chart are delegations of authority. Delegations of authority clarify the extent of authority of individuals and in that way serve to define assignments. That they are not means of control is apparent from the very fact that wherever there has been a delegation of authority, the need for control increases. This could hardly be expected to happen if delegations of authority were themselves means of control.

Manager's Responsibility

Control becomes necessary whenever a manager delegates authority to a subordinate because he cannot delegate and then simply sit back and forget all about it. A manager's accountability to his own superior has not diminished one whit as a result of delegating part of his authority to a subordinate. The manager must exercise control over actions taken under the authority so delegated. That means checking serves as a basis for possible corrective action.

Objectives, plans, programs, organizational charts, and other elements of the managerial system are not fruitfully regarded as either controls or means of control. They are pre-established standards or models of performance to which operations are adjusted by the exercise of management control. These standards or models of performance are dynamic in character for they are constantly altered, modified, or revised. Policies, organizational set-up, procedures, delegations, etc. are constantly altered but, like objectives and plans, they remain in force until they are either abandoned or revised. All of the elements (or standards or models of performance), objectives, plans and prpgrams, policies, organization, etc. can be regarded as a *framework of management*.

Control Techniques

Examples of control techniques:
1. Compare against established standards
2. Compare with a similar operation
3. Compare with past operations
4. Compare with predictions of accomplishment

Where Forecasts Fit

Control is after-the-fact while forecasts are before. Forecasts and projections are important for setting objectives and formulating plans.

Information for aiming and planning does not have to before-the-fact. It may be an after-the-fact analysis proving that a certain policy has been impolitic in its effect on the relation of the company or department with customer, employee, taxpayer, or stockholder; or that a certain plan is no longer practical, or that a certain procedure is unworkable.

The prescription here certainly would not be in control (in these cases, control would simply bring operations into conformity with obsolete standards) but the establishment of new standards, a new policy, a new plan, and a new procedure to be controlled too.

Information is, of course, the basis for all communication in addition to furnishing evidence to management of the need for reconstructing the framework of management.

PROBLEM SOLVING

The accepted concept in modern management for problem solving is the utilization of the following steps:

1. Identify the problem
2. Gather data
3. List possible solutions
4. Test possible solutions
5. Select the best solution
6. Put the solution into actual practice

Occasions might arise where you would have to apply the second step of gathering data before completing the first step.

You might also find that it will be necessary to work on several steps at the same time.

1. Identify the Problem

Your first step is to define as precisely as possible the problem to be solved. While this may sound easy, it is often the most difficult part of the process.

It has been said of problem solving that you are halfway to the solution when you can write out a clear statement of the problem itself.

Our job now is to get below the surface manifestations of the trouble and pinpoint the problem. This is usually accomplished by a logical analysis, by going from the general to the particular; from the obvious to the not-so-obvious cause.
Let us say that production is behind schedule. WHY? Absenteeism is high. Now, is absenteeism the basic problem to be tackled, or is it merely a symptom of low morale among the workforce? Under these circumstances, you may decide that production is not the problem; the problem is *employee morale*.

In trying to define the problem, remember there is seldom one simple reason why production is lagging, or reports are late, etc.

Analysis usually leads to the discovery that an apparent problem is really made up of several subproblems which must be attacked separately.

Another way is to limit the problem, and thereby ease the task of finding a solution, and concentrate on the elements which are within the scope of your control.

When you have gone this far, write out a tentative statement of the problem to be solved.

2. Gather Data

In the second step, you must set out to collect all the information that might have a bearing on the problem. Do not settle for an assumption when reasonable fact and figures are available.

If you merely go through the motions of problem-solving, you will probably shortcut the information-gathering step. Therefore, do not stack the evidence by confining your research to your own preconceived ideas.

As you collect facts, organize them in some form that helps you make sense of them and spot possible relationships between them. For example: Plotting cost per unit figures on a graph can be more meaningful than a long column of figures.

Evaluate each item as you go along. Is the source material: absolutely reliable, probably reliable, or not to be trusted.

One of the best methods for gathering data is to go out and look the situation over carefully. Talk to the people on the job who are most affected by this problem.

Always keep in mind that a primary source is usually better than a secondary source of information.

3. List Possible Solutions

This is the creative thinking step of problem solving. This is a good time to bring into play whatever techniques of group dynamics the agency or bureau might have developed for a joint attack on problems.

Now the important thing for you to do is: Keep an open mind. Let your imagination roam freely over the facts you have collected. Jot down every possible solution that occurs to you. Resist the temptation to evaluate various proposals as you go along. List seemingly absurd ideas along with more plausible ones. The more possibilities you list during this step, the less risk you will run of settling for merely a workable, rather than the best, solution.

Keep studying the data as long as there seems to be any chance of deriving additional - ideas, solutions, explanations, or patterns from it.

4. Test Possible Solutions

Now you begin to evaluate the possible solutions. Take pains to be objective. Up to this point, you have suspended judgment but you might be tempted to select a solution you secretly favored all along and proclaim it as the best of the lot.

The secret of objectivity in this phase is to test the possible solutions separately, measuring each against a common yardstick. To make this yardstick try to enumerate as many specific criteria as you can think of. Criteria are best phrased as questions which you ask of each possible solution. They can be drawn from these general categories:

> Suitability - Will this solution do the job?
> Will it solve the problem completely or partially?

Is it a permanent or a stopgap solution?

Feasibility   -   Will this plan work in actual practice?
Can we afford this approach?
How much will it cost?

Acceptability -   Will the boss go along with the changes required in the plan?
Are we trying to drive a tack with a sledge hammer?

5.   Select the Best Solution

This is the area of executive decision.

Occasionally, one clearly superior solution will stand out at the conclusion of the testing process. But often it is not that simple. You may find that no one solution has come through all the tests with flying colors.

You may also find that a proposal, which flunked miserably on one of the essential tests, racked up a very high score on others.

The best solution frequently will turn out to be a combination.

Try to arrange a marriage that will bring together the strong points of one possible solution with the particular virtues of another. The more skill and imagination that you apply, the greater is the likelihood that you will come out with a solution that is not merely adequate and workable, but is the best possible under the circumstances.

6.   Put the Solution Into Actual Practice
As every executive knows, a plan which works perfectly on paper may develop all sorts of bugs when put into actual practice.

Problem-solving does not stop with selecting the solution which looks best in theory. The next step is to put the chosen solution into action and watch the results. The results may point towards modifications.

If the problem disappears when you put your solution into effect, you know you have the right solution.

If it does not disappear, even after you have adjusted your plan to cover unforeseen difficulties that turned up in practice, work your way back through the problem-solving solutions.

Would one of them have worked better?
Did you overlook some vital piece of data which would have given you a different slant on the whole situation? Did you apply all necessary criteria in testing solutions? If no light dawns after this much rechecking, it is a pretty good bet that you defined the problem incorrectly in the first place.

You came up with the wrong solution because you tackled the wrong problem.

Thus, step six may become step one of a new problem-solving cycle.

COMMUNICATION

1. <u>What is Communication?</u>
    We communicate through writing, speaking, action or inaction. In speaking to people face-to-face, there is opportunity to judge reactions and to adjust the message. This makes the supervisory chain one of the most, and in many instances the most, important channels of communication.

    In an organization, communication means keeping employees informed about the organization's objectives, policies, problems, and progress. Communication is the free interchange of information, ideas, and desirable attitudes between and among employees and between employees and management.

2. <u>Why is Communication Needed?</u>
    a. People have certain social needs
    b. Good communication is essential in meeting those social needs
    c. While people have similar basic needs, at the same time they differ from each other
    d. Communication must be adapted to these individual differences

    An employee cannot do his best work unless he knows why he is doing it. If he has the feeling that he is being kept in the dark about what is going on, his enthusiasm and productivity suffer.

    Effective communication is needed in an organization so that employees will understand what the organization is trying to accomplish; and how the work of one unit contributes to or affects the work of other units in the organization and other organizations.

3. <u>How is Communication Achieved?</u>
    Communication flows downward, upward, sideways.

    a. Communication may come from top management down to employees. This is <u>downward communication</u>.

        Some means of downward communication are:
        (1) Training (orientation, job instruction, supervision, public relations, etc.)
        (2) Conferences
        (3) Staff meetings
        (4) Policy statements
        (5) Bulletins
        (6) Newsletters
        (7) Memoranda
        (8) Circulation of important letters

        In downward communication, it is important that employees be informed in advance of changes that will affect them.

    b. Communications should also be developed so that the ideas, suggestions, and knowledge of employees will flow <u>upward</u> to top management.

Some means of upward communication are:
(1)   Personal discussion conferences
(2)   Committees
(3)   Memoranda
(4)   Employees suggestion program
(5)   Questionnaires to be filled in giving comments and suggestions about proposed actions that will affect field operations

Upward communication requires that management be willing to listen, to accept, and to make changes when good ideas are present. Upward communication succeeds when there is no fear of punishment for speaking out or lack of interest at the top. Employees will share their knowledge and ideas with management when interest is shown and recognition is given.

c.   The *advantages* of downward communication:
(1)   It enables the passing down of orders, policies, and plans necessary to the continued operation of the station.
(2)   By making information available, it diminishes the fears and suspicions which result from misinformation and misunderstanding.
(3)   It fosters the pride people want to have in their work when they are told of good work.
(4)   It improves the morale and stature of the individual to be *in the know*.
(5)   It helps employees to understand, accept, and cooperate with changes when they know about them in advance.

d.   The *advantages* of upward communication:
(1)   It enables the passing upward of information, attitudes, and feelings.
(2)   It makes it easier to find out how ready people are to receive downward communication.
(3)   It reveals the degree to which the downward communication is understood and accepted.
(4)   It helps to satisfy the basic *social* needs.
(5)   It stimulates employees to participate in the operation of their organization.
(6)   It encourages employees to contribute ideas for improving the efficiency and economy of operations.
(7)   It helps to solve problem situations before they reach the explosion point.

4.   Why Does Communication Fail?
   a.   The technical difficulties of conveying information clearly
   b.   The emotional content of communication which prevents complete transmission
   c.   The fact that there is a difference between what management needs to say, what it wants to say, and what it does say
   d.   The fact that there is a difference between what employees would like to say, what they think is profitable or safe to say, and what they do say

5.   How to Improve Communication.
   As a supervisor, you are a key figure in communication. To improve as a communicator, you should:
   a.   Know - Knowing your subordinates will help you to recognize and work with individual differences.

b. <u>Like</u> - If you like those who work for you and those for whom you work, this will foster the kind of friendly, warm, work atmosphere that will facilitate communication.

c. <u>Trust</u> - Showing a sincere desire to communicate will help to develop the mutual trust and confidence which are essential to the free flow of communication.

d. <u>Tell</u> - Tell your subordinates and superiors *what's doing*. Tell your subordinates *why* as well as *how*.

e. <u>Listen</u> - By listening, you help others to talk and you create good listeners. Don't forget that listening implies action.

f. <u>Stimulate</u> - Communication has to be stimulated and encouraged. Be receptive to ideas and suggestions and motivate your people so that each member of the team identifies himself with the job at hand.

g. <u>Consult</u> - The most effective way of consulting is to let your people participate, insofar as possible, in developing determinations which affect them or their work.

6. <u>How to Determine Whether You are Getting Across</u>.
   a. Check to see that communication is received and understood
   b. Judge this understanding by actions rather than words
   c. Adapt or vary communication, when necessary
   d. Remember that good communication cannot cure all problems

7. <u>The Key Attitude</u>.
   Try to see things from the other person's point of view. By doing this, you help to develop the permissive atmosphere and the shared confidence and understanding which are essential to effective two-way communication.

   Communication is a two-way process.
   a. The basic purpose of any communication is to get action.
   b. The only way to get action is through acceptance.
   c. In order to get acceptance, communication must be humanly satisfying as well as technically efficient.

HOW ORDERS AND INSTRUCTIONS SHOULD BE GIVEN

<u>Characteristics of Good Orders and Instructions</u>

1. <u>Clear</u>
   Orders should be definite as to
   - <u>What</u> is to be done
   - <u>Who</u> is to do it
   - <u>When</u> it is to be done
   - <u>Where</u> it is to be done
   - <u>How</u> it is to be done

2. <u>Concise</u>
   Avoid wordiness. Orders should be brief and to the point.

3. <u>Timely</u>
   Instructions and orders should be sent out at the proper time and not too long in advance of expected performance.

4. Possibility of Performance
   Orders should be feasible:
   a. Investigate before giving orders
   b. Consult those who are to carry out instructions before formulating and issuing them

5. Properly Directed
   Give the orders to the people concerned. Do not send orders to people who are not concerned. People who continually receive instructions that are not applicable to them get in the habit of neglecting instructions generally.

6. Reviewed Before Issuance
   Orders should be reviewed before issuance:
   a. Test them by putting yourself in the position of the recipient
   b. If they involve new procedures, have the persons who are to do the work review them for suggestions

7. Reviewed After Issuance
   Persons who receive orders should be allowed to raise questions and to point out unforeseen consequences of orders.

8. Coordinated
   Orders should be coordinated so that work runs smoothly.

9. Courteous
   Make a request rather than a demand. There is no need to continually call attention to the fact that you are the boss.

10. Recognizable as an Order
    Be sure that the order is recognizable as such.

11. Complete
    Be sure recipient has knowledge and experience sufficient to carry out order. Give illustrations and examples.

A DEPARTMENTAL PERSONNEL OFFICE IS RESPONSIBLE FOR THE FOLLOWING FUNCTIONS

1. Policy
2. Personnel Programs
3. Recruitment and Placement
4. Position Classification
5. Salary and Wage Administration
6. Employee Performance Standards and Evaluation
7. Employee Relations
8. Disciplinary Actions and Separations
9. Health and Safety
10. Staff Training and Development
11. Personnel Records, Procedures, and Reports
12. Employee Services
13. Personnel Research

SUPERVISION

Leadership

All leadership is based essentially on authority. This comes from two sources: it is received from higher management or it is earned by the supervisor through his methods of supervision. Although effective leadership has always depended upon the leader's using his authority in such a way as to appeal successfully to the motives of the people supervised, the conditions for making this appeal are continually changing. The key to today's problem of leadership is flexibility and resourcefulness on the part of the leader in meeting changes in conditions as they occur.

Three basic approaches to leadership are generally recognized:

1. The Authoritarian Approach
    a. The methods and techniques used in this approach emphasize the *I* in leadership and depend primarily on the formal authority of the leader. This authority is sometimes exercised in a hardboiled manner and sometimes in a benevolent manner, but in either case the dominating role of the leader is reflected in the thinking, planning, and decisions of the group.
    b. Group results are to a large degree dependent on close supervision by the leader. Usually, the individuals in the group will not show a high degree of initiative or acceptance of responsibility and their capacity to grow and develop probably will not be fully utilized. The group may react with resentment or submission, depending upon the manner and skill of the leader in using his authority
    c. This approach develops as a natural outgrowth of the authority that goes with the leader's job and his feeling of sole responsibility for getting the job done. It is relatively easy to use and does not require much resourcefulness.
    d. The use of this approach is effective in times of emergencies, in meeting close deadlines as a final resort, in settling some issues, in disciplinary matters, and with dependent individuals and groups.

2. The Laissez-Faire or *Let 'em Alone* Approach
    a. This approach generally is characterized by an avoidance of leadership responsibility by the leader. The activities of the group depend largely on the choice of its members rather than the leader.
    b. Group results probably will be poor. Generally, there will be disagreements over petty things, bickering, and confusion. Except for a few aggressive people, individuals will not show much initiative and growth and development will be retarded. There may be a tendency for informal leaders to take over leadership of the group.
    c. This approach frequently results from the leader's dislike of responsibility, from his lack of confidence, from failure of other methods to work, from disappointment or criticism. It is usually the easiest of the three to use and requires both understanding and resourcefulness on the part of the leader.
    d. This approach is occasionally useful and effective, particularly in forcing dependent individuals or groups to rely on themselves, to give someone a chance to save face by clearing his own difficulties, or when action should be delayed temporarily for good cause.

3. The Democratic Approach
    a. The methods and techniques used in this approach emphasize the *we* in leadership and build up the responsibility of the group to attain its objectives. Reliance is placed largely on the earned authority of the leader.
    b. Group results are likely to be good because most of the job motives of the people will be satisfied. Cooperation and teamwork, initiative, acceptance of responsibility, and the individual's capacity for growth probably will show a high degree of development.
    c. This approach grows out of a desire or necessity of the leader to find ways to appeal effectively to the motivation of his group. It is the best approach to build up inside the person a strong desire to cooperate and apply himself to the job.
    It is the most difficult to develop, and requires both understanding and resourcefulness on the part of the leader.
    d. The value of this approach increases over a long period where sustained efficiency and development of people are important. It may not be fully effective in all situations, however, particularly when there is not sufficient time to use it properly or where quick decisions must be made.

All three approaches are used by most leaders and have a place in supervising people. The extent of their use varies with individual leaders, with some using one approach predominantly. The leader who uses these three approaches, and varies their use with time and circumstance, is probably the most effective. Leadership which is used predominantly with a democratic approach requires more resourcefulness on the part of the leader but offers the greatest possibilities in terms of teamwork and cooperation.

The one best way of developing democratic leadership is to provide a real sense of participation on the part of the group, since this satisfies most of the chief job motives. Although there are many ways of providing participation, consulting as frequently as possible with individuals and groups on things that affect them seems to offer the most in building cooperation and responsibility. Consultation takes different forms, but it is most constructive when people feel they are actually helping in finding the answers to the problems on the job.

There are some requirements of leaders in respect to human relations which should be considered in their selection and development. Generally, the leader should be interested in working with other people, emotionally stable, self-confident, and sensitive to the reactions of others. In addition, his viewpoint should be one of getting the job done through people who work cooperatively in response to his leadership. He should have a knowledge of individual and group behavior, but, most important of all, he should work to combine all of these requirements into a definite, practical skill in leadership.

Nine Points of Contrast Between *Boss* and *Leader*

1. The boss drives his men; the leader coaches them.
2. The boss depends on authority; the leader on good will.
3. The boss inspires fear; the leader inspires enthusiasm.
4. The boss says J; the leader says *We*.
5. The boss says *Get here on time;* the leader gets there ahead of time.
6. The boss fixes the blame for the breakdown; the leader fixes the breakdown.
7. The boss knows how it is done; the leader shows how.
8. The boss makes work a drudgery; the leader makes work a game.
9. The boss says *Go*; the leader says *Let's go.*

EMPLOYEE MORALE

Employee morale is the way employees feel about each other, the organization or unit in which they work, and the work they perform.

Some Ways to Develop and Maintain Good Employee Morale

1. Give adequate credit and praise when due.
2. Recognize importance of all jobs and equalize load with proper assignments, always giving consideration to personality differences and abilities.
3. Welcome suggestions and do not have an *all-wise* attitude. Request employees' assistance in solving problems and use assistants when conducting group meetings on certain subjects.
4. Properly assign responsibilities and give adequate authority for fulfillment of such assignments.
5. Keep employees informed about matters that affect them.
6. Criticize and reprimand employees privately.
7. Be accessible and willing to listen.
8. Be fair.
9. Be alert to detect training possibilities so that you will not miss an opportunity to help each employee do a better job, and if possible with less effort on his part.
10. Set a good example.
11. Apply the golden rule.

Some Indicators of Good Morale
1. Good quality of work
2. Good quantity
3. Good attitude of employees
4. Good discipline
5. Teamwork
6. Good attendance
7. Employee participation

MOTIVATION

Drives

A *drive,* stated simply, is a desire or force which causes a person to do or say certain things. These are some of the most usual drives and some of their identifying characteristics recognizable in people motivated by such drives:

1. Security (desire to provide for the future)
   Always on time for work
   Works for the same employer for many years
   Never takes unnecessary chances Seldom resists doing what he is told

2. Recognition (desire to be rewarded for accomplishment)
   Likes to be asked for his opinion
   Becomes very disturbed when he makes a mistake
   Does things to attract attention

Likes to see his name in print

3. <u>Position</u> (desire to hold certain status in relation to others)
   Boasts about important people he knows
   Wants to be known as a key man
   Likes titles
   Demands respect
   Belongs to clubs, for prestige

4. <u>Accomplishment</u> (desire to get things done)
   Complains when things are held up
   Likes to do things that have tangible results
   Never lies down on the job
   Is proud of turning out good work

5. <u>Companionship</u> (desire to associate with other people)
   Likes to work with others
   Tells stories and jokes
   Indulges in horseplay
   Finds excuses to talk to others on the job

6. <u>Possession</u> (desire to collect and hoard objects)
   Likes to collect things
   Puts his name on things belonging to him
   Insists on the same work location

Supervisors may find that identifying the drives of employees is a helpful step toward motivating them to self-improvement and better job performance. For example: An employee's job performance is below average. His supervisor, having previously determined that the employee is motivated by a drive for security, suggests that taking training courses will help the employee to improve, advance, and earn more money. Since earning more money can be a step toward greater security, the employee's drive for security would motivate him to take the training suggested by the supervisor. In essence, this is the process of charting an employee's future course by using his motivating drives to positive advantage.

EMPLOYEE PARTICIPATION

<u>What is Participation?</u>

Employee participation is the employee's giving freely of his time, skill and knowledge to an extent which cannot be obtained by demand.

<u>Why is it Important</u>?

The supervisor's responsibility is to get the job done through people. A good supervisor gets the job done through people who work willingly and well. The participation of employees is important because:

1. Employees develop a greater sense of responsibility when they share in working out operating plans and goals.
2. Participation provides greater opportunity and stimulation for employees to learn, and to develop their ability.

3. Participation sometimes provides better solutions to problems because such solutions may combine the experience and knowledge of interested employees who want the solutions to work.
4. An employee or group may offer a solution which the supervisor might hesitate to make for fear of demanding too much.
5. Since the group wants to make the solution work, they exert *pressure* in a constructive way on each other.
6. Participation usually results in reducing the need for close supervision.

<u>How May Supervisors Obtain It</u>?

Participation is encouraged when employees feel that they share some responsibility for the work and that their ideas are sincerely wanted and valued. Some ways of obtaining employee participation are:

1. Conduct orientation programs for new employees to inform them about the organization and their rights and responsibilities as employees.
2. Explain the aims and objectives of the agency. On a continuing basis, be sure that the employees know what these aims and objectives are.
3. Share job successes and responsibilities and give credit for success.
4. Consult with employees, both as individuals and in groups, about things that affect them.
5. Encourage suggestions for job improvements. Help employees to develop good suggestions. The suggestions can bring them recognition. The city's suggestion program offers additional encouragement through cash awards.

The supervisor who encourages employee participation is not surrendering his authority. He must still make decisions and initiate action, and he must continue to be ultimately responsible for the work of those he supervises. But, through employee participation, he is helping his group to develop greater ability and a sense of responsibility while getting the job done faster and better.

STEPS IN HANDLING A GRIEVANCE

1. <u>Get the facts</u>
   a. Listen sympathetically.
   b. Let him talk himself out.
   c. Get his story straight.
   d. Get his point of view.
   e. Don't argue with him.
   f. Give him plenty of time.
   g. Conduct the interview privately.
   h. Don't try to shift the blame or pass the buck.

2. <u>Consider the facts</u>
   a. Consider the employee's viewpoint.
   b. How will the decision affect similar cases.
   c. Consider each decision as a possible precedent.
   d. Avoid snap judgments - don't jump to conclusions.

3. <u>Make or get a decision</u>
   a. Frame an effective counter-proposal.
   b. Make sure it is fair to all.
   c. Have confidence in your judgment.
   d. Be sure you can substantiate your decision.

4. <u>Notify the employee of your decision</u>
   Be sure he is told; try to convince him that the decision is fair and just.

5. <u>Take action when needed and if within your authority</u>
   Otherwise, tell employee that the matter will be called to the attention of the proper person or that nothing can be done, and why it cannot.

6. <u>Follow through</u> to see that the desired result is achieved.

7. <u>Record key facts</u> concerning the complaint and the action taken.

8. <u>Leave the way open to him to appeal your decision</u> to a higher authority.

9. <u>Report all grievances to your superior</u>, whether they are appealed or not.

DISCIPLINE

Discipline is training that develops self-control, orderly conduct, and efficiency.

To discipline does not necessarily mean to punish.

To discipline does mean to train, to regulate, and to govern conduct.

<u>The Disciplinary Interview</u>

Most employees sincerely want to do what is expected of them. In other words, they are self-disciplined. Some employees, however, fail to observe established rules and standards, and disciplinary action by the supervisor is required.

The primary purpose of disciplinary action is to improve conduct without creating dissatisfaction, bitterness, or resentment in the process.

Constructive disciplinary action is more concerned with causes and explanations of breaches of conduct than with punishment. The disciplinary interview is held to get at the causes of apparent misbehavior and to motivate better performance in the future.

It is important that the interview be kept on as impersonal a basis as possible. If the supervisor lets the interview descend to the plane of an argument, it loses its effectiveness.

<u>Planning the Interview</u>

Get all pertinent facts concerning the situation so that you can talk in specific terms to the employee.

Review the employee's record, appraisal ratings, etc.

Consider what you know about the temperament of the employee. Consider your attitude toward the employee. Remember that the primary requisite of disciplinary action is fairness.

Don't enter upon the interview when angry.

Schedule the interview for a place which is private and out of hearing of others.

<u>Conducting the Interview</u>

1. Make an effort to establish accord.

2. Question the employee about the apparent breach of discipline. Be sure that the question is not so worded as to be itself an accusation.

3. Give the employee a chance to tell his side of the story. Give him ample opportunity to talk.

4. Use understanding-listening except where it is necessary to ask a question or to point out some details of which the employee may not be aware. If the employee misrepresents facts, make a plain, accurate statement of the facts, but don't argue and don't engage in personal controversy.

5. Listen and try to understand the reasons for the employee's (mis)conduct. First of all, don't assume that there has been a breach of discipline. Evaluate the employee's reasons for his conduct in the light of his opinions and feelings concerning the consistency and reasonableness of the standards which he was expected to follow. Has the supervisor done his part in explaining the reasons for the rules? Was the employee's behavior unintentional or deliberate? Does he think he had real reasons for his actions? What new facts is he telling? Do the facts justify his actions? What causes, other than those mentioned, could have stimulated the behavior?

6. After listening to the employee's version of the situation, and if censure of his actions is warranted, the supervisor should proceed with whatever criticism is justified. Emphasis should be placed on future improvement rather than exclusively on the employee's failure to measure up to expected standards of job conduct.

7. Fit the criticism to the individual. With one employee, a word of correction may be all that is required.

8. Attempt to distinguish between unintentional error and deliberate misbehavior. An error due to ignorance requires training and not censure.

9. Administer criticism in a controlled, even tone of voice, never in anger. Make it clear that you are acting as an agent of the department. In general, criticism should refer to the job or the employee's actions and not to the person. Criticism of the employee's work is not an attack on the individual.

10. Be sure the interview does not destroy the employee's self-confidence. Mention his good qualities and assure him that you feel confident that he can improve his performance.

11. Wherever possible, before the employee leaves the interview, satisfy him that the incident is closed, that nothing more will be said on the subject unless the offense is repeated.

———

Made in the USA
Columbia, SC
09 November 2022

70750764R00183